Teacher Resource Book C

VISIONS

Language ✧ Literature ✧ Content

Mary Lou McCloskey

Lydia Stack

THOMSON

HEINLE

Australia ✧ Canada ✧ Mexico ✧ Singapore ✧ United Kingdom ✧ United States

VISIONS TEACHER RESOURCE BOOK C
Mary Lou McCloskey and Lydia Stack

Publisher: *Phyllis Dobbins*
Director of Development: *Anita Raducanu*
Developmental Editor: *Tania Maundrell-Brown*
Associate Developmental Editor: *Yeny Kim*
Associate Developmental Editor: *Kasia Zagorski*
Editorial Assistant: *Audra Longert*
Production Supervisor: *Mike Burggren*
Marketing Manager: *Jim McDonough*
Manufacturing Manager: *Marcia Locke*
Director, ELL Training and Development: *Evelyn Nelson*
Photography Manager: *Sheri Blaney*
Development: *Proof Positive/Farrowlyne Associates, Inc.; Quest Language Systems, LLC*
Design and Production: *Proof Positive/Farrowlyne Associates, Inc.*
Cover Designer: *Studio Montage*
Printer: *Phoenix Color Corp.*

Printed in the United States of America.
4 5 6 7 8 9 10   08   07   06   05   04

For more information, contact Heinle, 25 Thomson Place, Boston, Massachusetts 02210 USA,
or you can visit our Internet site at http://www.heinle.com

For permission to use material from this text or product contact us:
Tel   1-800-730-2214
Fax   1-800-730-2215
Web   www.thomsonrights.com

ISBN: 0-8384-5348-1

Contents

LESSON PLANS

TEACHER RESOURCES

READING SUMMARIES (English, Spanish, Hmong, Vietnamese, Cantonese, Cambodian, Haitian Creole)

PARENT NEWSLETTERS (English, Spanish, Vietnamese, Hmong, Cantonese, Cambodian, Haitian Creole)

VIDEO SCRIPTS

VIDEO WORKSHEETS

UNIT 1 Mysteries

CHAPTER 1 • The Loch Ness Monster, by Malcolm Yorke

Chapter Materials

Activity Book: pp. 1–8
Audio: Unit 1, Chapter 1
Student Handbook
Student CD-ROM: Unit 1, Chapter 1
Teacher Resource Book: Lesson Plan, p. 1; Teacher
   Resources, pp. 35–64; Reading Summaries, pp. 65–66;
   Activity Book Answer Key

Teacher Resource CD-ROM
Assessment Program: Unit 1, Chapter 1 Quiz, pp. 7–8;
   Teacher and Student Resources, pp. 115–144
Assessment CD-ROM: Unit 1, Chapter 1 Quiz
Transparencies
The Heinle Newbury House Dictionary/CD-ROM
Web Site: www.heinle.visions.com

➤ See the Teacher's Edition wrap-around for complete teaching suggestions for each section.

Day 1

- **Unit Opener** (p. 1) 20 MIN.
  Preview unit reading selections. Complete "View the Picture" activity.
- **Objectives** (p. 2) 5 MIN.
  Present chapter objectives.
- **Use Prior Knowledge** (p. 2) 15 MIN.
  Activate prior knowledge about animals.
- **Build Background** (p. 3) 5 MIN.
  Provide the background information on dinosaurs.
- **Homework:** KWL (TRB, p. 42); Have students complete the first and second columns based on what they learned in class. Students will complete the third column at the end of the chapter.

Day 2

- **Check Homework** 5 MIN.
  OR
- **Warm Up** 5 MIN.
  Write on the board: Write down 3 things you learned about dinosaurs yesterday.
- **Build Vocabulary** (p. 3) 15 MIN.
  Introduce how to use language structure to find meaning.
- **Text Structure** (p. 4) 10 MIN.
  Present text features of an informational text.
- **Reading Strategy** (p. 4) 10 MIN.
  Teach the strategy of making inferences using text evidence.
- **Reading Selection Opener** (p. 5) 5 MIN.
  Preview chapter reading selection.
- **Homework:** Activity Book (p. 1)

Day 3

- **Check Homework** 5 MIN.
  OR
- **Warm Up** 5 MIN.
  Write on the board: List 3 features of an informational text.
- **Reading Selection** (pp. 6–9) 25 MIN.
  Have students read the selections and use the reading strategy. Teach spelling, capitalization, and punctuation points on TE pp. 6–9.
- **Reading Comprehension** (p. 10) 10 MIN.
  Have students answer questions.
- **Build Reading Fluency** (p. 10) 5 MIN.
  Introduce how to build reading fluency by doing repeated reading.
- **Homework:** Activity Book (p. 2)

Day 4

- **Check Homework** 5 MIN.
  OR
- **Warm Up** 5 MIN.
  Write on the board: Complete these sentences: Write 3 things you learned about the Loch Ness monster from the reading. How did you learn these things about the monster?
- **Listen, Speak, Interact** (p. 11) 15 MIN.
  Have students present an interview.
- **Elements of Literature** (p. 11) 15 MIN.
  Teach the role of visuals in understanding text.
- **Word Study** (p. 12) 10 MIN.
  Present compound words.
- **Homework:** Activity Book (pp. 3–4)

Day 5

- **Check Homework** 5 MIN.
  OR
- **Warm Up** 5 MIN.
  Write on the board: Find a rhyming word for each word.
a. cat	**c.** deer	**e.** shark
b. mouse	**d.** bear	
- **Grammar Focus** (p. 12) 15 MIN.
  Present the conjunction *but*.
- **From Reading to Writing** (p. 13) 15 MIN.
  Teach how to write a paragraph that describes.
- **Across Content Areas** (p. 13) 10 MIN.
  Provide related math content on understanding length.
- **Homework:** Activity Book (pp. 5–8); Have students complete the third column of the KWL chart from Day 1. Have students study for the Unit 1, Chapter 1 Quiz.

UNIT 1 Mysteries

CHAPTER 2 • Mystery of the Cliff Dwellers

Chapter Materials

Activity Book: pp. 9–16
Audio: Unit 1, Chapter 2
Student Handbook
Student CD-ROM: Unit 1, Chapter 2
Teacher Resource Book: Lesson Plan, p. 2; Teacher
  Resources, pp. 35–64; Reading Summaries, pp. 67–68;
  Activity Book Answer Key

Teacher Resource CD-ROM
Assessment Program: Unit 1, Chapter 2 Quiz, pp. 9–10;
  Teacher and Student Resources, pp. 115–144
Assessment CD-ROM: Unit 1, Chapter 2 Quiz
Transparencies
The Heinle Newbury House Dictionary/CD-ROM
Web Site: www.heinle.visions.com

➤ See the Teacher's Edition wrap-around for complete teaching suggestions for each section.

Day 1

- **Unit 1, Chapter 1 Quiz** (Assessment Program, pp. 7–8)
  20 MIN.
- **Objectives** (p. 14) 5 MIN.
  Present the chapter objectives.
- **Use Prior Knowledge** (p. 14) 15 MIN.
  Activate prior knowledge about students' community.
- **Build Background** (p. 15) 5 MIN.
  Provide background on archaeologists.
- **Homework:** KWL (TRB, p. 42); Have students
  complete the first and second columns based on what
  they learned in class. Students will complete the third
  column at the end of the chapter.

Day 2

- **Check Homework** 5 MIN.
  OR
- **Warm Up** 5 MIN.
  Write on the board: Archaeologists are _____ who
  study the ways people _____ long ago.
- **Build Vocabulary** (p. 15) 15 MIN.
  Introduce context words by grouping.
- **Text Structure** (p. 16) 10 MIN.
  Present the text features of an informational text.
- **Reading Strategy** (p. 16) 10 MIN.
  Teach the strategy of finding the main idea and
  supporting details.
- **Reading Selection Opener** (p. 17) 5 MIN.
  Preview the chapter reading selection.
- **Homework:** Activity Book (p. 9)

Day 3

- **Check Homework** 5 MIN.
  OR
- **Warm Up** 5 MIN.
  Write on the board: Quotes are _____ that people
  have said. Quotes usually have _____ _____ around
  them.
- **Reading Selection** (pp. 18–21) 25 MIN.
  Have students read the selection and use the reading
  strategy. Teach spelling, capitalization, and
  punctuation points on TE pp. 18–21.

- **Reading Comprehension** (p. 22) 10 MIN.
  Have students answer the questions.
- **Build Reading Fluency** (p. 22) 5 MIN.
  Teach how to build reading fluency by reading silently
  and aloud.
- **Homework:** Activity Book (p. 10)

Day 4

- **Check Homework** 5 MIN.
  OR
- **Warm Up** 5 MIN.
  Write on the board: True or false?
  a. The Anasazi people made their homes in high cliffs.
  b. A kiva is a room above the ground.
  c. We know why the Anasazi left their homes.
- **Listen, Speak, Interact** (p. 23) 15 MIN.
  Have students distinguish between fact and opinion.
- **Elements of Literature** (p. 23) 15 MIN.
  Teach how to write quotes.
- **Word Study** (p. 24) 10 MIN.
  Present root words and suffixes.
- **Homework:** Activity Book (pp. 11–12)

Day 5

- **Check Homework** 5 MIN.
  OR
- **Warm Up** 5 MIN.
  Write on the board: Add quotation marks to these
  quotes.
  a. I asked, Why did the Anasazi leave?
  b. We don't know exactly why the Anasazi left, the
    archaeologist said.
- **Grammar Focus** (p. 24) 15 MIN.
  Present prepositional phrases.
- **From Reading to Writing** (p. 25) 15 MIN.
  Teach how to write an informational text.
- **Across Content Areas** (p. 25) 10 MIN.
  Introduce related social studies content on reading a
  population map.
- **Homework:** Activity Book (pp. 13–16); Have students
  complete the third column of the KWL chart from
  Day 1. Have students study for the Unit 1, Chapter 2
  Quiz.

Class _____ Date _____

UNIT 1 Mysteries

CHAPTER 3 • Yawning, by Haleh V. Samiei

Chapter Materials

Activity Book: pp. 17–24
Audio: Unit 1, Chapter 3
Student Handbook
Student CD-ROM: Unit 1, Chapter 3
Teacher Resource Book: Lesson Plan, p. 3; Teacher
  Resources, pp. 35–64; Reading Summaries, pp. 69–70;
  Activity Book Answer Key

Teacher Resource CD-ROM
Assessment Program: Unit 1, Chapter 3 Quiz, pp. 11–12;
  Teacher and Student Resources, pp. 115–144
Assessment CD-ROM: Unit 1, Chapter 3 Quiz
Transparencies
The Heinle Newbury House Dictionary/CD-ROM
Web Site: www.heinle.visions.com

➤ See the Teacher's Edition wrap-around for complete teaching suggestions for each section.

Day 1

- **Unit 1, Chapter 2 Quiz** (Assessment Program, pp. 9–10) 20 MIN.
- **Objectives** (p. 26) 5 MIN.
  Present the chapter objectives.
- **Use Prior Knowledge** (p. 26) 15 MIN.
  Activate prior knowledge about yawning.
- **Build Background** (p. 27) 5 MIN.
  Provide the background information on oxygen.
- **Homework:** KWL (TRB, p. 42); Have students complete the first and second columns based on what they learned in class. Students will complete the third column at the end of the chapter.

Day 2

- **Check Homework** 5 MIN.
  OR
- **Warm Up** 5 MIN.
  Write on the board: List 3 facts about oxygen.
- **Build Vocabulary** (p. 27) 15 MIN.
  Introduce antonyms.
- **Text Structure** (p. 28) 10 MIN.
  Present the text features of an informational text.
- **Reading Strategy** (p. 28) 10 MIN.
  Teach the strategy of comparing the text to your own experiences.
- **Reading Selection Opener** (p. 29) 5 MIN.
  Preview the chapter reading selection.
- **Homework:** Activity Book (p. 17)

Day 3

- **Check Homework** 5 MIN.
  OR
- **Warm Up** 5 MIN.
  Write on the board: Write an antonym for each word.
  a. awake   **d.** loud
  b. easy   **e.** interesting
  c. hot
- **Reading Selection** (pp. 30–33) 25 MIN.
  Have students read the selection and use the reading strategy. Teach spelling, capitalization, and punctuation points on TE pp. 30–33.

- **Reading Comprehension** (p. 34) 10 MIN.
  Have students answer the questions.
- **Build Reading Fluency** (p. 34) 5 MIN.
  Teach how to build reading fluency by using rapid word recognition.
- **Homework:** Activity Book (p. 18)

Day 4

- **Check Homework** 5 MIN.
  OR
- **Warm Up** 5 MIN.
  Write on the board: True or false?
  a. Some animals yawn.
  b. Scientists agree on the reasons why we yawn.
- **Listen, Speak, Interact** (p. 35) 15 MIN.
  Have students give an informational presentation.
- **Elements of Literature** (p. 35) 15 MIN.
  Teach how to recognize direct address.
- **Word Study** (p. 36) 10 MIN.
  Present contractions.
- **Homework:** Activity Book (pp. 19–20)

Day 5

- **Check Homework** 5 MIN.
  OR
- **Warm Up** 5 min.
  Write on the board: Add apostrophes to these sentences.
  a. Its a fish. Its name is George.
  b. Shell yawn when shes sleepy.
- **Grammar Focus** (p. 36) 15 MIN.
  Present dependent clauses.
- **From Reading to Writing** (p. 37) 15 MIN.
  Teach how to write a paragraph using chronology.
- **Across Content Areas** (p. 37) 10 MIN.
  Introduce related math content on reading a bar graph.
- **Homework:** Activity Book (pp. 21–24); Have students complete the third column of the KWL chart from Day 1. Have students study for the Unit 1, Chapter 3 Quiz.

UNIT 1 Mysteries

CHAPTER 4 • The Sneak Thief, by Falcon Travis

Chapter Materials

Activity Book: pp. 25–32
Audio: Unit 1, Chapter 4
Student Handbook
Student CD-ROM: Unit 1, Chapter 4
Teacher Resource Book: Lesson Plan, p. 4; Teacher
    Resources, pp. 35–64; Reading Summaries, pp. 71–72;
    Activity Book Answer Key

Teacher Resource CD-ROM
Assessment Program: Unit 1, Chapter 4 Quiz, pp. 13–14;
    Teacher and Student Resources, pp. 115–144
Assessment CD-ROM: Unit 1, Chapter 4 Quiz
Transparencies
The Heinle Newbury House Dictionary/CD-ROM
Web Site: www.heinle.visions.com

➤ See the Teacher's Edition wrap-around for complete teaching suggestions for each section.

Day 1

- **Unit 1, Chapter 3 Quiz** (Assessment Program, pp. 11–12) 20 MIN.
- **Objectives** (p. 38) 5 MIN.
Present the chapter objectives.
- **Use Prior Knowledge** (p. 38) 15 MIN.
Activate prior knowledge about rules.
- **Build Background** (p. 39) 5 MIN.
Provide the background information on inspectors.
- **Homework:** KWL (TRB, p. 42); Have students complete the first and second columns based on what they learned in class. Students will complete the third column at the end of the chapter.

Day 2

- **Check Homework** 5 min.
OR
- **Warm Up** 5 MIN.
Write on the board: List 3 rules in your school.
- **Build Vocabulary** (p. 39) 15 MIN.
Introduce words related to train travel.
- **Text Structure** (p. 40) 10 MIN.
Present the text features of a mystery.
- **Reading Strategy** (p. 40) 10 MIN.
Teach the strategy of using chronology to locate and recall information.
- **Reading Selection Opener** (p. 41) 5 MIN.
Preview the chapter reading selection.
- **Homework:** Activity Book (p. 25)

Day 3

- **Check Homework** 5 MIN.
OR
- **Warm Up** 5 MIN.
Write on the board: List 4 features of a mystery.
- **Reading Selection** (pp. 42–45) 25 MIN.
Have students read the selection and use the reading strategy. Teach spelling, capitalization, and punctuation points on TE pp. 42–45.
- **Reading Comprehension** (p. 46) 10 MIN.
Have students answer the questions.
- **Build Reading Fluency** (p. 46) 5 MIN.
Teach how to build reading fluency by adjusting the

reading rate for quotations.
- **Homework:** Activity Book (p. 26)

Day 4

- **Check Homework** 5 MIN.
OR
- **Warm Up** 5 MIN.
Write on the board: In "The Sneak Thief," which of these facts helped the inspector solve the mystery?
  a. The thief didn't have a key to the briefcase in his pocket.
  b. He didn't have a return ticket.
  c. He didn't have any way of paying for books.
- **Listen, Speak, Interact** (p. 47) 10 MIN.
Have students interpret a text through dramatization.
- **Elements of Literature** (p. 47) 15 MIN.
Present problems and problem resolution.
- **Word Study** (p. 48) 15 MIN.
Present letter-sound correspondences.
- **Homework:** Activity Book (pp. 27–28)

Day 5

- **Check Homework** 5 MIN.
OR
- **Warm Up** 5 MIN.
Write on the board: Identify the problem and the resolution in these pairs of sentences.
  1. Alicia didn't understand how to do the writing assignment.
  Alicia asked her teacher for help.
  2. Wei-Man borrowed $5 from her brother.
  Wei-Man needed money to buy a birthday present for her mother.
- **Grammar Focus** (p. 48) 15 MIN.
Present simple, compound, and complex sentences.
- **From Reading to Writing** (p. 49) 15 MIN.
Teach how to write dialogue in a mystery.
- **Across Content Areas** (p. 49) 10 MIN.
Introduce related language arts content on the law.
- **Homework:** Activity Book (pp. 29–32); Have students complete the third column of the KWL chart from Day 1. Have students study for the Unit 1, Chapter 4 Quiz.

UNIT 1 Mysteries

CHAPTER 5 • The Legend of Sleepy Hollow, by Washington Irving, and adapted by Jack Kelly

Chapter Materials

Activity Book: pp. 33–40
Audio: Unit 1, Chapter 5
Student Handbook
Student CD-ROM: Unit 1, Chapter 5
Teacher Resource Book: Lesson Plan, p. 5; Teacher Resources, pp. 35–64; Reading Summaries, pp. 73–74; Activity Book Answer Key

Teacher Resource CD-ROM
Assessment Program: Unit 1, Chapter 5 Quiz, pp. 15–16; Teacher and Student Resources, pp. 115–144
Assessment CD-ROM: Unit 1, Chapter 5 Quiz
Transparencies
The Heinle Newbury House Dictionary/CD-ROM
Web Site: www.heinle.visions.com

➤ See the Teacher's Edition wrap-around for complete teaching suggestions for each section.

- **Unit 1, Chapter 4 Quiz** (Assessment Program, pp. 13–14) 20 MIN.
- **Objectives** (p. 50) 5 MIN.
  Present the chapter objectives.
- **Use Prior Knowledge** (p. 50) 15 MIN.
  Activate prior knowledge about oral traditions.
- **Build Background** (p. 51) 5 MIN.
  Provide background on Sleepy Hollow.
- **Homework:** KWL (TRB, p. 42); Have students complete the first and second columns based on what they learned in class. Students will complete the third column at the end of the chapter.

Day 2

- **Check Homework** 5 MIN.
  OR
- **Warm Up** 5 MIN.
  Write on the board: The stories of La Llorona, Atlantis, Rip Van Winkle, and El Dorado are from the _____ _____. They are told from grandparent to _____ to _____.
- **Build Vocabulary** (p. 51) 15 MIN.
  Introduce frequently misspelled words.
- **Text Structure** (p. 52) 10 MIN.
  Present the text features of a legend.
- **Reading Strategy** (p. 52) 10 MIN.
  Teach the strategy of identifying imagery.
- **Reading Selection Opener** (p. 53) 5 MIN.
  Preview the chapter reading selection.
- **Homework:** Activity Book (p. 33)

Day 3

- **Check Homework** 5 MIN.
  OR
- **Warm Up** 5 MIN.
  Write: Fill in the blanks with there, their, or they're.
  _____ is an interesting story about some children. _____ lost in a forest. The animals in the forest help them find _____ way home.
- **Reading Selection** (pp. 54–59) 25 MIN.
  Have students read the selection and use the reading strategy. Teach spelling, capitalization, and

punctuation points on TE pp. 54–59.
- **Reading Comprehension** (p. 60) 10 MIN.
  Have students answer the questions.
- **Build Reading Fluency** (p. 60) 5 MIN.
  Build reading fluency by reading silently.
- **Homework:** Activity Book (p. 34)

Day 4

- **Check Homework** 5 MIN.
  OR
- **Warm Up** 5 MIN.
  Write on the board: Ichabod Crane was a _____ who lived in Sleepy Hollow. He loved to hear the old _____ that people told. Sometimes he would feel very _____ when he was outside during a dark night.
- **Listen, Speak, Interact** (p. 61) 15 MIN.
  Have students talk about the five senses.
- **Elements of Literature** (p. 61) 15 MIN.
  Present setting and tone.
- **Word Study** (p. 62) 10 MIN.
  Present root words and the suffix -less.
- **Homework:** Activity Book (pp. 35–36)

Day 5

- **Check Homework** 5 MIN.
  OR
- **Warm Up** 5 MIN.
  Write on the board: Complete these sentences with the word tone or setting.
  The _____ of a story is where it takes place. An author's _____ shows an attitude toward a person or a topic.
- **Grammar Focus** (p. 62) 15 MIN.
  Present pronoun referents.
- **From Reading to Writing** (p. 63) 15 MIN.
  Teach how to write a character description.
- **Across Content Areas** (p. 63) 10 MIN.
  Introduce related social studies content on reading a timeline.
- **Homework:** Activity Book (pp. 37–40); Have students complete the third column of the KWL chart from Day 1. Have students study for the Unit 1, Chapter 5 Quiz.

UNIT 1 Mysteries

APPLY AND EXPAND

End-of-Unit Materials

Student Handbook
CNN Video: Unit 1
Teacher Resource Book: Lesson Plan, p. 6; Teacher
   Resources, pp. 35–64; Home-School Connection,
   pp. 119–125; Video Script, pp. 161–162; Video
   Worksheet, p. 173
Teacher Resource CD-ROM

Assessment Program: Unit 1 Test, pp. 17–22; Teacher
   and Student Resources, pp. 115–144
Assessment CD-ROM: Unit 1 Test
Transparencies
The Heinle Newbury House Dictionary/CD-ROM
Heinle Reading Library
Web Site: www.heinle.visions.com

➤ See the Teacher's Edition wrap-around for complete teaching suggestions for each section.

Day 1

- **Unit 1, Chapter 5 Quiz** (Assessment Program,
  pp. 15–16) 20 MIN.
- **Listening and Speaking Workshop** (pp. 64–65)
  25 MIN.
  Introduce the assignment of describing an animal.
  Have students prepare their presentations (steps 1–4).
- **Homework:** Have students become familiar with their
  sentences from Step 4 in preparation for Day 2.

Day 2

- **Listening and Speaking Workshop** (pp. 64–65)
  45 MIN.
  Have students practice and present their descriptions
  (steps 5 and 6).
- **Homework:** Have students present their descriptions
  at home.

Day 3

- **Viewing Workshop** (p. 65) 45 MIN.
  Play a mystery video and have students identify the
  problem and resolution and write a summary of the
  story. Show the Visions CNN video for this unit. Have
  students do the Video Worksheet.
- **Homework:** Have students exchange papers and
  evaluate each other's summaries.

Day 4

- **Writer's Workshop** (pp. 66–67) 45 MIN.
  Present the assignment of writing a report
  comparing and contrasting two texts from the unit.
  Have students do the pre-writing activities and write
  a draft (steps 1–4).
- **Homework:** Have students review their drafts in
  preparation for revising them on Day 5.

Day 5

- **Writer's Workshop** (pp. 66–67) 45 MIN.
  Have students revise, edit, and publish their writing
  (steps 5–6).
- **Homework:** Students should have another person
  read their work and get feedback on it.

Day 6

- **Review and Reteach** 45 MIN.
  In small groups, have students list major points from
  the unit. Ask students to choose three points that they
  are least clear on and would like to review. Based on
  results of chapter quizzes and student feedback,
  choose points from the unit to reteach to the class.
- **Homework:** Have students study for the Unit 1 Test.

Day 7

- **Unit 1 Test** (Assessment Program, pp. 17–22) 45 MIN.
  After the Unit 1 Test, reassess student learning.
  Record strong and weak areas based on the unit test.
  Review weak areas before the Mid-Book Exam.

Class _____ Date _____

UNIT 2 Survival

CHAPTER 1 • How I Survived My Summer Vacation, by Robin Friedman

Chapter Materials

Activity Book: pp. 41–48
Audio: Unit 2, Chapter 1
Student Handbook
Student CD-ROM: Unit 2, Chapter 1
Teacher Resource Book: Lesson Plan, p. 7; Teacher
    Resources, pp. 35–64; Reading Summaries, pp. 75–76;
    Activity Book Answer Key

Teacher Resource CD-ROM
Assessment Program: Unit 2, Chapter 1 Quiz, pp. 23–24;
    Teacher and Student Resources, pp. 115–144
Assessment CD-ROM: Unit 2, Chapter 1
Transparencies
The Heinle Newbury House Dictionary/CD–ROM
Web Site: www.heinle.visions.com

➤ See the Teacher's Edition wrap-around for complete teaching suggestions for each section.

Day 1

- **Unit Opener** (pp. 70–71) 20 MIN.
  Preview the unit reading selections. Complete the
  "View the Picture" activity.
- **Objectives** (p. 72) 5 MIN.
  Present the chapter objectives.
- **Use Prior Knowledge** (p. 72) 15 MIN.
  Activate prior knowledge about summer experiences.
- **Build Background** (p. 73) 5 MIN.
  Provide the background information on tofu.
- **Homework:** KWL (TRB, p. 42); Have students
  complete the first and second columns based on what
  they learned in class. Students will complete the third
  column at the end of the chapter.

Day 2

- **Check Homework** 5 MIN.
  OR
- **Warm Up** 5 MIN.
  Write on the board: Tofu is a food made of _____.
- **Build Vocabulary** (p. 73) 15 MIN.
  Introduce the use of precise wording.
- **Text Structure** (p. 74) 10 MIN.
  Present the text features of realistic fiction.
- **Reading Strategy** (p. 74) 10 MIN.
  Teach the strategy of making inferences using text
  evidence and experience.
- **Reading Selection Opener** (p. 75) 5 MIN.
  Preview the chapter reading selection.
- **Homework:** Activity Book (p. 41)

Day 3

- **Check Homework** 5 MIN.
  OR
- **Warm Up** 5 MIN.
  Write on the board: List 3 features of realistic fiction.
- **Reading Selection** (pp. 76–81) 25 MIN.
  Have students read the selection and use the reading
  strategy. Teach spelling, capitalization, and
  punctuation points on TE pp. 76–81.
- **Reading Comprehension** (p. 82) 10 MIN.
  Have students answer the questions.

- **Build Reading Fluency** (p. 82) 5 MIN.
  Teach how to build reading fluency by using audio
  reading practice.
- **Homework:** Activity Book (p. 42)

Day 4

- **Check Homework** 5 MIN.
  OR
- **Warm Up** 5 MIN.
  Write on the board: True or false?
  a. In the story, Jackie wants to write a biography.
  b. Jackie is having trouble writing.
  c. Jackie's parents want to send him to a camp for
      writers.
- **Listen, Speak, Interact** (p. 83) 15 MIN.
  Have students predict a part of the story.
- **Elements of Literature** (p. 83) 15 MIN.
  Present plot.
- **Word Study** (p. 84) 10 MIN.
  Present words with Latin roots.
- **Homework:** Activity Book (pp. 43–44)

Day 5

- **Check Homework** 5 MIN.
  OR
- **Warm Up** 5 MIN.
  Write on the board: Choose the correct meaning of
  predict.
  a. To tell the truth.
  b. To tell something that you think happened in the
      past.
  c. To tell something that you think will happen in the
      present.
- **Grammar Focus** (p. 84) 15 MIN.
  Present progressive tenses.
- **From Reading to Writing** (p. 85) 15 MIN.
  Teach how to write realistic fiction.
- **Across Content Areas** (p. 85) 10 MIN.
  Introduce related science content on food groups.
- **Homework:** Activity Book (pp. 45–48); Have students
  complete the third column of the KWL chart from Day
  1. Have students study for the Unit 2, Chapter 1 Quiz.

UNIT 2 Survival

CHAPTER 2 • The Voyage of the *Frog*, by Gary Paulsen

Chapter Materials

Activity Book: pp. 49–56
Audio: Unit 2, Chapter 2
Student Handbook
Student CD-ROM: Unit 2, Chapter 2
Teacher Resource Book: Lesson Plan, p. 8; Teacher
　Resources, pp. 35–64; Reading Summaries, pp. 77–78;
　Activity Book Answer Key

Teacher Resource CD-ROM
Assessment Program: Unit 2, Chapter 2 Quiz, pp. 25–26;
　Teacher and Student Resources, pp. 115–144
Assessment CD-ROM: Unit 2, Chapter 2
Transparencies
The Heinle Newbury House Dictionary/CD-ROM
Web Site: www.heinle.visions.com

➤ **See the Teacher's Edition wrap-around for complete teaching suggestions for each section.**

Day 1

- **Unit 2, Chapter 1 Quiz** (Assessment Program, pp. 23–24) 20 MIN.
- **Objectives** (p. 86) 5 MIN.
  Present the chapter objectives.
- **Use Prior Knowledge** (p. 86) 15 MIN.
  Activate prior knowledge about dangerous weather.
- **Build Background** (p. 87) 5 MIN.
  Provide the background information on sailboats.
- **Homework:** KWL (TRB, p. 42); Have students complete the first and second columns based on what they learned in class. Students will complete the third column at the end of the chapter.

Day 2

- **Check Homework** 5 MIN.
  OR
- **Warm Up** 5 MIN.
  Write on the board: List 3 kinds of dangerous weather.
- **Build Vocabulary** (p. 87) 15 MIN.
  Introduce using reference sources.
- **Text Structure** (p. 88) 10 MIN.
  Present the text features of an adventure story.
- **Reading Strategy** (p. 88) 10 MIN.
  Teach the strategy of recognizing tone and mood.
- **Reading Selection Opener** (p. 89) 5 MIN.
  Preview the chapter reading selection.
- **Homework:** Activity Book (p. 49)

Day 3

- **Check Homework** 5 MIN.
  OR
- **Warm Up** 5 MIN.
  Write on the board: List 3 features of an adventure story.
- **Reading Selection** (pp. 90–97) 25 MIN.
  Have students read the selection and use the reading strategy. Teach spelling, capitalization, and punctuation points on TE pp. 90–97.
- **Reading Comprehension** (p. 98) 10 MIN.
  Have students answer the questions.

- **Build Reading Fluency** (p. 98) 5 MIN.
  Teach how to build reading fluency by adjusting your reading rate for quotations.
- **Homework:** Activity Book (p. 50)

Day 4

- **Check Homework** 5 MIN.
  OR
- **Warm Up** 5 MIN.
  Write on the board: Do you think that the captain of the ship admired David? Why or why not?
- **Listen, Speak, Interact** (p. 99) 15 MIN.
  Have students conduct an interview.
- **Elements of Literature** (p. 99) 15 MIN.
  Present problem resolution.
- **Word Study** (p. 100) 10 MIN.
  Present the suffix -*ly*.
- **Homework:** Activity Book (pp. 51–52)

Day 5

- **Check Homework** 5 MIN.
  OR
- **Warm Up** 5 MIN.
  Write on the board:
  1. Complete these sentences with <u>soft</u> or <u>softly</u>.
  a. He spoke in a _____ voice.
  b. He spoke _____.
  2. Complete these sentences with <u>happy</u> or <u>happily</u>.
  a. Mom smiled _____.
  b. She was _____.
- **Grammar Focus** (p. 100) 10 MIN.
  Present the future tense.
- **From Reading to Writing** (p. 101) 20 MIN.
  Teach how to write a story to resolve a problem.
- **Across Content Areas** (p. 101) 10 MIN.
  Introduce related social studies content on finding compass directions.
- **Homework:** Activity Book (pp. 53–56); Have students complete the third column of the KWL chart from Day 1. Have students study for the Unit 2, Chapter 2 Quiz.

Class _____ Date _____

UNIT 2 Survival

CHAPTER 3 • To Risk or Not to Risk, by David Ropeik

Chapter Materials

Activity Book: pp. 57–64
Audio: Unit 2, Chapter 3
Student Handbook
Student CD-ROM: Unit 2, Chapter 3
Teacher Resource Book: Lesson Plan, p. 9; Teacher
   Resources, pp. 35–64; Reading Summaries, pp. 79–80;
   Activity Book Answer Key

Teacher Resource CD-ROM
Assessment Program: Unit 2, Chapter 3 Quiz, pp. 27–28;
   Teacher and Student Resources, pp. 115–144
Assessment CD-ROM: Unit 2, Chapter 3
Transparencies
The Heinle Newbury House Dictionary/CD-ROM
Web Site: www.heinle.visions.com

➤ See the Teacher's Edition wrap-around for complete teaching suggestions for each section.

Day 1

• **Unit 2, Chapter 2 Quiz** (Assessment Program,
  pp. 25–26) 20 MIN.
• **Objectives** (p. 102) 5 MIN.
  Present the chapter objectives.
• **Use Prior Knowledge** (p. 102) 15 MIN.
  Activate prior knowledge about risks.
• **Build Background** (p. 103) 5 MIN.
  Provide the background information on the brain.
• **Homework:** KWL (TRB, p. 42); Have students
  complete the first and second columns based on what
  they learned in class. Students will complete the third
  column at the end of the chapter.

Day 2

• **Check Homework** 5 MIN.
  OR
• **Warm Up** 5 MIN.
  Write on the board: List 1 thing that you think is very
  risky and 1 thing that you think is only a little risky.
• **Build Vocabulary** (p. 103) 15 MIN.
  Introduce learning vocabulary through reading.
• **Text Structure** (p. 104) 10 MIN.
  Present the text features of an informational text.
• **Reading Strategy** (p. 104) 10 MIN.
  Teach the strategy of distinguishing fact from opinion.
• **Reading Selection Opener** (p. 105) 5 MIN.
  Preview the chapter reading selection.
• **Homework:** Activity Book (p. 57)

Day 3

• **Check Homework** 5 MIN.
  OR
• **Warm Up** 5 MIN.
  Write on the board: True or false?
  a. An informational text explains a topic.
  b. A fact is something that might be true—we don't
     know for sure.
  c. Informational texts sometimes ask questions.
• **Reading Selection** (pp. 106–111) 25 MIN.
  Have students read the selection and use the reading

strategy. Teach spelling, capitalization, and
punctuation points on TE pp. 106–111.
• **Reading Comprehension** (p. 112) 10 MIN.
  Have students answer the questions.
• **Build Reading Fluency** (p. 112) 5 MIN.
  Build reading fluency by reading silently.
• **Homework:** Activity Book (p. 58)

Day 4

• **Check Homework** 5 MIN.
  OR
• **Warm Up** 5 MIN.
  Write on the board: The author of "To Risk or Not to
  Risk" says that our fears are more important than the
  facts. Do you agree or disagree?
• **Listen, Speak, Interact** (p. 113) 15 MIN.
  Have students compare personal experiences.
• **Elements of Literature** (p. 113) 15 MIN.
  Present transition words.
• **Word Study** (p. 114) 10 MIN.
  Present the prefixes *over-* and *under-*
• **Homework:** Activity Book (pp. 59–60)

Day 5

• **Check Homework** 5 MIN.
  OR
• **Warm Up** 5 MIN.
  Write on the board: Put <u>over</u> or <u>under</u> in the blanks.
  a. If a car gets too hot, it is _____ heated.
  b. If you are not paid enough, you are _____ paid.
  c. If food isn't cooked enough, it is _____ done.
  d. If you paid too much, you were _____ charged.
• **Grammar Focus** (p. 114) 15 MIN.
  Present subject-verb agreement in the present tense.
• **From Reading to Writing** (p. 115) 15 MIN.
  Teach how to write an informational text.
• **Across Content Areas** (p. 115) 10 MIN.
  Introduce related social studies content on
  psychology.
• **Homework:** Activity Book (pp. 61–64); Have students
  complete the third column of the KWL chart from
  Day 1. Have students study for the Unit 2,
  Chapter 3 Quiz.

Class _____ Date _____

UNIT 2 Survival

CHAPTER 4 • Island of the Blue Dolphins, by Scott O'Dell

Chapter Materials

Activity Book: pp. 65–72
Audio: Unit 2, Chapter 4
Student Handbook
Student CD-ROM: Unit 2, Chapter 4
Teacher Resource Book: Lesson Plan, p. 10; Teacher
   Resources, pp. 35–64; Reading Summaries, pp. 81–82;
   Activity Book Answer Key

Teacher Resource CD-ROM
Assessment Program: Unit 2, Chapter 4 Quiz, pp. 29–30;
   Teacher and Student Resources, pp. 115–144
Assessment CD-ROM: Unit 2, Chapter 4
Transparencies
The Heinle Newbury House Dictionary/CD-ROM
Web Site: www.heinle.visions.com

➤ See the Teacher's Edition wrap-around for complete teaching suggestions for each section.

Day 1

- **Unit 1, Chapter 3 Quiz** (Assessment Program, pp. 27–28) 20 MIN.
- **Objectives** (p. 116) 5 MIN.
  Present the chapter objectives.
- **Use Prior Knowledge** (p. 116) 15 MIN.
  Activate prior knowledge about needs and wants.
- **Build Background** (p. 117) 5 MIN.
  Provide the background information on the lost woman of San Nicolas Island.
- **Homework:** KWL (TRB, p. 42); Have students complete the first and second columns based on what they learned in class. Students will complete the third column at the end of the chapter.

Day 2

- **Check Homework** 5 MIN.
  OR
- **Warm Up** 5 MIN.
  Write on the board: Write 2 things you learned about the lost woman of San Nicolas Island.
- **Build Vocabulary** (p. 117) 15 MIN.
  Show how to locate pronunciations of words.
- **Text Structure** (p. 118) 10 MIN.
  Present the text features of fiction based on a true story.
- **Reading Strategy** (p. 118) 10 MIN.
  Teach the strategy of paraphrasing to recall information.
- **Reading Selection Opener** (p. 119) 5 MIN.
  Preview the chapter reading selection.
- **Homework:** Activity Book (p. 65)

Day 3

- **Check Homework** 5 MIN.
  OR
- **Warm Up** 5 MIN.
  Write on the board: You can find meanings and pronunciations of words in a _____. _____ are shown with symbols. Some _____ are like letters of the alphabet. Others are different. Some letters in words, like the _g_ in gnaw, are _____.

Day 4 (column)

- **Reading Selection** (pp. 120–125) 25 MIN.
  Have students read the selection and use the reading strategy. Teach spelling, capitalization, and punctuation points on TE pp. 120–125.
- **Reading Comprehension** (p. 126) 10 MIN.
  Have students answer the questions.
- **Build Reading Fluency** (p. 126) 5 MIN.
  Teach how to build reading fluency by reading aloud to engage listeners.
- **Homework:** Activity Book (p. 66)

Day 4

- **Check Homework** 5 MIN.
  OR
- **Warm Up** 5 MIN.
  Write on the board: List 3 things that she made to satisfy her needs on the island.
- **Listen, Speak, Interact** (p. 127) 15 MIN.
  Have students compare ways of working.
- **Elements of Literature** (p. 127) 15 MIN.
  Teach how to compare and contrast themes and ideas across texts.
- **Word Study** (p. 128) 10 MIN.
  Present the spelling of frequently misspelled words.
- **Homework:** Activity Book (pp. 67–68)

Day 5

- **Check Homework** 5 MIN.
  OR
- **Warm Up** 5 MIN.
  Write on the board: Write three sentences using the words _two, too,_ and _to._
- **Grammar Focus** (p. 128) 15 MIN.
  Present the past and past perfect tenses.
- **From Reading to Writing** (p. 129) 15 MIN.
  Teach how to write instructions.
- **Across Content Areas** (p. 129) 10 MIN.
  Introduce related arts content on game rules.
- **Homework:** Activity Book (pp. 69–72); Have students complete the third column of the KWL chart from Day 1. Have students study for the Unit 2, Chapter 4 Quiz.

UNIT 2 Survival

CHAPTER 5 • The Next Great Dying, by Karin Vergoth and Christopher Lampton

Chapter Materials

Activity Book: pp. 73–80
Audio: Unit 2, Chapter 5
Student Handbook
Student CD-ROM: Unit 2, Chapter 5
Teacher Resource Book: Lesson Plan, p. 11; Teacher
  Resources, pp. 35–64; Reading Summaries, pp. 83–84;
  Activity Book Answer Key

Teacher Resource CD-ROM
Assessment Program: Unit 2, Chapter 5 Quiz, pp. 31–32;
  Teacher and Student Resources, pp. 115–144
Assessment CD-ROM: Unit 2, Chapter 5
Transparencies
The Heinle Newbury House Dictionary/CD-ROM
Web Site: www.heinle.visions.com

➤ See the Teacher's Edition wrap-around for complete teaching suggestions for each section.

Day 1

- **Unit 2, Chapter 4 Quiz** (Assessment Program, pp. 29–30) 20 MIN.
- **Objectives** (p. 130) 5 MIN.
  Present the chapter objectives.
- **Use Prior Knowledge** (p. 130) 15 MIN.
  Activate prior knowledge about plants and animals.
- **Build Background** (p. 131) 5 MIN.
  Provide background on endangered species.
- **Homework:** KWL (TRB, p. 42); Have students complete the first and second columns based on what they learned in class. Students will complete the third column at the end of the chapter.

Day 2

- **Check Homework** 5 MIN.
  OR
- **Warm Up** 5 MIN.
  Write: Animals that are very rare and that might disappear completely are called _____ species. One example of an endangered species is the _____.
- **Build Vocabulary** (p. 131) 15 MIN.
  Introduce the use of a word wheel.
- **Text Structure** (p. 132) 10 MIN.
  Present the text features of an informational text.
- **Reading Strategy** (p. 132) 10 MIN.
  Teach the strategy of identifying cause and effect.
- **Reading Selection Opener** (p. 133) 5 MIN.
  Preview the chapter reading selection.
- **Homework:** Activity Book (p. 73)

Day 3

- **Check Homework** 5 MIN.
  OR
- **Warm Up** 5 MIN.
  Write on the board: Which of the following is NOT a part of most informational texts: facts, examples, rhyme, definitions, plot.
- **Reading Selection** (pp. 134–139) 25 MIN.
  Have students read the selection and use the reading strategy. Teach spelling, capitalization, and punctuation points on TE pp. 134–139.

- **Reading Comprehension** (p. 140) 10 MIN.
  Have students answer the questions.
- **Build Reading Fluency** (p. 140) 5 MIN.
  Build reading fluency by rapid word recognition.
- **Homework:** Activity Book (p. 74)

Day 4

- **Check Homework** 5 MIN.
  OR
- **Warm Up** 5 MIN.
  Write on the board: Write two sentences that the author would probably agree with.
- **Listen, Speak, Interact** (p. 141) 15 MIN.
  Have students talk about conserving natural resources.
- **Elements of Literature** (p. 141) 15 MIN.
  Present deductive and inductive organization and presentation.
- **Word Study** (p. 142) 10 MIN.
  Present the suffix -ion
- **Homework:** Activity Book (pp. 75–76)

Day 5

- **Check Homework** 5 MIN.
  OR
- **Warm Up** 5 MIN.
  Write: Fill in the blanks with <u>deductive</u> or <u>inductive</u>.
  a. If you give the facts first and state your point later, you are using _____ organization.
  b. If you state your point first and then give your facts, you are using _____ organization.
- **Grammar Focus** (p. 142) 15 MIN.
  Present dependent clauses.
- **From Reading to Writing** (p. 143) 15 MIN.
  Teach how to write an informational text.
- **Across Content Areas** (p. 143) 10 MIN.
  Introduce related social studies content on reading a timeline.
- **Homework:** Activity Book (pp. 77–80); Have students complete the third column of the KWL chart from Day 1. Have students study for the Unit 2, Chapter 5 Quiz.

UNIT 2 Survival

APPLY AND EXPAND

End of Unit Materials

Student Handbook
CNN Video: Unit 2
Teacher Resource Book: Lesson Plan, p. 12; Teacher Resources, pp. 35–64; Home-School Connection, pp. 126–132; Video Script, pp. 163–164; Video Worksheet, p. 174
Teacher Resource CD-ROM

Assessment Program: Unit 2 Test, pp. 33–38; Teacher and Student Resources, pp. 115–144
Assessment CD-ROM: Unit 2 Test
Transparencies
The Heinle Newbury House Dictionary/CD-ROM
Heinle Reading Library
Web Site: www.heinle.visions.com

➤ See the Teacher's Edition wrap-around for complete teaching suggestions for each section.

Day 1

- **Unit 2, Chapter 5 Quiz** (Assessment Program, pp. 31–32) 20 MIN.
- **Listening and Speaking Workshop** (pp. 144–145) 25 MIN.
  Introduce the assignment of role-playing an interview with a scientist. Have students gather information for their interviews (steps 1–3).
- **Homework:** Have students practice the questions and answers orally.

Day 2

- **Listening and Speaking Workshop** (pp. 144–145) 45 MIN.
  Have students practice and present their interviews (steps 4–5). Record each interview if possible.
- **Homework:** Have students take their recordings home to share with their families.

Day 3

- **Viewing Workshop** (p. 145) 45 MIN.
  Have students look at pictures and/or diagrams from the unit and analyze how these add to meaning. Show the Visions CNN video for this unit. Have students do the Video Worksheet.
- **Homework:** Have students write a paragraph in which they summarize their findings about the visuals that they chose to examine.

Day 4

- **Writer's Workshop** (pp. 146–147) 45 MIN.
  Present the assignment of writing a survival manual for new students at their school. Have students do pre-writing preparation and write a draft (steps 1–4).
- **Homework:** Have students review their drafts in preparation for revising them on Day 5.

Day 5

- **Writer's Workshop** (pp. 146–147) 45 MIN.
  Have students add pictures, revise, edit, and publish their writing (steps 5–7).
- **Homework:** Have students get feedback on their manuals from other students in the school.

Day 6

- **Review and Reteach** 45 MIN.
  In small groups, have students list major points from the unit. Ask students to choose three points that they are least clear on and would like to review. Based on results of chapter quizzes and student feedback, choose points from the unit to reteach to the class.
- **Homework:** Have students study for the Unit 2 Test.

Day 7

- **Unit 2 Test** (Assessment Program, pp. 33–38) 45 MIN.
  After the Unit 2 Test, reassess student learning. Record strong and weak areas based on the unit test. Review weak areas before the Mid-Book Exam.

UNIT 3 Journeys

CHAPTER 1 • I Have No Address, by Hamza El Din

Chapter Materials

Activity Book: pp. 81–92
Audio: Unit 3, Chapter 1
Student Handbook
Student CD-ROM: Unit 3, Chapter 1
Teacher Resource Book: Lesson Plan, p. 13; Teacher
    Resources, pp. 35–64; Reading Summaries, pp. 85–86;
    Activity Book Answer Key

Teacher Resource CD-ROM
Assessment Program: Unit 3, Chapter 1 Quiz, pp. 39–40;
    Teacher and Student Resources, pp. 115–144
Assessment CD-ROM: Unit 3, Chapter 1
Transparencies
The Heinle Newbury House Dictionary/CD-ROM
Web Site: www.heinle.visions.com

➤ See the Teacher's Edition wrap-around for complete teaching suggestions for each section.

Day 1

- **Unit Opener** (pp. 150–151) 20 MIN.
  Preview the unit reading selections. Complete the
  "View the Picture" activity.
- **Objectives** (p. 152) 5 MIN.
  Present the chapter objectives.
- **Use Prior Knowledge** (p. 152) 15 MIN.
  Activate prior knowledge about journeys.
- **Build Background** (p. 153) 5 MIN.
  Provide the background information on song
  sparrows.
- **Homework:** KWL (TRB, p. 42); Have students
  complete the first and second columns based on what
  they learned in class. Students will complete the third
  column at the end of the chapter.

Day 2

- **Check Homework** 5 MIN.
  OR
- **Warm Up** 5 MIN.
  Write on the board: List 3 facts about the kind of
  birds called sparrows.
- **Build Vocabulary** (p. 153) 15 MIN.
  Introduce multiple-meaning words.
- **Text Structure** (p. 154) 10 MIN.
  Present the text features of a poem.
- **Reading Strategy** (p. 154) 10 MIN.
  Teach the strategy of recognizing figurative language.
- **Reading Selection Opener** (p. 155) 5 MIN.
  Preview the chapter reading selection.
- **Homework:** Activity Book (p. 81)

Day 3

- **Check Homework** 5 MIN.
  OR
- **Warm Up** 5 MIN.
  Write on the board: True or false?
  a. Figurative language means exactly what the
     words say.
  b. A metaphor is a type of figurative language.
- **Reading Selection** (pp. 156–157) 25 MIN.
  Have students read the selection and use the reading

strategy. Teach spelling, capitalization, and
punctuation points on TE pp. 156–157.
- **Reading Comprehension** (p. 158) 10 MIN.
  Have students answer the questions.
- **Build Reading Fluency** (p. 158) 5 MIN.
  Teach how to build reading fluency by using echo
  read aloud.
- **Homework:** Activity Book (p. 82)

Day 4

- **Check Homework** 5 MIN.
  OR
- **Warm Up** 5 MIN.
  Write on the board: In the poem, "I Have No
  Address," the poet compares himself to a _____.
- **Listen, Speak, Interact** (p. 159) 20 MIN.
  Have students draw and present images.
- **Elements of Literature** (p. 159) 10 MIN.
  Teach how to recognize style, tone, and mood.
- **Word Study** (p. 160) 10 MIN.
  Present the suffix -ity.
- **Homework:** Activity Book (pp. 83–84)

Day 5

- **Check Homework** 5 MIN.
  OR
- **Warm Up** 5 MIN.
  Write on the board: Style is how authors use _____ to
  express themselves. _____ is the author's attitude
  towards the topic. Mood is the _____ you get from
  reading a text.
- **Grammar Focus** (p. 160) 15 MIN.
  Present apostrophes with possessive nouns.
- **From Reading to Writing** (p. 161) 15 MIN.
  Teach how to write a poem using figurative language.
- **Across Content Areas** (p. 161) 10 MIN.
  Introduce related science content on migration of
  birds.
- **Homework:** Activity Book (pp. 85–88); Have students
  complete the third column of the KWL chart from
  Day 1. Have students study for the Unit 3, Chapter 1
  Quiz.

Class _____ Date _____

UNIT 3 Journeys

CHAPTER 2 • The Voyage of the Lucky Dragon, by Jack Bennett

Chapter Materials

Activity Book: pp. 89–96
Audio: Unit 3, Chapter 2
Student Handbook
Student CD-ROM: Unit 3, Chapter 2
Teacher Resource Book: Lesson Plan, p. 14; Teacher
    Resources, pp. 35–64; Reading Summaries, pp. 87–88;
    Activity Book Answer Key

Teacher Resource CD-ROM
Assessment Program: Unit 3, Chapter 2 Quiz, pp. 41–42;
    Teacher and Student Resources, pp. 115–144
Assessment CD-ROM: Unit 3, Chapter 2
Transparencies
The Heinle Newbury House Dictionary/CD-ROM
Web Site: www.heinle.visions.com

➤ See the Teacher's Edition wrap-around for complete teaching suggestions for each section.

Day 1

- **Unit 3, Chapter 1 Quiz** (Assessment Program, pp. 39–40) 20 MIN.
- **Objectives** (p. 162) 5 MIN.
  Present the chapter objectives.
- **Use Prior Knowledge** (p. 162) 15 MIN.
  Activate prior knowledge about problems.
- **Build Background** (p. 163) 5 MIN.
  Provide the background information on Vietnam.
- **Homework:** KWL (TRB, p. 42); Have students complete the first and second columns based on what they learned in class. Students will complete the third column at the end of the chapter.

Day 2

- **Check Homework** 5 MIN.
  OR
- Warm Up 5 MIN.
  Write on the board: A war within a country is called a _____ _____. What are some countries that have had a war like this. Use the letters to help you.
  V _ _ _ _ _ _   K _ r _ _
  The U _ _ _ ed S _ _ _ _ s
- **Build Vocabulary** (p. 163) 15 MIN.
  Introduce words related to emotions.
- **Text Structure** (p. 164) 10 MIN.
  Present the text features of historical fiction.
- **Reading Strategy** (p. 164) 10 MIN.
  Teach the strategy of paraphrasing to recall information.
- **Reading Selection Opener** (p. 165) 5 MIN.
  Preview the chapter reading selection.
- **Homework:** Activity Book (p. 89)

Day 3

- **Check Homework** 5 MIN.
  OR
- **Warm Up** 5 MIN.
  Write on the board: List 3 features of historical fiction.
- **Reading Selection** (pp. 166–173) 25 MIN.
  Have students read the selection and use the reading

strategy. Teach spelling, capitalization, and punctuation points on TE pp. 166–173.
- **Reading Comprehension** (p. 174) 10 MIN.
  Have students answer the questions.
- **Build Reading Fluency** (p. 174) 5 MIN.
  Build reading fluency by reading silently and aloud.
- **Homework:** Activity Book (p. 90)

Day 4

- **Check Homework** 5 MIN.
  OR
- **Warm Up** 5 MIN.
  Write on the board: At the end of the excerpt from "The Voyage of the Lucky Dragon," what did the family decide to do? Why?
- **Listen, Speak, Interact** (p. 175) 15 MIN.
  Have students debate whether the family should stay.
- **Elements of Literature** (p. 175) 15 MIN.
  Present mood.
- **Word Study** (p. 176) 10 MIN.
  Present the prefix un-.
- **Homework:** Activity Book (pp. 91–92)

Day 5

- **Check Homework** 5 MIN.
  OR
- **Warm Up** 5 MIN.
  Write: When authors create a feeling such as suspense or fear, it is called _____. What moods did you feel as you read this selection?
- **Grammar Focus** (p. 176) 15 MIN.
  Present subject and object pronouns.
- **From Reading to Writing** (p. 177) 15 MIN.
  Teach how to write to solve a problem.
- **Across Content Areas** (p. 177) 10 MIN.
  Introduce related social studies content describing countries on a map.
- Homework: Activity Book (pp. 93–96); Have students complete the third column of the KWL chart from Day 1. Have students study for the Unit 3, Chapter 2 Quiz.

UNIT 3 Journeys

CHAPTER 3 • The Time Bike, by Jane Langton

Chapter Materials

Activity Book: pp. 97–104
Audio: Unit 3, Chapter 3
Student Handbook
Student CD-ROM: Unit 3, Chapter 3
Teacher Resource Book: Lesson Plan, p. 15; Teacher
  Resources, pp. 35–64; Reading Summaries, pp. 89–90;
  Activity Book Answer Key

Teacher Resource CD-ROM
Assessment Program: Unit 3, Chapter 3 Quiz, pp. 43–44;
  Teacher and Student Resources, pp. 115–144
Assessment CD-ROM: Unit 3, Chapter 3
Transparencies
The Heinle Newbury House Dictionary/CD-ROM
Web Site: www.heinle.visions.com

➤ See the Teacher's Edition wrap-around for complete teaching suggestions for each section.

Day 1

- **Unit 3, Chapter 2 Quiz** (Assessment Program, pp. 41–42) 20 MIN.
- **Objectives** (p. 178) 5 MIN.
  Present the chapter objectives.
- **Use Prior Knowledge** (p. 178) 15 MIN.
  Activate prior knowledge about gifts.
- **Build Background** (p. 179) 5 MIN.
  Provide the background information on time.
- **Homework:** KWL (TRB, p. 42); Have students complete the first and second columns based on what they learned in class. Students will complete the third column at the end of the chapter.

Day 2

- **Check Homework** 5 MIN.
  OR
- **Warm Up** 5 MIN.
  Write on the board: List 3 ways to find out what time it is.
- **Build Vocabulary** (p. 179) 15 MIN.
  Introduce using context to understand new words.
- **Text Structure** (p. 180) 10 MIN.
  Present the text features of science fiction.
- **Reading Strategy** (p. 180) 10 MIN.
  Teach the strategy of predicting.
- **Reading Selection Opener** (p. 181) 5 MIN.
  Preview the chapter reading selection.
- **Homework:** Activity Book (p. 97)

Day 3

- **Check Homework** 5 MIN.
  OR
- **Warm Up** 5 MIN.
  Write on the board: True or false?
  a. Science fiction sometimes shows how science can make life different in the future.
  b. In science fiction, all of the events and people are real.
- **Reading Selection** (pp. 182–187) 25 MIN.
  Have students read the selection and use the reading

strategy. Teach spelling, capitalization, and punctuation points on TE pp. 182–187.
- **Reading Comprehension** (p. 188) 10 MIN.
  Have students answer the questions.
- **Build Reading Fluency** (p. 188) 5 MIN.
  Teach how to build reading fluency by using repeated reading.
- **Homework:** Activity Book (p. 98)

Day 4

- **Check Homework** 5 MIN.
  OR
- **Warm Up** 5 MIN.
  Write on the board: Who gave the bike to Eddy? How is it different from other bikes?
- **Listen, Speak, Interact** (p. 189) 15 MIN.
  Have students give a presentation.
- **Elements of Literature** (p. 189) 15 MIN.
  Present foreshadowing.
- **Word Study** (p. 190) 10 MIN.
  Present the prefix *bi-*.
- **Homework:** Activity Book (pp. 99–100)

Day 5

- **Check Homework** 5 MIN.
  OR
- **Warm Up** 5 MIN.
  Write on the board: Sometimes authors give clues about what will happen later in the story. This is called _____.
- **Grammar Focus** (p. 190) 15 MIN.
  Present contractions.
- **From Reading to Writing** (p. 191) 15 MIN.
  Teach how to write a description.
- **Across Content Areas** (p. 191) 10 MIN.
  Introduce related social studies content on time zones.
- **Homework:** Activity Book (pp. 101–104); Have students complete the third column of the KWL chart from Day 1. Have students study for the Unit 3, Chapter 3 Quiz.

UNIT 3 Journeys

CHAPTER 4 • Why We Can't Get There From Here, by Neil de Grasse Tyson

Chapter Materials

Activity Book: pp. 105–112
Audio: Unit 3, Chapter 4
Student Handbook
Student CD-ROM: Unit 3, Chapter 4
Teacher Resource Book: Lesson Plan, p. 16; Teacher
Resources, pp. 35–64; Reading Summaries, pp. 91–92;
Activity Book Answer Key

Teacher Resource CD-ROM
Assessment Program: Unit 3, Chapter 4 Quiz, pp. 45–46;
Teacher and Student Resources, pp. 115–144
Assessment CD-ROM: Unit 3, Chapter 4
Transparencies
The Heinle Newbury House Dictionary/CD-ROM
Web Site: www.heinle.visions.com

➤ See the Teacher's Edition wrap-around for complete teaching suggestions for each section.

Day 1

- **Unit 3, Chapter 3 Quiz** (Assessment Program, pp. 43–44) 20 MIN.
- **Objectives** (p. 192) 5 MIN.
Present the chapter objectives.
- **Use Prior Knowledge** (p. 192) 15 MIN.
Activate prior knowledge about ways to travel.
- **Build Background** (p. 193) 5 MIN.
Provide the background information on space.
- **Homework:** KWL (TRB, p. 42); Have students complete the first and second columns based on what they learned in class. Students will complete the third column at the end of the chapter.

Day 2

- **Check Homework** 5 MIN.
OR
- **Warm Up** 5 MIN.
Write on the board: List 3 things that are in space.
- **Build Vocabulary** (p. 193) 15 MIN.
Introduce applying knowledge of root words.
- **Text Structure** (p. 194) 10 MIN.
Present the text features of an informational text.
- **Reading Strategy** (p. 194) 10 MIN.
Teach the strategy of using preview questions, rereading, and recording.
- **Reading Selection Opener** (p. 195) 5 MIN.
Preview the chapter reading selection.
- **Homework:** Activity Book (p. 105)

Day 3

- **Check Homework** 5 MIN.
OR
- **Warm Up** 5 MIN.
Write on the board: Copy these words and underline the root words.
  - **a.** unmanned   **c.** preview   **e.** disrespect
  - **b.** rewrite   **d.** unable
- **Reading Selection** (pp. 196–199) 25 MIN.
Have students read the selection and use the reading strategy. Teach spelling, capitalization, and punctuation points on TE pp. 194–199.

- **Reading Comprehension** (p. 200) 10 MIN.
Have students answer the questions.
- **Build Reading Fluency** (p. 200) 5 MIN.
Build reading fluency by adjusting reading rate to scan.
- **Homework:** Activity Book (p. 106)

Day 4

- **Check Homework** 5 MIN.
OR
- **Warm Up** 5 MIN.
Write on the board: Write 2 sentences that you think the author of "Why We Can't Get There From Here" would agree with.
- **Listen, Speak, Interact** (p. 201) 15 MIN.
Have students listen to an informational text.
- **Elements of Literature** (p. 201) 15 MIN.
Teach organization and presentation of ideas.
- **Word Study** (p. 202) 10 MIN.
Present the suffix -est.
- **Homework:** Activity Book (pp. 107–108)

Day 5

- **Check Homework** 5 MIN.
OR
- **Warm Up** 5 MIN.
Write on the board: Complete the sentences with the word contrast or compare.
When you show how things are the same, you _____ them. When you show how they are different, you _____ them.
- **Grammar Focus** (p. 202) 15 MIN.
Present superlative adjectives.
- **From Reading to Writing** (p. 203) 15 MIN.
Teach how to use multiple resources to write a research report.
- **Across Content Areas** (p. 203) 10 MIN.
Introduce related math content on solving a time problem.
- **Homework:** Activity Book (pp. 109–112); Have students complete the third column of the KWL chart from Day 1. Have students study for the Unit 3, Chapter 4 Quiz.

Class _____ Date _____

UNIT 3 Journeys

CHAPTER 5 • The California Gold Rush, by Pam Zollman
Dame Shirley and the Gold Rush, by Jim Rawls

Chapter Materials

Activity Book: pp. 113–120
Audio: Unit 3, Chapter 5
Student Handbook
Student CD-ROM: Unit 3, Chapter 5
Teacher Resource Book: Lesson Plan, p. 17; Teacher
  Resources, pp. 35–64; Reading Summaries, pp. 93–94;
  Activity Book Answer Key

Teacher Resource CD-ROM
Assessment Program: Unit 3, Chapter 5 Quiz, pp. 47–48;
  Teacher and Student Resources, pp. 115–144
Assessment CD-ROM: Unit 3, Chapter 5
Transparencies
The Heinle Newbury House Dictionary/CD-ROM
Web Site: www.heinle.visions.com

➤ See the Teacher's Edition wrap-around for complete teaching suggestions for each section.

Day 1

- **Unit 3, Chapter 4 Quiz** (Assessment Program,
  pp. 45–46) 20 MIN.
- **Objectives** (p. 204) 5 MIN.
  Present the chapter objectives.
- **Use Prior Knowledge** (p. 204) 15 MIN.
  Activate prior knowledge about challenges.
- **Build Background** (p. 205) 5 MIN.
  Provide the background information on the frontier.
- **Homework:** KWL (TRB, p. 42); Have students
  complete the first and second columns based on what
  they learned in class. Students will complete the third
  column at the end of the chapter.

Day 2

- **Check Homework** 5 MIN.
  OR
- **Warm Up** 5 MIN.
  Write on the board: List 3 natural resources.
- **Build Vocabulary** (p. 205) 15 MIN.
  Introduce systematic study of words.
- **Text Structure** (p. 206) 10 MIN.
  Present the text features of nonfiction and biography.
- **Reading Strategy** (p. 206) 10 MIN.
  Teach the strategy of comparing and contrasting.
- **Reading Selection Opener** (p. 207) 5 MIN.
  Preview the chapter reading selections.
- **Homework:** Activity Book (p. 113)

Day 3

- **Check Homework** 5 MIN.
  OR
- **Warm Up** 5 MIN.
  Write on the board: _____ is usually about real facts
  and events. A biography is a kind of nonfiction that is
  mostly about a person's _____ .
- **Reading Selections** (pp. 208–213) 25 MIN.
  Have students read the selections and use the reading
  strategy. Teach spelling, capitalization, and
  punctuation points on TE pp. 208–213.

- **Reading Comprehension** (p. 214) 10 MIN.
  Have students answer the questions.
- **Build Reading Fluency** (p. 214) 5 MIN.
  Teach how to build reading fluency by reading silently.
- **Homework:** Activity Book (p. 114)

Day 4

- **Check Homework** 5 MIN.
  OR
- **Warm Up** 5 MIN.
  Write on the board: List 2 things that are the same
  about "The California Gold Rush" and "Dame Shirley
  and the Gold Rush."
- **Listen, Speak, Interact** (p. 215) 15 MIN.
  Have students present the story of a journey.
- **Elements of Literature** (p. 215) 15 MIN.
  Teach how to analyze character traits and motivation.
- **Word Study** (p. 216) 10 MIN.
  Present learning words from context and experience.
  Homework: Activity Book (pp. 115–116)

Day 5

- **Check Homework** 5 MIN.
  OR
- **Warm Up** 5 MIN.
  Write on the board: Fill in the blanks with the words
  traits or motivation.
  a. _____ is why a character does something.
  b. _____ are what a character is like.
- **Grammar Focus** (p. 216) 10 MIN.
  Present adverbs.
- **From Reading to Writing** (p. 217) 20 MIN.
  Teach how to compare and contrast two reading
  selections.
- **Across Content Areas** (p. 217) 10 MIN.
  Introduce related science content on natural
  resources.
- **Homework:** Activity Book (pp. 117–120); Have
  students complete the third column of the KWL chart
  from Day 1. Have students study for the Unit 3,
  Chapter 5 Quiz.

Class _____ Date _____

UNIT 3 Journeys

APPLY AND EXPAND

End-of-Unit Materials

Student Handbook
CNN Video: Unit 3
Teacher Resource Book: Lesson Plan, p. 18; Teacher
  Resources, pp. 35–64; Home-School Connection,
  pp. 133–139; Video Script, pp. 165–166; Video
  Worksheet, p. 175
Teacher Resource CD-ROM
Assessment Program: Unit 3 Test, pp. 49–54; Mid-Book

Exam, pp. 55–60; Teacher and Student Resources,
  pp. 115–144
Assessment CD-ROM: Unit 3 Test, Mid-Book Exam
Transparencies
The Heinle Newbury House Dictionary/CD-ROM
Heinle Reading Library
Web Site: www.heinle.visions.com

➤ See the Teacher's Edition wrap-around for complete teaching suggestions for each section.

Day 1

- **Unit 3, Chapter 5 Quiz** (Assessment Program,
  pp. 47–48) 20 MIN.
- **Listening and Speaking Workshop** (pp. 218–219)
  25 MIN.
  Introduce the assignment of giving a presentation
  about a place. Have students do the preparation
  (steps 1–4).
- **Homework:** Have students familiarize themselves with
  their material in preparation for Day 2.

Day 2

- **Listening and Speaking Workshop** (pp. 218–219)
  45 MIN.
  Have students practice and give presentations (steps
  5–6). If possible, record the presentations on audio or
  video.
- **Homework:** Have students give their presentations to
  their families in person, or on video or audio.

Day 3

- **Viewing Workshop** (p. 219) 45 MIN.
  Show a video about another culture and have students
  analyze it. Show the Visions CNN video for this unit.
  Have students do the Video Worksheet.
- **Homework:** Have students write a paragraph in which
  they summarize their findings about the video.

Day 4

- **Writer's Workshop** (pp. 220–221) 45 MIN.
  Present the assignment of writing a report about a
  famous place that people made a journey to in the
  history of the United States. Have students do pre-
  writing preparation and write a draft (steps 1–4).
- **Homework:** Have students review their drafts in
  preparation for revising them on Day 5.

Day 5

- **Writer's Workshop** (pp. 220–221) 45 MIN.
  Have students revise, edit, and publish their writing
  (steps 5–7).
- **Homework:** Have students take their writing home to
  share with their families.

Day 6

- **Review and Reteach** 45 MIN.
  In small groups, have students list major points from
  the unit. Ask students to choose three points that they
  are least clear on and would like to review. Based on
  results of chapter quizzes and student feedback,
  choose points from the unit to reteach to the class.
- **Homework:** Have students study for the Unit 3 Test.

Day 7

- **Unit 3 Test** (Assessment Program, pp. 49–54) 45 MIN.
  After the Unit 3 Test, reassess student learning.
  Record strong and weak areas based on the unit test.
  Review weak areas before the Mid-Book Exam.
- **Homework:** Have students study for the Mid-Book
  Exam.

Day 8

- **Mid-Book Exam** (Assessment Program, pp. 55–60)
  45 MIN.

UNIT 4 Cycles

CHAPTER 1 • Water Dance, by Thomas Locker

Chapter Materials

Activity Book: pp. 121–128
Audio: Unit 4, Chapter 1
Student Handbook
Student CD-ROM: Unit 4, Chapter 1
Teacher Resource Book: Lesson Plan, p. 19; Teacher
   Resources, pp. 35–64; Reading Summaries, pp. 95–96;
   Activity Book Answer Key

Teacher Resource CD-ROM
Assessment Program: Unit 4, Chapter Quiz, pp. 61–62;
   Teacher and Student Resources, pp. 115–144
Assessment CD-ROM: Unit 4, Chapter 1
Transparencies
The Heinle Newbury House Dictionary/CD-ROM
Web Site: www.heinle.visions.com

➤ See the Teacher's Edition wrap-around for complete teaching suggestions for each section.

Day 1

- **Unit Opener** (pp. 224–225) 20 MIN.
  Preview the unit reading selections. Complete the
  "View the Picture" activity.
- **Objectives** (p. 226) 5 MIN.
  Present the chapter objectives.
- **Use Prior Knowledge** (p. 226) 15 MIN.
  Activate prior knowledge about uses of water.
- **Build Background** (p. 227) 5 MIN.
  Provide the background information on the water
  cycle.
- **Homework:** KWL (TRB, p. 42); Have students
  complete the first and second columns based on what
  they learned in class. Students will complete the third
  column at the end of the chapter.

Day 2

- **Check Homework** 5 MIN.
  OR
- **Warm Up** 5 MIN.
  Write on the board: Number these steps of the water
  cycle in order.
    __1__ The sun warms the earth.
    _____ The water falls back to the surface of the Earth
       as rain.
    _____ The water forms clouds in the sky.
    _____ The water on the Earth evaporates.
- **Build Vocabulary** (p. 227) 15 MIN.
  Introduce vivid verbs.
- **Text Structure** (p. 228) 10 MIN.
  Present the text features of a poem.
- **Reading Strategy** (p. 228) 10 MIN.
  Teach the strategy of describing mental images.
- **Reading Selection Opener** (p. 229) 5 MIN.
  Preview the chapter reading selection.
- **Homework:** Activity Book (p. 121)

Day 3

- **Check Homework** 5 MIN.
  OR
- **Warm Up** 5 MIN.
  Write on the board: What are the 5 senses?

- **Reading Selection** (pp. 230–233) 25 MIN.
  Have students read the selection and use the reading
  strategy. Teach spelling, capitalization, and
  punctuation points on TE pp. 230–233.
- **Reading Comprehension** (p. 234) 10 MIN.
  Have students answer the questions.
- **Build Reading Fluency** (p. 234) 5 MIN.
  Teach how to build reading fluency by reading aloud
  to engage listeners.
- **Homework:** Activity Book (p. 122)

Day 4

- **Check Homework** 5 MIN.
  OR
- **Warm Up** 5 MIN.
  Write on the board: In the poem "Water Dance," who
  is "I"?
- **Listen, Speak, Interact** (p. 235) 15 MIN.
  Have students respond to mood.
- **Elements of Literature** (p. 235) 15 MIN.
  Present figurative language.
- **Word Study** (p. 236) 10 MIN.
  Present denotative and connotative meanings.
- **Homework:** Activity Book (pp. 123–124)

Day 5

- **Check Homework** 5 MIN.
  OR
- **Warm Up** 5 MIN.
  Write on the board: When authors give something
  human characteristics, it is a figure of speech called
  _____.
- **Grammar Focus** (p. 236) 15 MIN.
  Present comparative adjectives.
- **From Reading to Writing** (p. 237) 15 MIN.
  Teach how to write a poem.
- **Across Content Areas** (p. 237) 10 MIN.
  Introduce related math content on calculating
  averages.
- **Homework:** Activity Book (pp. 125–128); Have
  students complete the third column of the KWL chart
  from Day 1. Have students study for the Unit 4,
  Chapter 1 Quiz.

UNIT 4 Cycles

CHAPTER 2 • Persephone and the Seasons, by Heather Amery

Chapter Materials

Activity Book: pp. 129–136
Audio: Unit 4, Chapter 2
Student Handbook
Student CD-ROM: Unit 4, Chapter 2
Teacher Resource Book: Lesson Plan, p. 20; Teacher
  Resources, pp. 35–64; Reading Summaries, pp. 97–98;
  Activity Book Answer Key

Teacher Resource CD-ROM
Assessment Program: Unit 4, Chapter 2 Quiz, pp. 63–64;
  Teacher and Student Resources, pp. 115–144
Assessment CD-ROM: Unit 4, Chapter 2
Transparencies
The Heinle Newbury House Dictionary/CD-ROM
Web Site: www.heinle.visions.com

➤ See the Teacher's Edition wrap-around for complete teaching suggestions for each section.

Day 1

• **Unit 4, Chapter 1 Quiz** (Assessment Program,
  pp. 61–62) 20 MIN.
• **Objectives** (p. 238) 5 MIN.
  Present the chapter objectives.
• **Use Prior Knowledge** (p. 238) 15 MIN.
  Activate prior knowledge about the seasons.
• **Build Background** (p. 239) 5 MIN.
  Provide the background information on hemispheres
  and the seasons.
• **Homework:** KWL (TRB, p. 42); Have students
  complete the first and second columns based on what
  they learned in class. Students will complete the third
  column at the end of the chapter.

Day 2

• **Check Homework** 5 MIN.
  OR
• **Warm Up** 5 MIN.
  Write on the board: Fill in the blank with <u>warmer</u> or
  <u>colder.</u>
  The hemisphere of the Earth that turns away from the
  sun is _____ than the hemisphere that turns toward
  the sun.
• **Build Vocabulary** (p. 239) 15 MIN.
  Introduce using a dictionary to find definitions,
  pronunciations, and derivations.
• **Text Structure** (p. 240) 10 MIN.
  Present the text features of a myth.
• **Reading Strategy** (p. 240) 10 MIN.
  Teach the strategy of using chronology to locate and
  recall information.
• **Reading Selection Opener** (p. 241) 5 MIN.
  Preview the chapter reading selection.
• **Homework:** Activity Book (p. 129)

Day 3

• **Check Homework** 5 MIN.
  OR
• **Warm Up** 5 MIN.
  Write on the board: List the features of a myth.
• **Reading Selection** (pp. 242–245) 25 MIN.

Have students read the selection and use the reading
strategy. Teach spelling, capitalization, and
punctuation points on TE pp. 242–245.
• **Reading Comprehension** (p. 246) 10 MIN.
  Have students answer the questions.
• **Build Reading Fluency** (p. 246) 5 MIN.
  Teach how to build reading fluency by reading silently
  and aloud.
• **Homework:** Activity Book (p. 130)

Day 4

• **Check Homework** 5 MIN.
  OR
• **Warm Up** 5 MIN.
  Write on the board: Summarize the story of
  Persephone in two or three sentences.
• **Listen, Speak, Interact** (p. 247) 15 MIN.
  Have students act out a story.
• **Elements of Literature** (p. 247) 15 MIN.
  Present foreshadowing.
• **Word Study** (p. 248) 10 MIN.
  Present contractions.
• **Homework:** Activity Book (pp. 131–132)

Day 5

• **Check Homework** 5 MIN.
  OR
• **Warm Up** 5 MIN.
  Write on the board: Add apostrophes to these
  sentences.
  a. Persephone didnt want to stay with Pluto.
  b. Pluto said, "You cant leave. I wont let you leave."
• **Grammar Focus** (p. 248) 15 MIN.
  Present irregular past tense verbs.
• **From Reading to Writing** (p. 249) 15 MIN.
  Teach how to summarize and paraphrase to inform.
• **Across Content Areas** (p. 249) 10 MIN.
  Introduce related language arts content on the
  meanings of *myth*.
• **Homework:** Activity Book (pp. 133–136); Have
  students complete the third column of the KWL chart
  from Day 1. Have students study for the Unit 4,
  Chapter 2 Quiz.

UNIT 4 Cycles

CHAPTER 3 • The Circuit, by Francisco Jiménez

Chapter Materials

Activity Book: pp. 137–144
Audio: Unit 4, Chapter 3
Student Handbook
Student CD-ROM: Unit 4, Chapter 3
Teacher Resource Book: Lesson Plan, p. 21; Teacher
  Resources, pp. 35–64; Reading Summaries,
  pp. 99–100; Activity Book Answer Key

Teacher Resource CD-ROM
Assessment Program: Unit 4, Chapter 3 Quiz, pp. 65–66;
  Teacher and Student Resources, pp. 115–144
Assessment CD-ROM: Unit 4, Chapter 3
Transparencies
The Heinle Newbury House Dictionary/CD-ROM
Web Site: www.heinle.visions.com

➤ See the Teacher's Edition wrap-around for complete teaching suggestions for each section.

Day 1

- **Unit 4, Chapter 2 Quiz** (Assessment Program, pp. 63–64) 20 MIN.
- **Objectives** (p. 250) 5 MIN.
  Present the chapter objectives.
- **Use Prior Knowledge** (p. 250) 15 MIN.
  Activate prior knowledge about moving.
- **Build Background** (p. 251) 5 MIN.
  Provide the background information on farming in the United States.
- **Homework:** KWL (TRB, p. 42); Have students complete the first and second columns based on what they learned in class. Students will complete the third column at the end of the chapter.

Day 2

- **Check Homework** 5 MIN.
  OR
- **Warm Up** 5 MIN.
  Write on the board: True or false.
  a. Machines can pick all of the crops that farmers grow.
  b. Migrant workers work on just one farm all year long.
- **Build Vocabulary** (p. 251) 15 MIN.
  Study word origins and guess meanings from context.
- **Text Structure** (p. 252) 10 MIN.
  Present the text features of an autobiographical short story.
- **Reading Strategy** (p. 252) 10 MIN.
  Teach the strategy of comparing the text to your own knowledge and experience.
- **Reading Selection Opener** (p. 253) 5 MIN.
  Preview the chapter reading selection.
- **Homework:** Activity Book (p. 137)

Day 3

- **Check Homework** 5 MIN.
  OR
- **Warm Up** 5 MIN.
  Write on the board: In an autobiographical short story, the author uses the pronouns _____, _____, _____, and _____. This is called _____ person point of view.

- **Reading Selection** (pp. 254–259) 25 MIN.
  Have students read the selection and use the reading strategy. Teach spelling, capitalization, and punctuation points on TE pp. 254–259.
- **Reading Comprehension** (p. 260) 10 MIN.
  Have students answer the questions.
- **Build Reading Fluency** (p. 260) 5 MIN.
  Teach how to build reading fluency by using rapid word recognition.
- **Homework:** Activity Book (p. 138)

Day 4

- **Check Homework** 5 MIN.
  OR
- **Warm Up** 5 MIN.
  Write on the board: List 3 things that happened to the author in "The Circuit."
- **Listen, Speak, Interact** (p. 261) 10 MIN.
  Have students present an experience.
- **Elements of Literature** (p. 261) 20 MIN.
  Present language use to show characterization.
- **Word Study** (p. 262) 10 MIN.
  Present applying letter-sound correspondences.
- **Homework:** Activity Book (pp. 139–140)

Day 5

- **Check Homework** 5 MIN.
  OR
- **Warm Up** 5 MIN.
  Write on the board: Sometimes you can tell if a person is educated or not by the way he or she uses _____.
- **Grammar Focus** (p. 262) 15 MIN.
  Present dependent clauses.
- **From Reading to Writing** (p. 263) 15 MIN.
  Teach how to write a letter to an author.
- **Across Content Areas** (p. 263) 10 MIN.
  Introduce related language arts content on the influence of other languages on English.
- **Homework:** Activity Book (pp. 141–144); Have students complete the third column of the KWL chart from Day 1. Have students study for the Unit 4, Chapter 3 Quiz.

UNIT 4 Cycles

CHAPTER 4 • The Elements of Life, by Paul Bennett

Chapter Materials

Activity Book: pp. 145–152
Audio: Unit 4, Chapter 4
Student Handbook
Student CD-ROM: Unit 4, Chapter 4
Teacher Resource Book: Lesson Plan, p. 22; Teacher
    Resources, pp. 35–64; Reading Summaries,
    pp. 101–102; Activity Book Answer Key

Teacher Resource CD-ROM
Assessment Program: Unit 4, Chapter 4 Quiz, pp. 67–68;
    Teacher and Student Resources, pp. 115–144
Assessment CD-ROM: Unit 4, Chapter 4
Transparencies
The Heinle Newbury House Dictionary/CD-ROM
Web Site: www.heinle.visions.com

➤ See the Teacher's Edition wrap-around for complete teaching suggestions for each section.

Day 1

- **Unit 4, Chapter 3 Quiz** (Assessment Program, pp. 65–66) 20 MIN.
- **Objectives** (p. 264) 5 MIN.
  Present the chapter objectives.
- **Use Prior Knowledge** (p. 264) 15 MIN.
  Activate prior knowledge about living and nonliving things.
- **Build Background** (p. 265) 5 MIN.
  Provide the background information on elements.
- **Homework:** KWL (TRB, p. 42); Have students complete the first and second columns based on what they learned in class. Students will complete the third column at the end of the chapter.

Day 2

- **Check Homework** 5 MIN.
  OR
- **Warm Up** 5 MIN.
  Write on the board: Write 2 things you learned about the elements.
- **Build Vocabulary** (p. 265) 15 MIN.
  Introduce science terms.
- **Text Structure** (p. 266) 10 MIN.
  Present the text features of an informational text.
- **Reading Strategy** (p. 266) 10 MIN.
  Teach the strategy of finding the main idea and supporting details.
- **Reading Selection Opener** (p. 267) 5 MIN.
  Preview the chapter reading selection.
- **Homework:** Activity Book (p. 145)

Day 3

- **Check Homework** 5 MIN.
  OR
- **Warm Up** 5 MIN.
  Write on the board: A process tells how something _____ and in what _____ order.
- **Reading Selection** (pp. 268–271) 25 MIN.
  Have students read the selection and use the reading strategy. Teach spelling, capitalization, and punctuation points on TE pp. 268–271.

- **Reading Comprehension** (p. 272) 10 MIN.
  Have students answer the questions.
- **Build Reading Fluency** (p. 272) 5 MIN.
  Teach how to build reading fluency by adjusting your reading rate to scan.
- **Homework:** Activity Book (p. 146)

Day 4

- **Check Homework** 5 MIN.
  OR
- **Warm Up** 5 MIN.
  Write on the board: The author of "The Elements of Life" says that in nature the elements are recycled. What does he mean by this? Choose the correct answer.
  a. We will run out of them in the future.
  b. They are used over and over again.
  c. They are not important.
- **Listen, Speak, Interact** (p. 273) 15 MIN.
  Have students listen and take notes.
- **Elements of Literature** (p. 273) 15 MIN.
  Teach how to use a diagram.
- **Word Study** (p. 274) 10 MIN.
  Present word origins and roots.
- **Homework:** Activity Book (pp. 147–148)

Day 5

- **Check Homework** 5 MIN.
  OR
- **Warm Up** 5 MIN.
  Write on the board: What root word is the same in all of these words? What does the root word mean? bicycle, recycle, motorcycle
- **Grammar Focus** (p. 274) 15 MIN.
  Present the active and passive voices.
- **From Reading to Writing** (p. 275) 15 MIN.
  Teach how to write a process and create a diagram.
- **Across Content Areas** (p. 275) 10 MIN.
  Introduce related science content on symbols for elements.
- **Homework:** Activity Book (pp. 149–152); Have students complete the third column of the KWL chart from Day 1. Have students study for the Unit 4, Chapter 4 Quiz.

UNIT 4 Cycles

APPLY AND EXPAND

End-of-Unit Materials

Student Handbook
CNN Video: Unit 4
Teacher Resource Book: Lesson Plan; p. 23; Teacher
   Resources, pp. 35–64; Home-School Connection,
   pp. 140–146; Video Script, pp. 167–168; Video
   Worksheet, p. 176
Teacher Resource CD-ROM

Assessment Program: Unit 4 Test, pp. 69–74; Teacher
   and Student Resources, pp. 115–144
Assessment CD-ROM: Unit 4 Test
Transparencies
The Heinle Newbury House Dictionary/CD-ROM
Heinle Reading Library
Web Site: www.heinle.visions.com

➤ See the Teacher's Edition wrap-around for complete teaching suggestions for each section.

Day 1

- **Unit 4, Chapter 4 Quiz** (Assessment Program,
  pp. 67–68) 20 MIN.
- **Listening and Speaking Workshop** (pp. 276–277)
  25 MIN.
  Introduce the assignment of giving a presentation
  about a cycle. Have students organize and prepare
  their presentations (steps 1–4).
- **Homework:** Have students review and practice their
  reports to present the next day.

Day 2

- **Listening and Speaking Workshop** (pp. 276–277)
  45 MIN.
  Have students practice and give their presentations
  to the class (steps 5–6).
- **Homework:** Have students give their presentations at
  home to their families.

Day 3

- **Viewing Workshop** (p. 277) 45 MIN.
  Explain the week-long survey of television and
  internet weather news. Have students conduct their
  surveys and report. Show the Visions CNN video for
  this unit. Have students do the Video Worksheet.
- **Homework:** Students should conduct their surveys as
  homework.

Day 4

- **Writer's Workshop** (pp. 278–279) 45 MIN.
  Present the writing assignment of comparing and
  contrasting the stories "Persephone and the Seasons"
  and "The Circuit." Have students do pre-writing
  preparation and write a draft (steps 1–2).
- **Homework:** Have students review their drafts in
  preparation for revising them on Day 5.

Day 5

- **Writer's Workshop** (pp. 278–279) 45 MIN.
  Have students revise, edit, and publish their writing
  (steps 3–5).
- **Homework:** Have students take their writing home to
  share with their families.

Day 6

- **Review and Reteach** 45 MIN.
  In small groups, have students list major points from
  the unit. Ask students to choose three points that they
  are least clear on and would like to review. Based on
  results of chapter quizzes and student feedback,
  choose points from the unit to reteach to the class.
- **Homework:** Have students study for the Unit 4 Test.

Day 7

- **Unit 4 Test** (Assessment Program, pp. 69–74) 45 MIN.
  After the Unit 4 Test, reassess student learning.
  Record strong and weak areas based on the unit test.
  Review weak areas before the End-of-Book Exam.

UNIT 5 Freedom

CHAPTER 1 • Rosa Parks, by Andrea Davis Pinkney

Chapter Materials

Activity Book: pp. 153–160
Audio: Unit 5, Chapter 1
Student Handbook
Student CD-ROM: Unit 5, Chapter 1
Teacher Resource Book: Lesson Plan, p. 24; Teacher
   Resources, pp. 35-64; Reading Summaries,
   pp. 103–104; Activity Book Answer Key

Teacher Resource CD-ROM
Assessment Program: Unit 5, Chapter 1 Quiz, pp. 75–76;
   Teacher and Student Resources, pp. 115–144
Assessment CD-ROM: Unit 5, Chapter 1
Transparencies
The Heinle Newbury House Dictionary/CD-ROM
Web Site: www.heinle.visions.com

➤ See the Teacher's Edition wrap-around for complete teaching suggestions for each section.

Day 1

- **Unit Opener** (pp. 282–283) 20 MIN.
  Preview the unit reading selections. Complete the
  "View the Picture" activity.
- **Objectives** (p. 284) 5 MIN.
  Present the chapter objectives.
- **Use Prior Knowledge** (p. 284) 15 MIN.
  Activate prior knowledge about fairness.
- **Build Background** (p. 285) 5 MIN.
  Provide background on segregation in the U.S.
- **Homework:** KWL (TRB, p. 42); Have students
  complete the first and second columns based on what
  they learned in class. Students will complete the third
  column at the end of the chapter.

Day 2

- **Check Homework** 5 MIN.
  OR
- **Warm Up** 5 MIN.
  Write on the board: Write 2 sentences about
  segregation.
- **Build Vocabulary** (p. 285) 15 MIN.
  Introduce using note cards to remember meaning.
- **Text Structure** (p. 286) 10 MIN.
  Present the text features of a biography.
- **Reading Strategy** (p. 286) 10 MIN.
  Teach the strategy of making inferences using text
  evidence.
- **Reading Selection Opener** (p. 287) 5 MIN.
  Preview the chapter reading selection.
- **Homework:** Activity Book (p. 153)

Day 3

- **Check Homework** 5 MIN.
  OR
- **Warm Up** 5 MIN.
  Write on the board: Which of these features is NOT
  usually in a biography?
  dates, events, important people, made-up people
- **Reading Selection** (pp. 288–295) 25 MIN.
  Have students read the selection and use the reading

strategy. Teach spelling, capitalization, and
punctuation points on TE pp. 288–295.
- **Reading Comprehension** (p. 296) 10 MIN.
  Have students answer the questions.
- **Build Reading Fluency** (p. 296) 5 MIN.
  Build reading fluency by reading silently and aloud.
- **Homework:** Activity Book (p. 154)

Day 4

- **Check Homework** 5 MIN.
  OR
- **Warm Up** 5 MIN.
  Write on the board: Write 2 facts about Rosa Parks.
- **Listen, Speak, Interact** (p. 297) 15 MIN.
  Have students present reactions.
- **Elements of Literature** (p. 297) 15 MIN.
  Present style.
- **Word Study** (p. 298) 10 MIN.
  Present the suffix -ment.
- **Homework:** Activity Book (pp. 155–156)

Day 5

- **Check Homework** 5 MIN.
  OR
- **Warm Up** 5 MIN.
  Write on the board: Choose the best completion for
  this sentence:
  The author's style in "Rosa Parks" sounds like . . .
  a. she is telling a story.
  b. she is giving an important speech.
  c. she is writing something for school.
- **Grammar Focus** (p. 298) 15 MIN.
  Present regular and irregular past tense verbs.
- **From Reading to Writing** (p. 299) 15 MIN.
  Teach how to write a biography.
- **Across Content Areas** (p. 299) 10 MIN.
  Introduce related social studies content on
  constitutional amendments.
- **Homework:** Activity Book (pp. 157–160); Have
  students complete the third column of the KWL
  chart from Day 1. Have students study for the
  Unit 5, Chapter 1 Quiz.

Class _____ Date _____

UNIT 5 Freedom

CHAPTER 2 • The Gettysburg Address, by Kenneth Richards

Chapter Materials

Activity Book: pp. 161–168
Audio: Unit 5, Chapter 2
Student Handbook
Student CD-ROM: Unit 5, Chapter 2
Teacher Resource Book: Lesson Plan, p. 25; Teacher
  Resources, pp. 35–64; Reading Summaries,
  pp. 105–106; Activity Book Answer Key

Teacher Resource CD-ROM
Assessment Program: Unit 5, Chapter 2 Quiz, pp. 77–78;
  Teacher and Student Resources, pp. 115–144
Assessment CD-ROM: Unit 5, Chapter 2
Transparencies
The Heinle Newbury House Dictionary/CD-ROM
Web Site: www.heinle.visions.com

➤ See the Teacher's Edition wrap-around for complete teaching suggestions for each section.

Day 1

- **Unit 5, Chapter 1 Quiz** (Assessment Program, pp. 75–76) 20 MIN.
- **Objectives** (p. 300) 5 MIN.
  Present the chapter objectives.
- **Use Prior Knowledge** (p. 300) 15 MIN.
  Activate prior knowledge about civil wars.
- **Build Background** (p. 301) 5 MIN.
  Provide the background information on the U.S. Civil War.
- **Homework:** KWL (TRB, p. 42); Have students complete the first and second columns based on what they learned in class. Students will complete the third column at the end of the chapter.

Day 2

- **Check Homework** 5 MIN.
  OR
- **Warm Up** 5 MIN.
  Write on the board: List 3 facts about the U.S. Civil War.
- **Build Vocabulary** (p. 301) 15 MIN.
  Introduce using Word Squares to remember meaning.
- **Text Structure** (p. 302) 10 MIN.
  Present the text features of a historical narrative and a speech.
- **Reading Strategy** (p. 302) 10 MIN.
  Teach the strategy of summarizing and paraphrasing.
- **Reading Selection Opener** (p. 303) 5 MIN.
  Preview the chapter reading selection.
- **Homework:** Activity Book (p. 161)

Day 3

- **Check Homework** 5 MIN.
  OR
- **Warm Up** 5 MIN.
  Write on the board: List 2 features of a historical narrative and 2 features of a speech.
- **Reading Selection** (pp. 304–311) 25 MIN.
  Have students read the selection and use the reading strategy. Teach spelling, capitalization, and punctuation points on TE pp. 304–311.

- **Reading Comprehension** (p. 312) 10 MIN.
  Have students answer the questions.
- **Build Reading Fluency** (p. 312) 5 MIN.
  Teach how to build reading fluency by adjusting your rate to memorize.
- **Homework:** Activity Book (p. 162)

Day 4

- **Check Homework** 5 MIN.
  OR
- **Warm Up** 5 MIN.
  Write on the board: Lincoln opens the Gettysburg Address with the words "Four score and seven years ago." What does this mean? Choose the correct answer.
  a. 97 years   **c.** 87 years
  b. 40 years
- **Listen, Speak, Interact** (p. 313) 15 MIN.
  Have students give a speech.
- **Elements of Literature** (p. 313) 15 MIN.
  Teach how to analyze the delivery of a speech.
- **Word Study** (p. 314) 10 MIN.
  Present the suffix -or.
- **Homework:** Activity Book (pp. 163–164)

Day 5

- **Check Homework** 5 MIN.
  OR
- **Warm Up** 5 MIN.
  Write on the board: Complete these sentences.
  a. A person who creates is a <u>creator</u>.
  b. A person who acts is an _____.
  c. A person who decorates is a _____.
- **Grammar Focus** (p. 314) 15 MIN.
  Present verb + object + infinitive phrases.
- **From Reading to Writing** (p. 315) 15 MIN.
  Teach how to write a news article.
- **Across Content Areas** (p. 315) 10 MIN.
  Introduce related math vocabulary content.
- **Homework:** Activity Book (pp. 165–168); Have students complete the third column of the KWL chart from Day 1. Have students study for the Unit 5, Chapter 2 Quiz.

UNIT 5 Freedom

CHAPTER 3 • So Far from the Bamboo Grove, by Yoko Kawashima Watkins

Chapter Materials

Activity Book: pp. 169–176
Audio: Unit 5, Chapter 3
Student Handbook
Student CD-ROM: Unit 5, Chapter 3
Teacher Resource Book: Lesson Plan, p. 26; Teacher
   Resources, pp. 35–64; Reading Summaries,
   pp. 107–108; Activity Book Answer Key

Teacher Resource CD-ROM
Assessment Program: Unit 5, Chapter 3 Quiz, pp. 79–80;
   Teacher and Student Resources, pp. 115–144
Assessment CD-ROM: Unit 5, Chapter 3
Transparencies
The Heinle Newbury House Dictionary/CD-ROM
Web Site: www.heinle.visions.com

➤ **See the Teacher's Edition wrap-around for complete teaching suggestions for each section.**

Day 1

- **Unit 5, Chapter 2 Quiz** (Assessment Program, pp. 77–78) 20 MIN.
- **Objectives** (p. 316) 5 MIN.
  Present the chapter objectives.
- **Use Prior Knowledge** (p. 316) 15 MIN.
  Activate prior knowledge about getting help.
- **Build Background** (p. 317) 5 MIN.
  Provide the background information on World War II and Korea.
- **Homework:** KWL (TRB, p. 42); Have students complete the first and second columns based on what they learned in class. Students will complete the third column at the end of the chapter.

Day 2

- **Check Homework** 5 MIN.
  OR
- **Warm Up** 5 MIN.
  Write on the board: Complete the sentences with these words: difficult, Korea, like, Japanese, World War II. During _____, Japan controlled Korea. Most Koreans did not _____ this. Many _____ people tried to get out of _____, but this was _____.
- **Build Vocabulary** (p. 317) 15 MIN.
  Introduce using text features.
- **Text Structure** (p. 318) 10 MIN.
  Present the text features of fiction based on a true story.
- **Reading Strategy** (p. 318) 10 MIN.
  Teach the strategy of predicting.
- **Reading Selection Opener** (p. 319) 5 MIN.
  Preview the chapter reading selection.
- **Homework:** Activity Book (p. 169)

Day 3

- **Check Homework** 5 MIN.
  OR
- **Warm Up** 5 MIN.
  Write on the board: In "So Far from the Bamboo Grove," there are words in Korean. These words are printed in _____ type. Words from another language are usually printed in italic _____.

- **Reading Selection** (pp. 320–325) 25 MIN.
  Have students read the selection and use the reading strategy. Teach spelling, capitalization, and punctuation points on TE pp. 320–325.
- **Reading Comprehension** (p. 326) 10 MIN.
  Have students answer the questions.
- **Build Reading Fluency** (p. 326) 5 MIN.
  Teach how to build reading fluency by doing repeated reading.
- **Homework:** Activity Book (p. 170)

Day 4

- **Check Homework** 5 MIN.
  OR
- **Warm Up** 5 MIN.
  Write on the board: True or false?
  a. Hideo was a Korean boy.
  b. A Korean family was kind to him.
  c. In the end, he was able to escape.
- **Listen, Speak, Interact** (p. 327) 15 MIN.
  Have students present a story about danger.
- **Elements of Literature** (p. 327) 15 MIN.
  Present character motivation.
- **Word Study** (p. 328) 10 MIN.
  Present the Latin root word *grat*.
- **Homework:** Activity Book (pp. 171–172)

Day 5

- **Check Homework** 5 MIN.
  OR
- **Warm Up** 5 MIN.
  Write on the board: The reasons why a character does something is his or her _____.
- **Grammar Focus** (p. 328) 15 MIN.
  Present the conjunction *so that* to connect ideas.
- **From Reading to Writing** (p. 329) 15 MIN.
  Teach how to write a historical fiction story.
- **Across Content Areas** (p. 329) 10 MIN.
  Introduce related language arts content on punctuation and intonation.
- **Homework:** Activity Book (pp. 173–176); Have students complete the third column of the KWL chart from Day 1. Have students study for the Unit 5, Chapter 3 Quiz.

UNIT 5 Freedom

CHAPTER 4 • Alone & Samantha's Story, by Samantha Abeel

Chapter Materials

Activity Book: pp. 177–184
Audio: Unit 5, Chapter 4
Student Handbook
Student CD-ROM: Unit 5, Chapter 4
Teacher Resource Book: Lesson Plan, p. 27; Teacher Resources, pp. 35–64; Reading Summaries, pp. 109–110; Activity Book Answer Key

Teacher Resource CD-ROM
Assessment Program: Unit 5, Chapter 4 Quiz, pp. 81–82; Teacher and Student Resources, pp. 115–144
Assessment CD-ROM: Unit 5, Chapter 4
Transparencies
The Heinle Newbury House Dictionary/CD-ROM
Web Site: www.heinle.visions.com

➤ See the Teacher's Edition wrap-around for complete teaching suggestions for each section.

Day 1

- **Unit 5, Chapter 3 Quiz** (Assessment Program, pp. 79–80) 20 MIN.
- **Objectives** (p. 330) 5 MIN.
  Present the chapter objectives.
- **Use Prior Knowledge** (p. 330) 15 MIN.
  Activate prior knowledge about strengths and weaknesses.
- **Build Background** (p. 331) 5 MIN.
  Provide background on learning disabilities.
- **Homework:** KWL (TRB, p. 42); Have students complete the first and second columns based on what they learned in class. Students will complete the third column at the end of the chapter.

Day 2

- **Check Homework** 5 MIN.
  OR
- **Warm Up** 5 MIN.
  Write on the board: Fill in the blanks with these words: learning disability, trouble, smart, help. Some people who have _____ learning have a _____. They can be very _____, but they need _____ to overcome their disability.
- **Build Vocabulary** (p. 331) 15 MIN.
  Introduce correct spelling of frequently misspelled words.
- **Text Structure** (p. 332) 10 MIN.
  Present the text features of poem and an autobiography.
- **Reading Strategy** (p. 332) 10 MIN.
  Teach the strategy of comparing and contrasting different texts.
- **Reading Selection Opener** (p. 333) 5 MIN.
  Preview the chapter reading selection.
- **Homework:** Activity Book (p. 177)

Day 3

- **Check Homework** 5 MIN.
  OR
- **Warm Up** 5 MIN.
  Write on the board: A _____ is the story of a person's life written by another person. An _____ is the story of a person's life written by that person.

- **Reading Selections** (pp. 334–337) 25 MIN.
  Have students read the selections and use the reading strategy. Teach spelling, capitalization, and punctuation points on TE pp. 334–337.
- **Reading Comprehension** (p. 338) 10 MIN.
  Have students answer the questions.
- **Build Reading Fluency** (p. 338) 5 MIN.
  Teach how to build reading fluency by reading aloud to engage listeners.
- **Homework:** Activity Book (p. 178)

Day 4

- **Check Homework** 5 MIN.
  OR
- **Warm Up** 5 MIN.
  How did Samantha feel in the seventh grade? How did she feel in the eighth grade? What made the difference?
- **Listen, Speak, Interact** (p. 339) 15 MIN.
  Have students respond to literature.
- **Elements of Literature** (p. 339) 15 MIN.
  Present figurative language.
- **Word Study** (p. 340) 10 MIN.
  Present related words.
- **Homework:** Activity Book (pp. 179–180)

Day 5

- **Check Homework** 5 MIN.
  OR
- **Warm Up** 5 MIN.
  Write on the board: Fill in the blanks with the words metaphor or figure of speech. A _____ is a kind of _____. It presents one thing as something else.
- **Grammar Focus** (p. 340) 15 MIN.
  Present superlative adjectives.
- **From Reading to Writing** (p. 341) 15 MIN.
  Teach how to write a poem.
- **Across Content Areas** (p. 341) 10 MIN.
  Introduce related language arts content on genres.
- **Homework:** Activity Book (pp. 181–184); Have students complete the third column of the KWL chart from Day 1. Have students study for the Unit 5, Chapter 4 Quiz.

UNIT 5 Freedom

APPLY AND EXPAND

End-of-Unit Materials

Student Handbook
CNN Video: Unit 5
Teacher Resource Book: Lesson Plan, p. 28; Teacher
  Resources, pp. 35–64; Home-School Connection,
  pp. 147–153; Video Script, pp. 169–170; Video
  Worksheet, p. 177
Teacher Resource CD-ROM

Assessment Program: Unit 5 Test, pp. 83–88; Teacher
  and Student Resources, pp. 115–144
Assessment CD-ROM: Unit 5 Test
Transparencies
The Heinle Newbury House Dictionary/CD-ROM
Heinle Reading Library
Web Site: www.heinle.visions.com

➤ See the Teacher's Edition wrap-around for complete teaching suggestions for each section.

Day 1

- **Unit 5, Chapter 4 Quiz** (Assessment Program,
  pp. 81–82) 20 MIN.
- **Listening and Speaking Workshop** (pp. 342–343)
  25 MIN.
  Introduce the assignment of presenting an
  autobiographical narrative. Have students plan and
  prepare their narratives (steps 1–3).
- **Homework:** Have students review and practice their
  reports to present the next day.

Day 2

- **Listening and Speaking Workshop** (pp. 342–343)
  45 MIN.
  Have students practice and present their television
  news reports to the class (step 4).
- **Homework:** In preparation for Day 3, have students
  look for pictures and videos about Korea during
  World War II.

Day 3

- **Viewing Workshop** (p. 343) 45 MIN.
  Show pictures and a video about Korea during World
  War II. Have students compare and contrast the two
  media with "So Far from the Bamboo Grove." Show
  the Visions CNN video for this unit. Have students do
  the Video Worksheet.
- **Homework:** Have students write a paragraph in which
  they summarize their findings about the similarities
  and differences between the images and the reading.

Day 4

- **Writer's Workshop** (pp. 344–345) 45 MIN.
  Present the assignment of writing a biographical
  narrative. Have students do pre-writing preparation
  and write a draft (steps 1–2).
- **Homework:** Have students review their drafts in
  preparation for revising them on Day 5.

Day 5

- **Writer's Workshop** (pp. 344–345) 45 MIN.
  Have students revise, edit, and publish their writing
  (steps 3–6).
- **Homework:** Have students take their writing home to
  share with their families.

Day 6

- **Review and Reteach** 45 MIN.
  In small groups, have students list major points from
  the unit. Ask students to choose three points that they
  are least clear on and would like to review. Based on
  results of chapter quizzes and student feedback,
  choose points from the unit to reteach to the class.
- **Homework:** Have students study for the Unit 5 Test.

Day 7

- **Unit 5 Test** (Assessment Program, pp. 83–88) 45 MIN.
  After the Unit 5 Test, reassess student learning.
  Record strong and weak areas based on the unit test.
  Review weak areas before the End-of-Book Exam.

Class _____ Date _____

UNIT 6 Visions

CHAPTER 1 • Mr. Scrooge Finds Christmas, by Aileen Fisher, adapted from
A Christmas Carol, by Charles Dickens

Chapter Materials

Activity Book: pp. 185–192
Audio: Unit 6, Chapter 1
Student Handbook
Student CD-ROM: Unit 6, Chapter 1
Teacher Resource Book: Lesson Plan, p. 29; Teacher
Resources, pp. 35–64; Reading Summaries,
pp. 111–112; Activity Book Answer Key

Teacher Resource CD-ROM
Assessment Program: Unit 6, Chapter 1 Quiz, pp. 89–90;
Teacher and Student Resources, pp. 115–144
Assessment CD-ROM: Unit 6, Chapter 1
Transparencies
The Heinle Newbury House Dictionary/CD-ROM
Web Site: www.heinle.visions.com

➤ See the Teacher's Edition wrap-around for complete teaching suggestions for each section.

Day 1

- **Unit Opener** (pp. 348–349) 20 MIN.
  Preview the unit reading selections. Complete the
  "View the Picture" activity.
- **Objectives** (p. 350) 5 MIN.
  Present the chapter objectives.
- **Use Prior Knowledge** (p. 350) 15 MIN.
  Activate knowledge about past, present, and future.
- **Build Background** (p. 351) 5 MIN.
  Provide the background information on Scrooge.
- **Homework:** KWL (TRB, p. 42); Have students
  complete the first and second columns based on what
  they learned in class. Students will complete the third
  column at the end of the chapter.

Day 2

- **Check Homework** 5 MIN.
  OR
- **Warm Up** 5 MIN.
  Write on the board: List 3 facts about Christmas.
- **Build Vocabulary** (p. 351) 15 MIN.
  Introduce denotative and connotative meanings.
- **Text Structure** (p. 352) 10 MIN.
  Present the text features of a play.
- **Reading Strategy** (p. 352) 10 MIN.
  Teach the strategy of using chronology to locate and
  recall information.
- **Reading Selection Opener** (p. 353) 5 MIN.
  Preview the chapter reading selection.
- **Homework:** Activity Book (p. 185)

Day 3

- **Check Homework** 5 MIN.
  OR
- **Warm Up** 5 MIN.
  Write on the board: Fill in the blanks in the sentences
  with these words: stage directions, dialogue, scenes.
  a. A play is divided into _____, which are different
  parts of the story.
  b. _____ is what the characters say to each other.

- **c.** _____ tell the actors what to do on the stage.
- **Reading Selection** (pp. 354–359) 25 MIN.
  Have students read the selection and use the reading
  strategy. Teach spelling, capitalization, and
  punctuation points on TE pp. 354–359.
- **Reading Comprehension** (p. 360) 10 MIN.
  Have students answer the questions.
- **Build Reading Fluency** (p. 360) 5 MIN.
  Teach how to build reading fluency by doing audio
  CD reading practice.
- **Homework:** Activity Book (p. 186)

Day 4

- **Check Homework** 5 MIN.
  OR
- **Warm Up** 5 MIN.
  Write: What kind of person is Ebenezer Scrooge?
- **Listen, Speak, Interact** (p. 361) 15 MIN.
  Have students present a scene from a play.
- **Elements of Literature** (p. 361) 15 MIN.
  Present dialogue and stage directions.
- **Word Study** (p. 362) 10 MIN.
  Present contractions.
- **Homework:** Activity Book (pp. 187–188)

Day 5

- **Check Homework** 5 MIN.
  OR
- **Warm Up** 5 MIN.
  Write on the board: In "Mr. Scrooge Finds Christmas,"
  the stage directions are written in _____.
- **Grammar Focus** (p. 362) 15 MIN.
  Present the present perfect tense.
- **From Reading to Writing** (p. 363) 15 MIN.
  Teach how to write a persuasive letter.
- **Across Content Areas** (p. 363) 10 MIN.
  Introduce related math content on currency.
- **Homework:** Activity Book (pp. 189–192); Have
  students complete the third column of the KWL chart
  from Day 1. Have students study for the Unit 6,
  Chapter 1 Quiz.

UNIT 6 Visions

CHAPTER 2 • The House on Mango Street, by Sandra Cisneros

Chapter Materials

Activity Book: pp. 193–200
Audio: Unit 6, Chapter 2
Student Handbook
Student CD-ROM: Unit 6, Chapter 2
Teacher Resource Book: Lesson Plan, p. 30; Teacher
Resources, pp. 35–64; Reading Summaries,
pp. 113–114; Activity Book Answer Key

Teacher Resource CD-ROM
Assessment Program: Unit 6, Chapter 2 Quiz, pp. 91–92;
Teacher and Student Resources, pp. 115–144
Assessment CD-ROM: Unit 6, Chapter 2
Transparencies
The Heinle Newbury House Dictionary/CD-ROM
Web Site: www.heinle.visions.com

➤ See the Teacher's Edition wrap-around for complete teaching suggestions for each section.

Day 1

- **Unit 6, Chapter 1 Quiz** (Assessment Program,
pp. 89–90) 20 MIN.
- **Objectives** (p. 364) 5 MIN.
Present the chapter objectives.
- **Use Prior Knowledge** (p. 364) 15 MIN.
Activate prior knowledge about the meanings of *home*.
- **Build Background** (p. 365) 5 MIN.
Provide the background information on Chicago.
- **Homework:** KWL (TRB, p. 42); Have students
complete the first and second columns based on what
they learned in class. Students will complete the third
column at the end of the chapter.

Day 2

- **Check Homework** 5 MIN.
OR
- **Warm Up** 5 MIN.
Write on the board: List 3 facts about Chicago.
- **Build Vocabulary** (p. 365) 15 MIN.
Introduce antonyms.
- **Text Structure** (p. 366) 10 MIN.
Present the text features of fiction.
- **Reading Strategy** (p. 366) 10 MIN.
Teach the strategy of paraphrasing to recall
information.
- **Reading Selection Opener** (p. 367) 5 MIN.
Preview the chapter reading selection.
- **Homework:** Activity Book (p. 193)

Day 3

- **Check Homework** 5 MIN.
OR
- **Warm Up** 5 MIN.
Write on the board: Write an antonym for each word.
a. changing   c. plain
b. back
- **Reading Selection** (pp. 368–371) 25 MIN.
Have students read the selection and use the reading
strategy. Teach spelling, capitalization, and
punctuation points on TE pp. 368–371.

- **Reading Comprehension** (p. 372) 10 MIN.
Have students answer the questions.
- **Build Reading Fluency** (p. 372) 5 MIN.
Teach how to build reading fluency by reading aloud
to engage listeners.
- **Homework:** Activity Book (p. 194)

Day 4

- **Check Homework** 5 MIN.
OR
- **Warm Up** 5 MIN.
Write on the board: What kind of house did the
author want? What kind did she get?
- **Listen, Speak, Interact** (p. 373) 15 MIN.
Have students talk about mental images.
- **Elements of Literature** (p. 373) 15 MIN.
Teach how to recognize first-person narratives.
- **Word Study** (p. 374) 10 MIN.
Present English words from other languages.
- **Homework:** Activity Book (pp. 195–196)

Day 5

- **Check Homework** 5 MIN.
OR
- **Warm Up** 5 MIN.
Write on the board: True or false?
If a character in a story tells the story and uses the
pronouns *I, me, we,* and *us,* the story is a third-person
narrative.
- **Grammar Focus** (p. 374) 15 MIN.
Present the spelling of frequently misspelled words.
- **From Reading to Writing** (p. 375) 15 MIN.
Teach how to write a descriptive paragraph.
- **Across Content Areas** (p. 375) 10 MIN.
Introduce related science content on animal habitats.
- **Homework:** Activity Book (pp. 197–200); Have
students complete the third column of the KWL chart
from Day 1. Have students study for the Unit 6,
Chapter 2 Quiz.

UNIT 6 Visions

CHAPTER 3 • The Pearl, by John Steinbeck

Chapter Materials

Activity Book: pp. 201–208
Audio: Unit 6, Chapter 3
Student Handbook
Student CD-ROM: Unit 6, Chapter 3
Teacher Resource Book: Lesson Plan, p. 31; Teacher
   Resources, pp. 35–64; Reading Summaries,
   pp. 115–116; Activity Book Answer Key

Teacher Resource CD-ROM
Assessment Program: Unit 6, Chapter 3 Quiz, pp. 93–94;
   Teacher and Student Resources, pp. 115–144
Assessment CD-ROM: Unit 6, Chapter 3
Transparencies
The Heinle Newbury House Dictionary/CD-ROM
Web Site: www.heinle.visions.com

➤ See the Teacher's Edition wrap-around for complete teaching suggestions for each section.

Day 1

- **Unit 6, Chapter 2 Quiz** (Assessment Program, pp. 91–92) 20 MIN.
- **Objectives** (p. 376) 5 MIN.
Present the chapter objectives.
- **Use Prior Knowledge** (p. 376) 15 MIN.
Activate prior knowledge about the ocean.
- **Build Background** (p. 377) 5 MIN.
Provide the background information on oysters.
- **Homework:** KWL (TRB, p. 42); Have students complete the first and second columns based on what they learned in class. Students will complete the third column at the end of the chapter.

Day 2

- **Check Homework** 5 MIN.
OR
- **Warm Up** 5 MIN.
Write on the board: List 3 facts about oysters.
- **Build Vocabulary** (p. 377) 15 MIN.
Introduce locating pronunciations and derivations.
- **Text Structure** (p. 378) 10 MIN.
Present the text features of realistic fiction.
- **Reading Strategy** (p. 378) 10 MIN.
Teach the strategy of making inferences using text evidence.
- **Reading Selection Opener** (p. 379) 5 MIN.
Preview the chapter reading selection.
- **Homework:** Activity Book (p. 201)

Day 3

- **Check Homework** 5 MIN.
OR
- **Warm Up** 5 MIN.
Write on the board: True or false?
  a. In a dictionary, the derivation of a word tells you the language that it came from.
  b. In a dictionary, the pronunciation of a word tells you its meaning.

- **Reading Selection** (pp. 380–387) 25 MIN.
Have students read the selection and use the reading strategy. Teach spelling, capitalization, and punctuation points on TE pp. 380–387.
- **Reading Comprehension** (p. 388) 10 MIN.
Have students answer the questions.
- **Build Reading Fluency** (p. 388) 5 MIN.
Teach how to build reading fluency by doing repeated reading.
- **Homework:** Activity Book (p. 202)

Day 4

- **Check Homework** 5 MIN.
OR
- **Warm Up** 5 MIN.
Write on the board: Write a summary of "The Pearl" in two or three sentences.
- **Listen, Speak, Interact** (p. 389) 15 MIN.
Have students listen to and present the story.
- **Elements of Literature** (p. 389) 15 MIN.
Present plot and problem resolution.
- **Word Study** (p. 390) 10 MIN.
Present words from Latin.
- **Homework: Activity Book** (pp. 203–204)

Day 5

- **Check Homework** 5 MIN.
OR
- **Warm Up** 5 MIN.
Write on the board: The _____ is the main events of a story. It usually has a _____, a _____, and an _____.
- **Grammar Focus** (p. 390) 15 MIN.
Present conjunctions in forming compound sentences.
- **From Reading to Writing** (p. 391) 15 MIN.
Teach how to write a fiction story.
- **Across Content Areas** (p. 391) 10 MIN.
Introduce related social studies content on bodies of water.
- **Homework:** Activity Book (pp. 205–208); Have students complete the third column of the KWL chart from Day 1. Have students study for the Unit 6, Chapter 3 Quiz.

UNIT 6 Visions

CHAPTER 4 • What Will Our Towns Look Like?, by Martha Pickerill

---

Chapter Materials

Activity Book: pp. 209–216
Audio: Unit 6, Chapter 4
Student Handbook
Student CD-ROM: Unit 6, Chapter 4
Teacher Resource Book: Lesson Plan, p. 32; Teacher
  Resources, pp. 35–64; Reading Summaries,
  pp. 117–118; Activity Book Answer Key

Teacher Resource CD-ROM
Assessment Program: Unit 6, Chapter 4 Quiz, pp. 95–96;
  Teacher and Student Resources, pp. 115–144
Assessment CD-ROM: Unit 6, Chapter 4
Transparencies
The Heinle Newbury House Dictionary/CD-ROM
Web Site: www.heinle.visions.com

➤ See the Teacher's Edition wrap-around for complete teaching suggestions for each section.

Day 1

• **Unit 6, Chapter 3 Quiz** (Assessment Program,
  pp. 93–94) 20 MIN.
• **Objectives** (p. 392) 5 MIN.
  Present the chapter objectives.
• **Use Prior Knowledge** (p. 392) 15 MIN.
  Activate prior knowledge about natural resources.
• **Build Background** (p. 393) 5 MIN.
  Provide the background information on fossil fuels.
• **Homework:** KWL (TRB, p. 42); Have students
  complete the first and second columns based on what
  they learned in class. Students will complete the third
  column at the end of the chapter.

Day 2

• **Check Homework** 5 MIN.
  OR
• **Warm Up** 5 MIN.
  Write on the board: List 3 facts about fossil fuels.
• **Build Vocabulary** (p. 393) 15 MIN.
  Introduce putting words into groups.
• **Text Structure** (p. 394) 10 MIN.
  Present the text features of an informational text.
• **Reading Strategy** (p. 394) 10 MIN.
  Teach the strategy of summarizing text to recall ideas.
• **Reading Selection Opener** (p. 395) 5 MIN.
  Preview the chapter reading selection.
• **Homework: Activity Book** (p. 209)

Day 3

• **Check Homework** 5 MIN.
  OR
• **Warm Up** 5 MIN.
  Write on the board: Headings are _____ to organize
  text. Examples are details that show how something is
  _____.
• **Reading Selection** (pp. 396–399) 25 MIN.
  Have students read the selection and use the reading
  strategy. Teach spelling, capitalization, and
  punctuation points on TE pp. 396–399.

• **Reading Comprehension** (p. 400) 10 MIN.
  Have students answer the questions.
• **Build Reading Fluency** (p. 400) 5 MIN.
  Teach how to build reading fluency by adjusting your
  reading rate to scan.
• **Homework: Activity Book** (p. 210)

Day 4

• **Check Homework** 5 MIN.
  OR
• **Warm Up** 5 MIN.
  Write on the board: Does the author of "What Will
  Our Towns Look Like?" think that the future is good
  or bad for our towns?
• **Listen, Speak, Interact** (p. 401) 15 MIN.
  Have students give a persuasive speech.
• **Elements of Literature** (p. 401) 15 MIN.
  Teach how to identify an author's purpose.
• **Word Study** (p. 402) 10 MIN.
  Present the Latin prefix *co-*.
• **Homework:** Activity Book (pp. 211–212)

Day 5

• **Check Homework** 5 MIN.
  OR
• **Warm Up** 5 MIN.
  Write on the board: What are the three main
  purposes for writing?
• **Grammar Focus** (p. 402) 15 MIN.
  Present using *will* to predict future events.
• **From Reading to Writing** (p. 403) 15 MIN.
  Teach how to create a form, interview, and
  summarize.
• **Across Content Areas** (p. 403) 10 MIN.
  Introduce related science content on acid rain.
• **Homework:** Activity Book (pp. 213–216); Have
  students complete the third column of the KWL chart
  from Day 1. Have students study for the Unit 6,
  Chapter 4 Quiz.

UNIT 6 Visions

APPLY AND EXPAND

End-of-Unit Materials

Student Handbook
CNN Video: Unit 6
Teacher Resource Book: Lesson Plan, p. 33; Teacher
  Resources, pp. 35–64; Home-School Connection,
  pp. 154–160; Video Script, pp. 171–172; Video
  Worksheet, p. 178
Teacher Resource CD-ROM
Assessment Program: Unit 6 Test, pp. 97–102;

End-of-Book Exam, pp. 103–108; Teacher and
  Student Resources, pp. 115–144
Assessment CD-ROM: Unit 6 Test, End-of-Book Exam
Transparencies
The Heinle Newbury House Dictionary/CD-ROM
Heinle Reading Library
Web Site: www.heinle.visions.com

➤ See the Teacher's Edition wrap-around for complete teaching suggestions for each section.

Day 1

- **Unit 6, Chapter 4 Quiz** (Assessment Program,
  pp. 95–96) 20 MIN.
- **Listening and Speaking Workshop** (pp. 404–405)
  25 MIN.
  Introduce the assignment of writing and presenting a
  persuasive role play between Mr. Scrooge and the
  solicitor. Have students write the role play (steps 1–4).
- **Homework:** Have students review and practice their
  role plays to present the next day.

Day 2

- **Listening and Speaking Workshop** (pp. 404–405)
  45 MIN.
  Have students practice and present their role plays to
  the class (steps 5–6).
- **Homework:** If possible, record the role plays on audio
  or video. Have students take their recordings home to
  share with their families.

Day 3

- **Viewing Workshop** (p. 405) 45 MIN.
  Show a film or video version of "A Christmas Carol."
  Have students compare and contrast the film or video
  version with the play version that they have read.
  Show the Visions CNN video for this unit. Have
  students do the Video Worksheet.
- **Homework:** Have students write a paragraph in which
  they summarize their findings about the similarities
  and differences between the film or video and the
  reading.

Day 4

- **Writer's Workshop** (pp. 406–407) 45 MIN.
  Present the assignment of collaborating to write a
  persuasive letter. Have students do pre-writing
  preparation and write a draft (steps 1–5).
- **Homework:** Have students review their drafts in
  preparation for revising them on Day 5.

Day 5

- **Writer's Workshop** (pp. 406–407) 45 MIN.
  Have students revise, edit, and publish their writing
  (steps 6–9).
- **Homework:** Have students take their writing home to
  share with their families.

Day 6

- **Review and Reteach** 45 MIN.
  In small groups, have students list major points from
  the unit. Ask students to choose three points that they
  are least clear on and would like to review. Based on
  results of chapter quizzes and student feedback,
  choose points from the unit to reteach to the class.
- **Homework:** Have students study for the Unit 6 Test.

Day 7

- **Unit 6 Test** (Assessment Program, pp. 97–102)
  45 MIN.
  After the Unit 6 Test, reassess student learning.
  Record strong and weak areas based on the unit test.
  Review weak areas before the End-of-Book Exam.
- **Homework:** Have students study for the End-of-Book
  Exam.

Day 8

- **End-of-Book Exam** (Assessment Program,
  pp. 103–108) 45 MIN.

Venn Diagram

Compare and Contrast

➤ Use a Venn Diagram for listening and speaking, writing, and viewing activities.

1. Write the two things you are comparing on the lines in the two circles.
2. List ways the two things are different under the lines.
3. List ways the two things are alike in the space where the circles overlap.

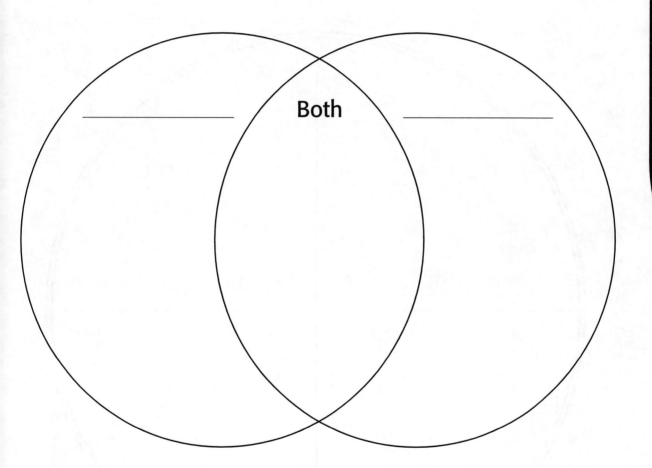

Both

Word or Concept Wheel

➤ Use a Word (Concept) Wheel to help build your vocabulary and better understand word meanings.

1. Write the key word or concept on the line in the wheel.
2. Write the dictionary definition of the key word or concept below the line.
3. Write related words in the other sections.

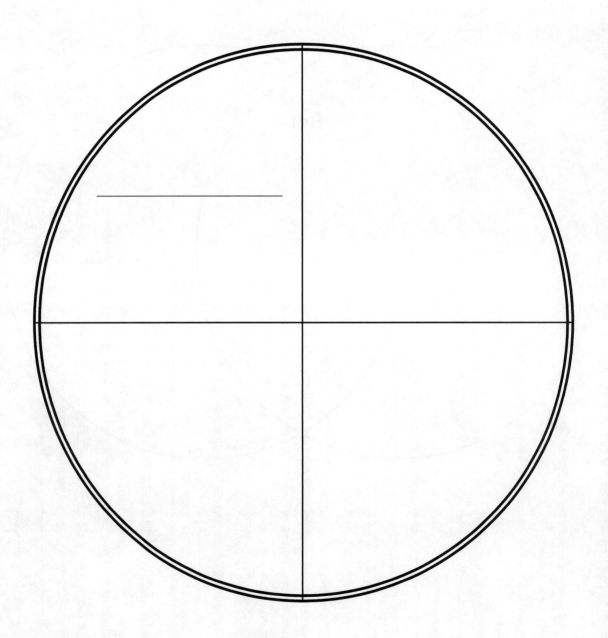

Name _____ Date _____

Web

➤ A Web is useful for building vocabulary or for main idea and details.

1. Write the main vocabulary word or main idea in the large oval in the middle.
2. Write related vocabulary words or details in the smaller ovals.
3. Add or delete ovals as needed.

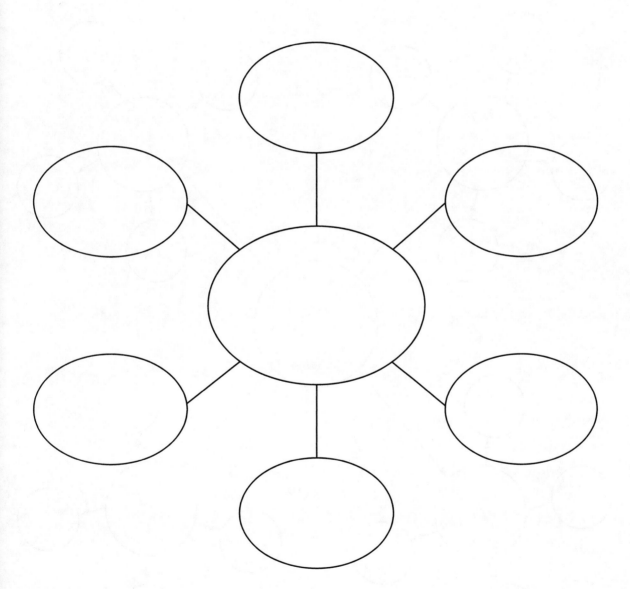

Cluster Map

Compare and Contrast

➤ Use a Cluster Map to help you organize your ideas.

1. Write the topic in the largest circle.
2. Write the main ideas about the topic in the medium circles.
3. Write details about the main ideas in the smallest circles.

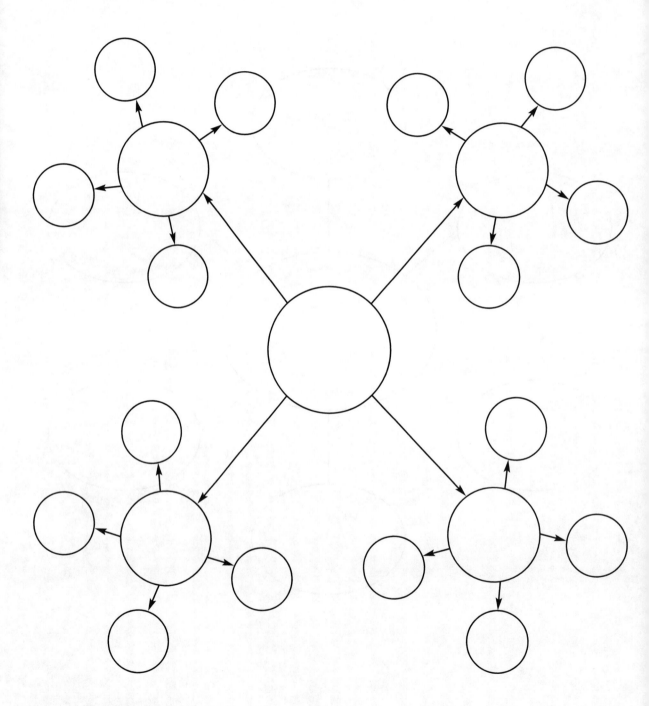

Name _____ Date _____

Timelines

➤ Select one of the timelines to show order of events.

1. Write the events in the order they took place.
2. On the left, write the first event and the date.
3. On the right, put the latest event and the date.

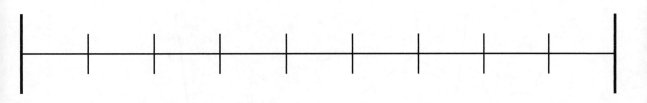

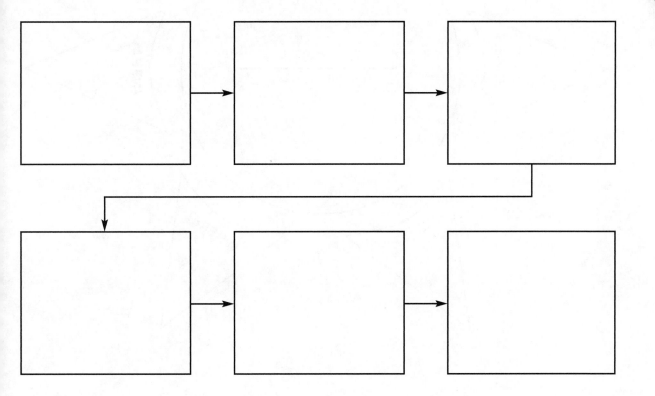

Sunshine Organizer

Reporting

➤ Use a Sunshine Organizer to help you answer questions about a story or to write a report.

1. Write the topic in the circle in the middle.
2. Write answers to the *wh-* questions next to the triangles.

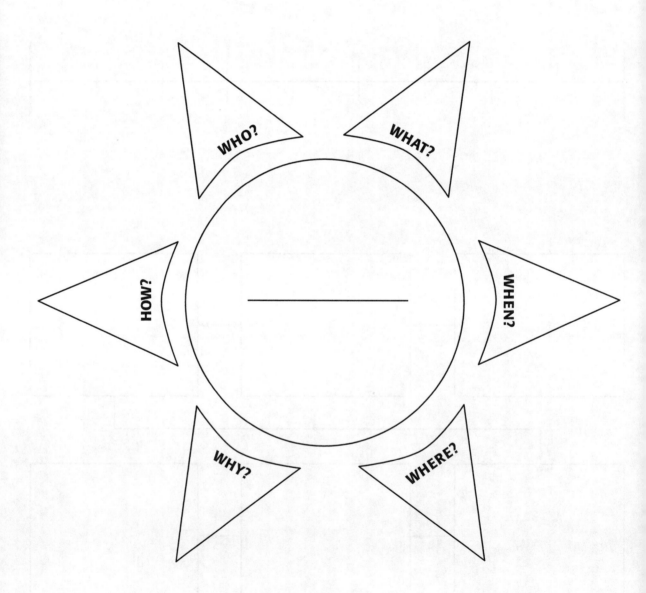

Name _____ Date _____

Word Squares

Build Vocabulary

➤ Use Word Squares to help you remember the meanings of new words.

1. Write a new word you do not know in the **Word** box.
2. Use a dictionary or glossary. Write the meaning of the word in the **Meaning** box.
3. Draw a symbol to remember the word in the **Symbol** box.
4. Write a sentence with the word in the **Sentence** box.

Word	Symbol	Word	Symbol
Meaning	**Sentence**	**Meaning**	**Sentence**
Word	**Symbol**	**Word**	**Symbol**
Meaning	**Sentence**	**Meaning**	**Sentence**
Word	**Symbol**	**Word**	**Symbol**
Meaning	**Sentence**	**Meaning**	**Sentence**

Know/Want to Know/Learned Chart (KWL)

1. Write the topic in the top box.
2. Write things you **know** in the first column.
3. Write things you **want to know** in the second column.
4. Write things you **learned** in the third column.

Topic:

Know What do I already know about the topic?	Want to Know What do I want to know about the topic?	Learned What did I learn about the topic?

Name _____ Date _____

Storyboard

➤ Use a Storyboard to summarize, outline, and show sequence with pictures and words.

1. Write a sequence of the most important events in a story.
2. Put the events in the order in which they happened.
3. Draw a simple picture above each sentence if you wish.

1.

First, _____

_____

_____

2.

Second, _____

_____

_____

3.

Third, _____

_____

_____

4.

Fourth, _____

_____

_____

5.

Fifth, _____

_____

_____

6.

Finally, _____

_____

_____

Two-Column Chart

Taking Notes

➤ Use this chart when you read and take notes on Main Idea/Details, Fact/Opinion, Cause/Effect, Problem/Resolution, Words/Synonyms (or Antonyms), and Advantage/Disadvantages.

1. Write the topic or title in the top box.
2. In the left column, write the first word; for example: Main Idea.
3. In the right column, write the second word; for example: Details.

Three-Column Chart

Categorize or Classify

➤ Use this chart for analyzing characters, style, mood and tone, or for vocabulary words and their connotative and denotative meanings.

1. Write the topic or title in the top box.
2. Write the names of the three categories in the next box.
3. List words in the three categories as appropriate.

Paragraph

1. Write in a notebook or on the computer.
2. Write a topic sentence, supporting details, and a closing sentence.
3. Use a dictionary or computer software for help with words and spelling.

Title

Indent

(Topic Sentence)

(Details, Supporting Facts, Examples)

(Closing Sentence: topic sentence with different words)

Open Mind Diagram

Characterization

➤ Use an Open Mind Diagram to analyze characters. Choose from the **Topics** in the chart and write what the character is thinking.

Topics				
Describe the character's **traits**.	Write what the character is thinking. **(motivation)**	Write about the character's **conflicts**.	Describe a character's **point of view**.	Write about the character's **relationships**.

Narrative

Brainstorming

➤ Use this graphic organizer for listening/speaking presentations and for writing.

Headings	Notes or drawings to help you plan your presentation/writing
Title	
Who? What? When? Where? Why? How?	
First Event	
Complication	
Resolution	
Summary or Conclusion	

VISIONS TEACHER RESOURCE

Narrative

Draft

➤ Use this graphic organizer when you write your first draft. Use transition words.

Title Page	**Title** **Name** **Date**

Beginning

Indent   **Introduction**

Indent   **Body**

Middle

Indent

Indent

End

Indent   **Conclusion or Resolution**

Chronological Order

Narrative or Informational Text

➤ Use this graphic organizer when you write in chronological order.

Title

Beginning

| Indent | **Setting**
Who? What? When? Where? Why? How? |

| Indent | **Events in Time Order**
Event 1 |

| Indent | Event 2 |

Middle

| Indent | Event 3 |

| Indent | Event 4 |

| Indent | **Conclusion/Ending** |

End

Name _____ Date _____

Persuasive – Debate and Writing

For and Against

➤ Use this graphic organizer when preparing an oral or a written persuasive presentation.

ARGUMENTS FOR	SUPPORTING EVIDENCE
1.	
2.	
3.	

ARGUMENTS AGAINST	SUPPORTING EVIDENCE
1.	
2.	
3.	

CONCLUSION or SUMMARY

Persuasive Essay

Three Paragraphs

➤ Use this graphic organizer for oral presentations or writing assignments.

1. Write in a notebook or on the computer.
2. Write a thesis stating your position.
3. Give reasons with examples and a conclusion.
4. Use words such as *first of all, next,* and *in conclusion.*
5. Use a dictionary or computer software to help with words and spelling.

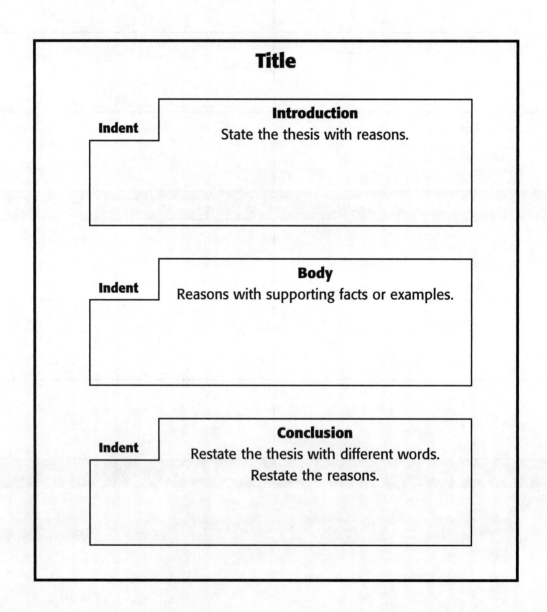

Title

Indent

Introduction
State the thesis with reasons.

Indent

Body
Reasons with supporting facts or examples.

Indent

Conclusion
Restate the thesis with different words.
Restate the reasons.

Persuasive Essay

Five Paragraphs

➤ Use this graphic organizer for oral presentations or writing assignments.

1. Write in a notebook or on the computer.
2. Write a thesis stating your position.
3. Give three reasons with examples and a conclusion.
4. Use words such as *first of all, next, finally,* and *in conclusion.*
5. Use a dictionary or computer software to help with words and spelling.

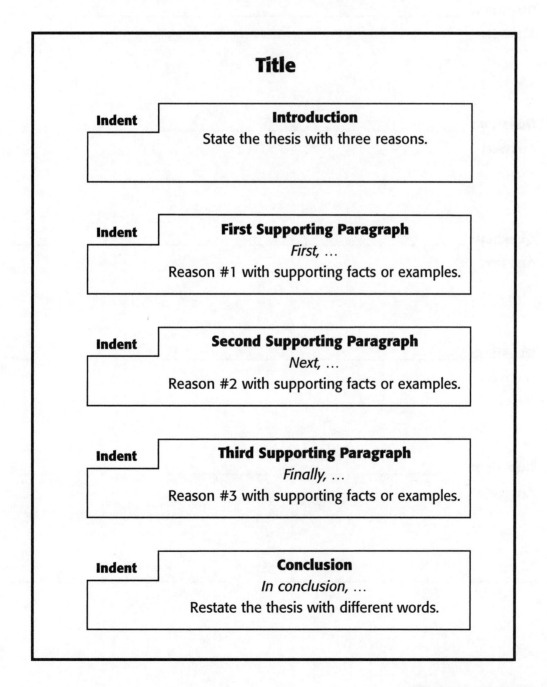

Name _____ Date _____

Interview

1. Write a list of questions.
2. Record the interviewee's answers.

Interview questions for _____

(Name of interviewee)

1. Question: _____ **?**

Answer:

2. Question: _____ **?**

Answer:

3. Question: _____ **?**

Answer:

4. Question: _____ **?**

Answer:

5. Question: _____ **?**

Answer:

Name _____ Date _____

Step-by-Step Instructions
Procedural

➤ Use this graphic organizer for directions, recipes, and games.

1. Write information in each section.
2. Use this during your first draft of oral presentations or writing assignments.

INTRODUCTION Tell about the process. What is to be done?
REQUIREMENTS What is needed to complete the task? (tools, parts, materials, utensils)
INSTRUCTIONS What is to be done? **1.** **2.** **3.** **4.** **5.** **6.** **7.** **8.**
CONCLUSION Summarize the process.

Friendly Letter

➤ This format is used for writing a letter to a friend.

1. Write on an 8 $\frac{1}{2}$ by 11 inch piece of paper or on personal stationery.
2. Write using good penmanship.
3. Proofread your spelling and punctuation.

_____
(Date)

Dear _____ **,**

Indent

Describe yourself and where you are.

Indent

Describe your daily life.

Indent

Talk about the person you are writing to.

Yours truly,

(Your name)

Business Letter/Letter to the Editor

➤ A business letter is different from a friendly letter. It is brief, direct, and limited to one or two points.

1. In the first paragraph, clearly state what you want or why you are writing.
2. Add supporting information in the second paragraph.
3. Write a polite closing.
4. If possible, use a computer for your final draft.
5. Proofread for spelling, grammar, capital letters, and proper business form.

VISIONS TEACHER RESOURCE

Your Street
City, State/Country
Date

Company Name
Address

Dear _____ :

Indent

Indent

Explain what you introduced in the first paragraph.

Indent

Closing (Conclusion)

Sincerely,

(signature)

Note-Taking

Research Report

1. Use 4 x 6 inch cards.
2. Use a variety of resources: encyclopedias, the Internet, books, magazines, software resources, experts, etc.
3. Think of three or four questions about the topic.
4. Write each question at the top of a different note card.
5. Paraphrase an idea or copy a "quotation" on each card.
6. In the bottom left-hand corner, identify the source and page number.
7. In the upper right-hand corner, write the general heading of the information.

Question: _____   **General Heading:** _____
(What do you want to know?)

Paraphrase your source.

or

Summarize from your source.

or

"Quote" your source.

Source, page

Outline

Informational Texts and Research Papers

1. Sort your note cards before you do your outline.
2. Organize topics and subtopics into logical order.
3. Keep it simple. Write a topic or a thesis—not complete sentences.
4. List major headings after a Roman numeral and a period.
5. List subtopics after a capital letter and a period.
6. List supporting details and examples after a number and a period.

Title

I. Topic 1 or Thesis
   A. Subtopic 1
      1. Detail/Example
      2. Detail/Example

   B. Subtopic 2
      1. Detail/Example
      2. Detail/Example

II. Topics or Thesis
   A. Subtopic 1
      1. Detail/Example
      2. Detail/Example

   B. Subtopic 2
      1. Detail/Example
      2. Detail/Example

III. Conclusion (Restate thesis)

Research Report
Final Draft

Title Page

> **Title**
>
> **Name**
> **Date**

Thesis (an opening paragraph)
A statement that clearly and briefly says why you chose this topic to research.

Topic (the two to three subtopics you researched)
The information should be relevant to the topic.

Subtopic 1
Start a new page.

Subtopic 2
Start a new page.

Conclusion
A paragraph that summarizes your report and tells how your research helped you achieve the purpose of your report.

---

1. **Visuals:** You may want to include pictures, graphs, tables, or photos.
2. **Bibliography:** Check with your teacher for a copy of the correct format required for a bibliography. Also see your Student Handbook.
3. **Format:** If you use a computer, use double space and use 12–14 point font with one inch margins around the paper. If you write by hand, use black or blue pen and cursive writing.
4. **Proofread:** Check for spelling and grammar mistakes. Remember that computer software spell-check only catches words that are spelled incorrectly. It does not catch words that are spelled correctly but used incorrectly.

Name _____ Date _____

Sense Chart
Description

1. Write the name of the object or thing in the first column.
2. Write down what you see, hear, smell, and touch.

Title:				
Name of Thing	**See**	**Hear**	**Smell**	**Touch**

Problem/Resolution Chart

➤ This chart can be used for listening/speaking presentations and for writing assignments.

1. Write a problem. List two possible resolutions and two results of those resolutions. Write an end result.
2. Use a dictionary or computer software for help with words and spelling.

Title:	
State Problem: (Include some of this information: Who? What? When? Where? Why? How?)	
Resolution 1:	**Result 1:**
Resolution 2:	**Result 2:**
End Result:	

Personal Dictionary

➤ Use a Personal Dictionary for building your vocabulary.

1. Organize your Personal Dictionary into two sections.
2. One section will have pages for taking notes or for vocabulary activities from the chapter.
3. The other section will have a page for each letter of the alphabet. As you learn new words, write them on the correct pages.

Unit and Chapter *or* **Letter of the Alphabet:** _____

Name _____ Date _____

Reading Log

➤ Use a Reading Log for recording information about your reading.

1. Organize your Reading Log by date.
2. Write the date you are making the entry. Then write the title of the reading.

Date: _____ **Title:** _____

_____

_____

_____

_____

_____

_____

_____

_____

_____

_____

_____

_____

_____

_____

_____

_____

Name _____ Date _____

The Loch Ness Monster, by Malcom Yorke

ENGLISH

This informational text is about the mystery of the Loch Ness monster. Loch Ness is a lake in Scotland. Many people think a giant monster lives there. In 1963, Jim Ayton and his father saw a strange animal in the lake. Its body was as long as a bus. Other people have seen the monster, too. It was seen for the first time over 1,400 years ago. Since then, people have told many stories and made pictures of the monster. Scientists have not been able to solve this mystery. They cannot take clear underwater pictures because the water in the lake is cloudy. Some people think the Loch Ness monster is from the age of dinosaurs. Others think it is just a joke.

SPANISH

Este texto informativo es acerca del misterio del monstruo de Loch Ness. Loch Ness es un lago de Escocia en el que mucha gente piensa que vive un monstruo gigante. En 1963, Jim Ayton y su padre dijeron haber visto en el lago un animal extraño que tenía un cuerpo del largo de un autobús. Muchos otros también han dicho haber visto al monstruo. La primera vez que alguien mencionó haberlo visto fue hace más de 1,400 años. Desde entonces, se han divulgado muchas historias y se han hecho muchos bosquejos del supuesto monstruo. Los científicos no han podido resolver este misterio. Como el agua del lago es muy turbia, no se han podido tomar fotografías nítidas en el agua. Algunos piensan que el monstruo de Loch Ness existe de la era de los dinosaurios, mientras que otros afirman que tan sólo es una broma.

HMONG

Zaj lus ntawm no yog hais txog ib tug dab Loch Ness uas tseem tsi tau paub zoo txog. Loch Ness yog is lub pasdej tuag nyob rau tebchaws Scotland. Coob leej ntau tug xav hais tias yog ib tug dab loj heev nyob rau hauv lub pasdej ntawd. Nyob rau xyoo 1963, Jim Ayton thiab nws txiv pom ib tug tsiaj txawv kawg li nyob rau hauv lub pasdej. Nws lub cev ntev npaum li lub tsheb npav. Lwm tug lawv kuj tau pom tug dab ntawd lawm thiab. Thawj zaug tau pom yog li ntawm 1,400 xyoo dhau los lawm. Txij thaum ntawd los, tej tib neeg tau piav ntau yam dab neeg thiab tau kos duab txog tus dab ntawd. Cov scientists los sis cov kws tshawb nrhiav tseem tsi tau nrhiav pom hais tias qhov tseem tsi tau nkagsiab zoo ntawm no yog dabtsi li. Lawv nkag rau hauv qabthu dej thaij duab tiam sis cov dej pos fuab ces thaij pom tsi zoo. It txhia cov tib neeg lawv xav hais tias tus dab Loch Ness no yog los ntawm tiam cov tsiaj dinosaurs los. Lwm leej lwm tug ho xav hais tias qhov no tsua yog tib neeg lam hais xwb tsi muaj tseeb.

VIETNAMESE

Bài viết mang tính chất tài liệu này kể về bí mật con quái vật Loch Ness. Loch Ness là tên của một hồ ở Scotland. Nhiều người nghĩ rằng có một quái vật khổng lồ sống ở đó. Vào năm 1963, Jim Ayton và cha trông thấy một con vật quái dị dưới hồ. Cơ thể của nó dài bằng một chiếc xe buýt. Những người khác cũng thấy quái vật này. Quái vật được trông thấy lần đầu tiên cách đây trên 1,400 năm. Kể từ đó, người ta kể nhiều câu chuyện và vẽ nhiều tranh hình về con quái vật. Các nhà khoa học chưa tìm được giải đáp cho điều bí ẩn này. Vì nước hồ đục nên những tấm hình do các nhà khoa học chụp dưới nước không được rõ. Một số người nghĩ rằng quái vật hồ Loch Ness thuộc dòng khủng long. Những người khác nghĩ rằng đây chỉ là một trò đùa.

CANTONESE

這篇知識性文章講的是尼斯湖水怪．尼斯湖是位於蘇格蘭的一個湖，很多人認為有一隻大水怪生活在那裏．一九六三年，占·阿頓和他的父親曾在湖中看到一隻怪異的動物，身體有一輛公車那麼長．其他人亦曾見過這個怪物．一千四百多年前，有人第一次看到這個水怪．從此以後，人們講過很多關於水怪的故事，還繪製過圖片．科學家尚未能解開這個神秘疑團．他們無法拍攝到清楚的水下照片，因為湖水很渾濁．有些人認為尼斯湖水怪是恐龍時代的遺物，其他人則認為這只是一個玩笑．

CAMBODIAN

សេៀវភៅព័ត៌មាន៖ស្ដីពីអាថិកំបាំងនៃសត្វទឹកមនៗ ឡុច ណែស។ ឡុច ណែស ជាបឹងមួយនៅក្នុងប្រទេស ស្កុតឡែន។ មនុស្សជាច្រើនគិតថាសត្វទឹកមនៗធំមួយនៅទីនោះ។ ក្នុងឆ្នាំ ១៩៦៣ ជីម អាយតុន និងឪពុកគាត់បានឃើញសត្វទឹកមនៗមួយនៅក្នុងបឹង។ ខ្លួនវាវែងស្មើនឹងឡានៗ។ មនុស្សឯទៀតក៏បានឃើញសត្វទឹកមនៗ។ ថៃ។ គេឃើញវាជាលើកដំបូង ជាង ១៤០០ ឆ្នាំមុន។ តាំងពីនោះមក មនុស្សបាននិយាយរឿងជាច្រើន ហើយគូររូបសត្វនោះ។ ពួកវិទ្យាសាស្ត្រនៅមិនទាន់ភាគនោះ៖ស្រាយអាថិកំបាំងនោះៗនៅឡើយទៀត។ គេមិនអាច ថតរូបក្នុងទឹកឲ្យ ច្បាស់ឡើយ ព្រោះទឹកនៅបឹងនោះៗលក់ៗ។ មនុស្ស៖គិតថា សត្វទឹក ឡុច ណែស នោះៗមកពីជំនាន់ដាយណូស័រ។ នៅៗគិតថា វាគ្រាន់់ តែជាការកំប្លែងប៉ុណ្ណោះ។

HAITIAN CREOLE

Tèks enfòmasyonèl sa pale konsènan mistè mons Loch Ness lan. Loch Ness se yon lak nan peyi Scotland. Anpil moun panse gen yon mons jeyan ki rete la. An 1963, Jim Ayton ak papa li te wè yon animal etranj nan lak lan. Kò li te long menm jan ak yon otobis. Lòt te wè mons lan tou. Yo te wè mons lan pou lapremyè fwa sa fè deja 1 400 zan. Depi lè sa a, moun ap rakonte anpil istwa epi pran foto mons lan. Syantifik yo poko kapab rezoud mistè sa a. Yo paka pran foto klè anba dlo an paske dlo ki nan lak lan yon ti jan twoub. Kèk moun panse mons Loch Ness lan la depi epòk dinozò yo. Gen kèk lòt moun ki panse tout sa se blag.

UNIT 1 • CHAPTER 2
Mystery of the Cliff Dwellers

ENGLISH

This textbook article is about the ancient Pueblo Indians. The Pueblo settled in what is now Colorado around A.D. 550. At first, they lived in houses dug into hills. Then they began moving their homes high up in the cliffs. Many people think the Pueblo moved to protect themselves from enemies. Others think they moved to have more farmland. The Pueblo grew their own food, such as squash, corn, and beans. They held religious ceremonies in an underground area. They called this area a kiva. By 1300, the Pueblo left their cliff homes. Nobody knows why. Some people think the Pueblo left because of a war or disease.

SPANISH

Este artículo de un libro de texto es acerca de los indígenas de la tribu Pueblo. Los Pueblo vivieron en lo que ahora es Colorado desde cerca del año 550 a.c. En un principio, los Pueblo vivieron en casas que escababan en la parte baja de los barrancos. Luego, comenzaron a construir sus viviendas más alto en los barrancos. Muchos piensan que los Pueblo construyeron en lo alto de los barrancos para protegerse de sus enemigos y otros creen que lo hicieron para tener más campo para labrar. Para alimentarse, los Pueblo cultivaban calabazillas, maíz o elote, y frijoles o judías para alimentarse. Llevaban a cabo ceremonias religiosas en un área subterránea que llamaban una kiva. Hacia el año 1300, Los Pueblo dejaron sus viviendas en los barrancos, pero nadie sabe por qué. Muchos piensan que se fueron de esa área a causa de enfermedad o de una guerra.

HMONG

Zaj lus ntawm no yog hais txog cov Khab Pueblo thaum ntau txheej thaum ub los lawm. Cov neeg Pueblo ua zej zos rau tam sim no uas yog Colorado cheeb tsam xyoo a.d. 550. Yav ua ntej no, cov tsev lawv nyob yog khawb qhov rau tej pob roob xwb. Ces tauj ntxiv ntawd los mus rau tom qab no lawv khawb qhov nce mus siab zuj zug rau puag saum ib ntaj roob zeb roob a li lawm. Coob leej ntau tug tej tib neeg xav tias qhov cov Pueblo khiav yog lawv tiv thaiv lawv tus kheej xwb los ntawm lawv cov yeebncuab xwb. Lwm leej lwm tug lawv ho xav hais tias qhov khiav no yog mus nrhiav liaj av ua teb. Cov neeg Pueblo no lawv muaj lawv qoob loo cog, xws li taub, pobkws, thiab taum pauv. Lawv muab tej kevcai ntseeg coj mus ua nyob rau hauv qhov av. Lawv hu qhov chaw no ua kiva. Txog rau xyoo 1300 ces cov neeg Pueblo no lawv khiav tawm cov tsev siab saum ib nta roob zeb a mus lawm. Tsi muaj leej twg paub hais tias yog vim li cas. Tej tib neeg ib txhia xav hais tias qhov lawv khiav yog vim kev sib ntaus sib tua los sis vim muaj kab mob nkeeg.Others believe they just moved south.

VIETNAMESE

Bài giáo khoa này nói về dân Da Đỏ Pueblo cổ xưa. Vào khoảng năm 550 sau Công Nguyên, người Pueblo định cư tại vùng đất giờ đây được gọi là bang Colorado. Trước tiên, họ sống trong các hang tự khoét trên sườn đồi. Sau đó họ bắt đầu dời nơi ở lên đỉnh cao của các vách đá. Nhiều người nghĩ rằng người Pueblo dời nơi ở để khỏi bị kẻ thù tấn công. Một số người khác cho rằng họ dời nơi ở để mở rộng đất đai trồng trọt. Dân Pueblo đã tự nuôi trồng thức ăn, chẳng hạn như bí, bắp, và đậu. Họ tổ chức các buổi lễ tôn giáo tại một khu vực dưới mặt đất. Họ gọi vùng này là "kiva". Vào khoảng năm 1300, người Pueblo rời bỏ các căn nhà xây trên vách đá. Không một ai biết lý do. Một số người nghĩ rằng người Pueblo rời bỏ nhà cửa vì chiến tranh hay bệnh tật.

CANTONESE

這篇教科書文章是關於古時的晉布印第安人．晉布人約於西元後550年定居於現在的科羅拉多州．最初，他們居住在挖出的山洞中．後來，他們開始把家遷往懸崖上．很多人認為晉布人搬家是為了躲避敵人，其他人則認為他們搬家是為了得到更多農地．晉布人自己種植食物，例如南瓜、玉米及豆類．他們在地底下舉行宗教儀式，他們稱這些場地為「奇瓦」．一三零零年，晉布人離開了他們在懸崖上的家．沒有人知道他們離開的原因．有些人認為，晉布人是為了躲避戰爭或疾病而離開的．

CAMBODIAN

សៀវភៅនេះវាគឺអំពី ៖ ស្តីពី ជនជាតិបុរាណ។ ឬ ក្លាប់មានទីតាំងនៅកន្លែងក្រោម កម្ពុជ៍ម្ព សូឡៃខ ក្នុងកំឡុង ព្រឹស្រាការ ៥៥០។ ដំបូងរេសស្មៅនៅក្នុងរូង្គ បរិលោកក្នុងភ័ណ្ឌភា។ បន្ទាប់មក រេវាបានផ្សេមឬស្លៃនៅនៅនៅខ្ពស់ៗ លោកញុំ អ្នកសុៗជាច្រើនគិតថា ឬ ក្លាស់ព្យូរ ម៉ើ ម្បីការពោយនេះពីសត្រូវ ឬ គិតថា គេម្យេវោរ៉េកម៍ការ ឬ ម្យាវ៉ើ ឬ ដាំដំណាំខ្លួនឯង យូចថា ស្នោះ, ពោត, ៩ឥសវណ្ណត៍។ ទៅឥ្បុណ្ណសាសនាៗនៅនៅកន្លែងក្រោមដី។ ទៅហៅនេ ពោះ ៖ ខា គីវ៉ា។ មុន្តេ ១៣០០ ឬ ធាការធាណល៍នៅ ខាឡូក៍ខ្លួឡ បល់។ ៗនោណណាណ៍ងានៃហេតុស្លីវៗ។ អ្នកសុៗ ៖ គិតថា ឬ ធាការឥ្ញី៌ព្រោះសង្គ្រាម ឬ ជម្ងឺ។

HAITIAN CREOLE

Atik manyèl sa a pale konsènan ansyen endyen Pueblo yo. Pèp Pueblo an te rete kote yo rele kounye a Colorado ozanviwon 550 epòk nou an. Okòmansman yo te rete nan kay ki anba kolin yo. Aprè sa yo te vin kòmanse mete kay yo anwo soutèt falèz yo. Anpil moun kwè pèp Pueblo an te fè sa pou yo te ka pwoteje tèt yo kont enmi yo. Gen lòt moun ki panse yo te deplase pou yo te ka gen plis tè pou fè fèm. Pèp Pueblo an te fè pwòp manje l, tankou joumou, mayi, ak kèk pwa. Yo te konn fè seremoni relijye nan yon twou anbatè. Yo te rele zòn sa a yon kiva. Rive 1300, pèp Pueblo an te abandone kay sou tèt falèz yo. Pèsonn pa konnen pou ki rezon. Kèk moun panse pèp Pueblo an te pati akòz lagè oswa yon maladi.

UNIT 1 • CHAPTER 3

Yawning, by Haleh V. Samiei

ENGLISH

"Yawning" is an informational text about why people yawn. Many people think feeling tired or bored causes yawning. A scientist named Robert Provine completed tests to show that people do yawn when they are bored or tired. People also yawn when they stretch. Tired or bored people are not the only ones who yawn. If they are nervous before an event, athletes and musicians may yawn. Yawning helps them feel more alert. This is because yawning stretches the muscles in the face. Stretching brings more blood to the brain. Even with these tests and explanations, some scientists think that there is no reason for yawning.

SPANISH

"Yawning" es un texto informativo acerca del por qué la gente bosteza. Muchos piensan que el bostezo indica cansancio o aburrimiento. Un científico llamado Robert Provine hizo unas pruebas para demostrar que la gente sí bosteza cuando está aburrida o cansada y también cuando se estira. Pero la gente no sólo bosteza cuando está aburrida o cansada. Por ejemplo, los atletas y los músicos pueden bostezar antes de un juego o un concierto si están nerviosos, porque el bostezar los pone más alerta. Eso sucede, porque al bostezar se estiran los músculos de la cara, y al estirar la cara llega más sangre al cerebro. Aun con esas pruebas y explicaciones, algunos científicos consideran que no existe una razón específica para bostezar.

HMONG

"Yawning" yog ib zaj lus hais qhia txog tias yog vim li cas tib neeg ho rua lo. Coob leej ntau tug tib neeg xav hais tias thaum nkees thiab dhuav lawd ces nws ua rau yus rua lo. Ib tug kws tshawb nrhiav los sis scientist uas muaj lub npe hu ua Robert Provine tau tshawb nrhiav sim ntau seem qhia tau tias tej tib neeg rua lo thaum lub sib hawm lawv nkees thiab dhuav lawd. Tej tib neeg kuj rua lo rau thaum lawv xyab hluab thiab. Kuj tsi yog tib co tib neeg uas nkees thiab dhua thiaj yog cov rua lo xwb. Cov neeg kislas thiab cov tub qoj paj nduag tej zaum lawv kuj rua lo thiab yog tias lawv muaj qhov ntshai ua ntej yuav mus koom kev sib ntsib tej. Qhov rua lo no pab tau rau lawv ib nyuag meejpem zog tuaj. Nws pab tau li no vim tias thaum rua lo ces nws rub cov nqaij ntawm ntsej muag lawm. Kev xyab hluab ua tau rau cov ntshav nce ntau zog mus rau lub hlwb. Txawm yog tias twb muaj cov kev kawm tshawb nrhiav no los qhia piav txog lawm los, ib txhia cov kws tshawb nrhiav tseem xav tias qhov rua lo no nws tsi muaj qhov tseem ceeb dabtsi li.

VIETNAMESE

"Yawning" là một bài viết mang tính chất tài liệu giải thích tại sao con người ngáp. Nhiều người nghĩ rằng cảm giác mệt mỏi hay chán chường là nguyên nhân gây ngáp. Một nhà khoa học tên Robert Provine tiến hành những cuộc thử nghiệm để chứng tỏ rằng đúng là con người ngáp khi chán hay mệt mỏi. Chúng ta cũng ngáp khi vươn người. Không phải chỉ có những người mệt hay chán mới ngáp. Nếu hồi hộp trước một cuộc thi đấu hay buổi diễn, các vận động viên và nhạc sĩ có thể ngáp. Ngáp làm cho họ tỉnh táo hơn. Nói như vậy là vì khi ngáp các cơ mặt căng giãn ra. Việc vươn giãn cơ bắp làm cho máu huyết chảy vào não nhiều hơn. Tuy nhiên, dù đã có những cuộc thử nghiệm và giải thích này, một số nhà khoa học nghĩ rằng không có lý do gì khiến cho ta ngáp.

CANTONESE

Yawning 是一篇知識性文章，講述人們為何打呵欠．很多人認為，疲倦或沈悶是打呵欠的原因．有位名叫羅拔‧普溫的科學家，完成了一些實驗，結果顯示人在感到疲倦或沈悶時，確實會打呵欠．人在舒展身體時亦會打呵欠．疲倦及沈悶的人不是唯一會打呵欠的人．如果對比賽或演出感到緊張，運動員及音樂家亦會打呵欠．打呵欠有助於他們提高警覺，這是因為打呵欠舒展了面部的肌肉，能為腦部帶來更多血液．雖然有這些實驗及解釋，部份科學家認為打呵欠並不需要甚麼理由．

CAMBODIAN

"Yawning" ជាសៀវភៅដែលមាន មួយអំពី មនុស្សរៀលស្លាបៗ. មនុស្សជាច្រើនគិតថា ការអស់កំលាំងឬ អផ្សុក បណ្ដាល ឱ្យស្លាបៗ. អ្នកវិទ្យាសាស្ត្រម្នាក់ឈ្មោះ រ៉ូប៊ីត ប្រូវីន ធ្វើការសាកល្បងដើម្បីបង្ហាញថា មនុស្ស ពិតជាស្លាបនៅពេលណាអស់កំលាំងឬ អផ្សុក. មនុស្សកំស្លាបដែរ ពេលណាគេចង់ទ្រនិចខ្លួន. មនុស្សអស់កំលាំងឬ អផ្សុក មិនមែនជាអ្នកស្លាបតែម្នាក់នោះ. បើពេល ជ្រាល ថ្ងៃមុន ព្រឹត្តិការណ៍ណីមួយ អ្នកកីឡាឬអ្នកភ្លេង អាច ស្លាបៗ. ការស្លាបធ្វើឱ្យគេ មានការ មុ៉ល្អ ប្រុងប្រៀបមុខៗ. ដ៏ព្រោះការស្លាបវាពាញសាច់ដុំលើថ្ងៃមុខៗ. ការទ្រនិច ធ្វើឱ្យ ធ្លាយ ឈាម ថ្ងៃនៅខ្ញុំ ស្កាល់ ថៃ មាតៀ៉ៗ. បើនោះៈ ជាមាន ។ របស់ និងការ ពន្យល់ ទាំងនេះៈ ភ្នំ អ្នកវិទ្យាសាស្ត្រ ៥ៈ គិតថា ឆ្អាបារហុតុលភ្ទីបញ្ហាក់ពីការស្លា បនៈ ។

HAITIAN CREOLE

"Yawning" se yon tèks enfòmasyonèl konsènan rezon ki fè moun baye. Anpil moun panse se fatig oswa lè yon moun annuiye ki fè moun baye. Yon syantifik yo rele Robert Provine te fè yon tès pou l montre moun baye vre lè yo annuiye oswa fatige. Moun baye tou lè y ap detire. Se pa sèlman moun ki fatige oswa annuiye ki baye. Si yo nève anvan yon aktivite, atlèt ak mizisyen ka baye tou. Lè yo baye sa ede yo rete pi alèt. Se paske lè w baye sa detire misk ki nan figi w yo. Lè w detire sa fè plis san ale nan sèvo w. Menm avèk tout tès sa yo ak eksplikasyon sa yo, kèk syantifik panse pa gen okenn rezon ki eksplike poukisa moun baye.

UNIT 1 • CHAPTER 4

The Sneak Thief, by Falcon Travis

ENGLISH

In this mystery, Inspector Will Ketchum asks Mr. Fink questions. The Inspector thinks Mr. Fink took a briefcase holding papers and money. Mr. Fink tells the Inspector that someone gave him the wrong briefcase. He says his briefcase contains magazines only. Then Mr. Fink tells the Inspector why he is in town. Mr. Fink says that he has a ticket to travel to town for one day and then he is returning home that night. He says he is in town to buy books. He also says he has plans to leave town that night. Then, Mr. Fink empties his pockets. He does not have a key for his briefcase, a return ticket home, or enough money to buy books. These missing things prove that the briefcase does not belong to Mr. Fink.

SPANISH

En este misterio, el inspector Will Ketchum hace preguntas al señor Fink. El inspector piensa que el señor Fink se tomó un maletín en el que hay dinero y papeles importantes. El señor Fink asegura al inspector que alguien le dio el maletín equivocado y que en su maletín sólo hay revistas. También le dice que vino a la ciudad a comprar libros y que tiene un boleto para regresar esa misma noche a casa. Cuando el señor Fink desocupa sus bolsillos, el inspector se da cuenta de que Fink no tiene la llave para abrir el maletín, no tiene su boleto de regreso y tampoco tiene suficiente dinero para comprar libros. Estas cosas confirman que el maletín no es del señor Fink.

HMONG

Nyob rau qhov dab neeg uas nkagsiab tsi zoo txog no, tug kws xwj uas yog Will Ketchum nug Mr. Fink ntau yam. Tug kws xwj xav hais tias lub hnabtawv Mr. Fink nqa ntawd yog ntim ntaub ntawv thiab nyiaj. Mr. Fink hais rau tus kws xwj ntawd tias leejtwg tau muab lub hnabtawv yuamkev rau nws lawm. Nws hais tias nws lub ruas muaj cov ntawv magazines xwb. Ces Mr. Fink nug tug kws xwj hais tias yog vim li cas nws ho tuaj rau hauv lub zos ntawd. Mr. Fink hais tias nws muaj ib daim tivkev tuaj nyob ib hnub hauv zos xwb thiab yuav tau rov qab mus tsev hmo ntawd. Nws hais tias nws tuaj hauv zos yog tuaj yuav ib co ntawv. Tsi tag li ntawd nws kuj hais tias nws yuav mus tsev mo ntawd thiab. Ces Mr. Fink thau nws tej hnab tsis hnab tshos. Nws tsi muaj tug yuamsij rau lub hnabtawv, tsi muaj tivkev rov mus tsev, thiab tsi muaj nyiaj txaus yuav ntawv li. Qhov tsi muaj cov khoom ntawm no ua tau pov thawj qhia tias lub hnabtawv no tsi yog Mr. Fink li.

VIETNAMESE

Trong truyện trinh thám này, Thanh Tra Viên Will Ketchum thẩm vấn Ông Fink. Thanh Tra Viên nghi rằng Ông Fink đánh cắp chiếc vali đựng giấy tờ và tiền bạc. Ông Fink nói với Thanh Tra Viên rằng có người đưa lộn cho ông cái vali. Ông nói rằng chiếc vali của mình chỉ đựng tạp chí mà thôi. Rồi Ông Fink cho Thanh Tra Viên biết lý do ông có mặt tại thành phố. Ông Fink đã mua vé du lịch tới thành phố rồi sẽ trở về nhà vào buổi tối cùng ngày. Ông nói rằng ông đến thành phố để mua sách. Ông cũng nói rằng ông dự định rời thành phố vào tối hôm đó. Sau đó, Ông Fink dốc hết các túi ra. Ông không có chìa khóa vali, vé khứ hồi, cũng không đủ tiền mua sách. Điều này chứng minh rằng chiếc vali không thuộc về Ông Fink.

CANTONESE

在這個懸疑故事中，警官威·傑臣盤問芬格先生．這位警官認為芬格先生拿了一個內有文件及金錢的公文箱．芬格先生告訴警官，有人錯給他這個公文箱．他說他的公文箱內只有雜誌．然後芬格先生告訴警官他到該鎮的原因．芬格先生說，他有一張前往該鎮的即日車票，他會在當天晚上回家．他說他來這裏是為了買書，還說他計劃當晚離開．然後，芬格先生把衣袋中的所有東西取出來．他並沒有公文箱的鎖匙，也沒有回程車票或足夠買書的錢．缺少這些東西，便証明這個公文箱不是芬格先生的．

CAMBODIAN

នៅក្នុងរឿងអាថិកំបាំងនេះ អធិការប៉ូលីស វីល ខេទ្សុម ស្ទង់ស្ទើរលោក ហ្វីង។ អធិការ គិតថាលោក ហ្វីង យកការប៉ូបដែលមាក់ក្រោសស្ថា មធិឈលចប។ លោក ហ្វីង ប្រាប់ទៅអធិការ ថា មានមនុស្សឲ្យការប៉ុនុស មកគាត់។ គាត់ថា ការប៉ូមានទេស្ស្យាឆ្ងាឌ្បដៃប៉ុណ្ណោះ។ បន្ទាប់មកលោក ហ្វីង ប្រាប់ទៅអធិការដ៍មូលហេតុដែលគាត់មកគ្រុងនេះ។ លោក ហ្វីង ថាវាសនាគាត់មានសំបុត្រធ្វើដំណើរ មុក មកគាត់ឆ្ងឺក្រុងស៉ាវាប់ម្ងយ៉ៃ ហើយគាត់ត្រូវ្រ្រឡប់ទៅផ្ទះវិញនៅពេលយប់នោះ។ បន្ទាប់មក លោក ហ្វីង ពាមាកមាំនោភាវិភាគ់ទេញ។ គាត់ ឋានក្ងោះសាសំរាប់ការប៉ូនោះ១ម, មានទៃស៉ីបុត្រធ្វើដំណើរ មកផ្ទះវិញ ឬក៍លុយសល្យមទិញាសុ្រវគ្រាំ។ ការឧ្ងវ្តុំនៃ នេះ បញ្ជាក់ថា ការប៉ុម៉ឺនៃមែនជារបស់លោក ហ្វីង ឡើយ។

HAITIAN CREOLE

Nan mistè sa a, Enspektè Will Ketchum ap poze mesye Fink kèk kesyon. Enspektè a panse mesye Fink te volè yon valiz ki te gen kèk papye ak kòb ladan l. Mesye Fink di Enspektè a se yon moun ki te ba li move valiz lan. Li di valiz pa l lan sèlman gen revi ladan l. Aprè sa mesye Fink eksplike Enspektè a pouki rezon ki fè li nan vil lan. Mesye Fink di li te gen yon tikè pou l vwayaje pase nan vil lan pou yon jou epi li gen pou li retounen lakay li nan aswè. Li di li vin nan vil lan pou achte kèk liv. Li di tou li gen entansyon kite vil lan nan menm aswè an. Aprè sa, mesye Fink vide tout pòch li yo. Li pa gen yon kle pou valiz li an, yon tikè retou, oswa ase lajan pou li achete liv yo. Tout bagay sa yo ki manke yo pwouve valiz lan pa pou pou mesye Fink.

Name _____ Date _____

UNIT 1 • CHAPTER 5
The Legend of Sleepy Hollow, by Washington Irving

ENGLISH

In this legend, the people of Sleepy Hollow tell stories about the Headless Horseman. Some people think the Horseman is a ghost. People say the Horseman lost his head in the Revolutionary War. One man says the Headless Horseman is looking for his missing head when he rides at night. Ichabod Crane enjoys stories about the Headless Horseman. When Crane walks home at night, these stories come to life. He sees shapes and shadows that he thinks are signs of the Headless Horseman. Sometimes he hears something rushing through the trees. Crane tells himself that it is just the wind, but he is always scared that it may be the Headless Horseman.

SPANISH

En ésta leyenda, los habitantes del pueblo de Sleepy Hollow cuentan historias acerca del Cabalgante Descabezado. Algunos creen que el Cabalgante es un fantasma, y que perdió su cabeza en una batalla en la Guerra de la Independencia. Un hombre dice que el Cabalgante sale de noche en busca de su cabeza. Ichabod Crane disfruta éstas historias acerca del Cabalgante Descabezado. Cuando Crane camina hacia su casa de noche, las historias toman vida. Ve figuras y sombras que lo hacen pensar que son señales del Cabalgante. A veces escucha algo que pasa por los árboles y Crane se dice a sí mismo que es tan sólo el viento; sin embargo, siempre siente temor de que realmente sea el Cabalgante Descabezado.

HMONG

Nyob rau zaj dab neeg no, cov tib neeg nyob rau hauv lub zos Sleepy Hollow piav tej dab neeg txog tus Txivneej Tsi Muaj Taubhau caij nees. Tej tib neeg ib txhia xav hais tias tug txivneej caij nees no yog ib tug ntsujduab dab. Tej tib neeg hais tias tug txivneej caij nees ntawd lub taub hau poob thaum tsov rog ncaws nom tswv uas yog Revolutionary War lawm. Muaj ib tug txivneej hais tias tug txivneej tsi muaj taub hau ntawd pheej nrhiav nws lub taub hau thaum nws caij nees yav raus ntuj. Thaum Crane mus taw mus tsev yav tsaus ntuj, cov dab neeg no txawm muaj tshwm tiag li. Nws pom tej yam thiab tej tug duab uas nws xav tias yuav yog tus txivneej caij nees uas tsi muaj taub hau ntawd ntag. Tej thaum nws hnov tej yam nrov phoom cuagtsi tom tej ntoo los. Crane xav twbywm rau nws tus kheej hais tias nws tsuas yog cua xwb, tiam sis nws ntshai tas mus li hais tias tsam ib ntsis nws ho yog tug txivneej caij nees uas tsi muaj taub hau.

VIETNAMESE

Trong truyền thuyết này, cư dân thị trấn Sleepy Hollow kể chuyện về Kỵ Sĩ Không Đầu. Một số người cho rằng Kỵ Sĩ là một con ma. Người ta nói rằng Kỵ Sĩ bị mất đầu tại Trận Chiến Cách Mạng. Một người đàn ông kể rằng khi cưỡi ngựa vào ban đêm, Kỵ Sĩ Không Đầu đi tìm chiếc đầu bị chặt đi của mình. Ichbod Crane thích thú với những câu chuyện về Kỵ Sĩ Không Đầu. Khi Crane đi bộ về nhà vào ban đêm, những câu chuyện này sống lại. Ông thấy những hình bóng trông như dấu hiệu của Kỵ Sĩ Không Đầu. Đôi khi ông nghe tiếng vật gì đó lao xuyên qua cây cối. Crane tự nhủ rằng chắc chỉ là gió thôi, nhưng cậu luôn lo sợ có thể đó là Kỵ Sĩ Không Đầu.

CANTONESE

在這個傳奇中，Sleepy Hollow 的居民講述了關於「無頭騎士」的故事。有些人認為這名騎士是個幽靈。人們說，騎士在獨立戰爭中掉了頭顱。有一個人說，無頭騎士在深夜出沒，是要尋找他失去的頭顱。伊查保·關尼很喜歡無頭騎士的故事。當關尼深夜步行回家時，這些故事變成了活生生的事。他看到人影或黑影，便以為看到了無頭騎士的縮影。有時他聽到樹林中有東西在奔走。關尼告訴自己，那只是刮風而已，但他時常都感到驚慌，以為那可能就是無頭騎士。

CAMBODIAN

เเอ็ก្នុงเรឿงเเรยฎบุราณ មនุស្សเเอ็ស្រុก Sleepy Hollow ธิឋาฮาเริฎๆฎีอ็กฏๅ็เร็ะ ฎา้ก็ฐาฮกญาญฯ มนุស្ស่เ้ยฎ ฎกญ:เร็ะ์ฏ้ฮ้ณាฎ่ฯ ฎกស្រุก้ยฎ ฎกฯ:เร็ะ ฎา้ก็ฯาฎเเอ็ฎ็เฎฮ้ฮฎບ้ฮ็ฯฏฏ็ฯ มนุ ฎก้ฮ้ฮขา ฎกญ:เร็ะ:อ็ก็ฯาฎ ฎฉฮฎก็ฯาฎ้ฎญฮา้ฮบณ์กฏ็ญ เฮณณฏฮ่ฎ็:เร็ะ:ฮบ่ฆ็ฆๅ ฎีฮฎบ่ 1ฎฎ ฮฉ้ฮฎ่เฮฮๆฎ็เรช:ฮฉฮฎก็ฯาฎเ:ณ้ฯฯ เฮณ 1ฎฎ เฮฎฆฏๅฎฎฮ่ เฮฮฏบ่ฎเฎฮเ:ฮาญ็ ฎฮฎฎ่ฯฯ ฎฮฎฮบ็ฯฯเฮฏ็่ฮฮฏ:ฮฯฎ เฮฮฮฮๆฮ้ฮฎ เฮ็ฎ็ฯฯฮา ฎฮบๅฯำฮฮฏฮฮฎฯบ่ฮฎกฎฮ:ฮฮฎก็ฯาฎฯ เฮณฎฮฮฮฮฏฮฮฮฮฎฎฮฮฮฆ็ฯฯฏฮฮฮฮฮฮฮ้ฮ฿ฮฮฆ 1ฎฎ ธิฮฮฮฯฯฯำฎ฿ฮเอฮ ฮฮฎฮเฮฎฮฮฮฎฮๅฮฮฆฮๆฎ: เฮฮฮ เฮฮฮเฮฮฮ็ฮฮ ฮฯฎฮฮฮฮฆฮฮฮฮฎฮฮ:ฮฮฮฎฯฯาฎ้ยฯฯฮฎฎฯ

HAITIAN CREOLE

Nan lejann sa a, abitan Sleepy Hollow yo rakonte istwa sou Chevalye San Tèt. Kèk moun panse Chevalye a se yon fantom li ye. Moun rakonte Chevalye a te pèdi tèt li nan Lagè Revolisyonè a. Yon mesye fè konnen Chevalye San Tèt ap chèche tèt li lè yo wè l ap galope lèswa. Ichabod Crane renmen tande istwa sou Chevalye San Tèt. Lè Crane ap mache nannuit pral lakay li, istwa sa yo vin tounen yon reyalite. Li wè kèk fòm ak lombraj li panse ki se siy Chevalye San Tèt lan. Kèlkefwa li tande yon bagay k ap kouri pase nan bwa yo. Crane di tèt li se sèlman van k ap vante, men li toujou pè pou se pa Chevalye San Tèt lan k ap pase.

Name _____   Date _____

UNIT 2 • CHAPTER 1

How I Survived My Summer Vacation, by Robin Friedman

ENGLISH

Jackie is on summer vacation. He is trying to write a book. He is having a hard time thinking of things to write. He smells coffee. This means his father is making breakfast. He does not like Saturday breakfasts with his parents. At breakfast, Jackie tells his parents he does not like this weekly meal. His father tells him to relax and to have a muffin. This upsets Jackie. Jackie's parents tell him that they are sending him to a computer camp. Jackie tells his parents that they always send him to places he does not want to go. Jackie says he will not go, and he leaves the room.

SPANISH

Jackie está en vacaciones de verano y está tratando de escribir un libro, pero aún no sabe acerca de qué escribir. Hay un olor a café, lo que significa que su papá está preparando el desayuno. A Jackie no le gusta el desayuno de los sábados con sus padres y se los hace saber en este día. Su papá le dice que se relaje y que más bien se coma un panecillo. Eso hace enojar a Jackie. Luego sus padres le dicen que lo van a enviar a un campamento para que aprenda a manejar computadores. Jackie les reclama que ellos siempre lo envían a lugares a los que a él no le gusta ir. Jackie dice que él no quiere ir y se va del cuarto donde estaban hablando.

HMONG

Jackie mus so rau lub caij ntuj qhua. Nws tabtom sim sau ib phau ntawv. Nyuaj rau nws kawg li xav tsi tau ib yam los sau li. Nws hnov ntxhiab kasfes tsw. Qhov ntawm no txhais hais tias nws txiv tabtom ua tshais. Nws tsi nyiam noj tshais Vasxaum nrog nws niam thiab nws txiv. Thaum noj tshais, tug tub Jackie qhia rau nws niam thiab nws txiv hais tias nws tsi nyiam pluas mov ib asthiv muaj ib zaug no. Nws txiv hais tias kom nws nyob twbywm es cia li noj nws lub qhaubcij muffin. Qhov no cia li ua rau Jackie chim. Jackie niam thiab txiv hais tias obtug yuav muab nws xa mus rau ib lub chaw xyaum computer. Jackie hais rau nws niam thiab nws txiv hais tias nkawv yeej ibtxwm xa nws mus rau tej chaw uas nws tsi xav mus. Jackie hais tias nws yuav tsi kam mus, no ces nws txawm tawm lub hoob ntawd mus lawm.

VIETNAMESE

Jackie đang nghỉ hè. Cậu cố gắng viết một cuốn sách. Cậu gặp khó khăn trong việc nghĩ ra một chủ đề để viết. Cậu ngửi thấy mùi cà phê. Điều này có nghĩa là cha cậu đang nấu bữa sáng. Cậu không thích ăn sáng với cha mẹ vào Thứ Bảy. Vào bữa sáng, Jackie nói với cha mẹ rằng cậu không thích bữa ăn này trong tuần. Cha bảo cậu nên bớt nóng và hãy ăn một miếng bánh nướng xốp. Jackie rất bực mình. Cha mẹ Jackie nói với cậu là họ sẽ gởi cậu đến một trại học vi tính. Jackie nói rằng lúc nào cha mẹ cũng gởi cậu đến những nơi cậu không muốn đến. Jackie nói cậu sẽ không đi, rồi đi ra khỏi phòng.

CANTONESE

積奇正在放暑假，他想嘗試寫一本書，卻發現很難找到寫作題材。他聞到咖啡香味，說明父親正在弄早餐。他不喜歡與他的父母在星期六一起吃早餐。在吃早餐時，積奇告訴父母，他不喜歡這種每週例行的早餐。父親讓他放輕鬆，並叫他吃一個鬆餅。這令積奇很不開心。積奇的父母告訴他，要送他去參加一個電腦學習營。積奇告訴父母說，他們經常送他去他不想去的地方。積奇說他不會去學習營，說完便離開了房間。

CAMBODIAN

តាកគី មានវិស្សមកាលសួរវត្តៗ។ វាកំពុងសាកល្បងចងសរសេរសៀវភៅមួយ។ វាមានការលំបាកក្នុងការគិតឱសរសេរអំពីអ្វី។ វាកំពុងនៅហ្ញូ ១ នៈមានន៍ធនា ឧ្ពុកវាកំពុងធ្វើអាហារស្រល់ស្រុបពេលព្រឹក។ វាមិនចូលចិត្តស្រល់ស្រុបព្រឹកៃថ្ងៃសៅរ៍ជាមួយឧ្ពុកម្តាយវា។ ពេលស្រល់ស្រុប តាកគី និងាយប្រាប់ឧ្ពុកម្តាយ វា មិនចូលចិត្តអាហារ ប្រចាំសប្តាហ៍នេះទេ។ ឧ្ពុកវាប្រាប់វាឱ្យស្ងប់ស្ងាត់បន្តិច ហើយឱ្យញ៉ាំ់ម៉ុតម្តាយ។ វាធ្វើ តាកគី មិនសប្បាយចិត្ត។ ឧ្ពុកម្តាយតាកគី ប្រាប់វាថា ពួកគាត់និងបញ្ជូនវាទៅជំរុំហ្វឹកហ្វឺនខាងកំព្យូរ។ តាកគី និងាយថា ពួកគាត់តែងតែបញ្ជូនវាទៅតីណាៃដលវាមិនចង់ទៅ។ តាកគី និងាយថា វាមិនទៅៃទ ហើយវា ក៍ងើ់របេញ៉ញ័ពីបន្ទប់នៈទៅ។

HAITIAN CREOLE

Jackie nan vakans ete. Tigason an ap eseye ekri yon liv. Li gen anpil pwoblèm pou l reflechi sou kisa li pral ekri. Li pran sant kafe. Sa vle di papa l ap prepare ti dejene. Li pa renmen pran ti dejene le samdi ak paran l yo. Pandan ti dejene a, Jackie fè paran l yo konnen li pa renmen afè manje chak semèn sa a. Papa l di li pou l kalme l epi manje yon mòfenn (muffin). Jackie vin move. Paran Jackie yo di li yo pral voye l nan yon kan pou zafè òdinatè. Jackie di paran l yo toujou renmen voye l ale kote li pa renmen ale. Jackie di li pa prale, epi li vire kite pyès lan.

Name _____   Date _____

UNIT 2 • CHAPTER 2

The Voyage of the *Frog*, by Gary Paulsen

ENGLISH

This story is about David and his boat. The boat is called *Frog*. A storm pushed the *Frog* off course and now David is lost at sea. He does not know how he will survive. He sees a small ship in front of him. He gets the attention of the ship's crew. David sails the *Frog* to the ship. The ship's captain tells David to leave his boat and get on the ship. David does not want to leave his boat, the *Frog*, behind. David learns that his home is 350 miles away. He decides to sail the *Frog* home anyway. The ship's crew gives David food and supplies. David begins his long journey home.

SPANISH

Esta historia es acerca de David y su bote, llamado *Frog*. Durante uno de sus viajes, una tormenta sacó a *Frog* de su curso y ahora David está perdido en mar abierto. David no sabe cómo sobrevivirá, pero de pronto ve un barco cerca y hace señas para que lo vean. David navega a *Frog* hacia el barco y, cuando se acerca, el capitán del barco le dice que deje su bote y se suba al barco. Pero David no quiere abandonar a *Frog*. David se entera de que está a 350 millas de su destino y decide navegar a *Frog* de vuelta. Los marineros del barco le dan comestibles y provisiones a David y él emprende su largo viaje a casa.

HMONG

Zaj dab neeg no yog hais txog David thiab nws lub nkoj. Lub nkoj nws hu ua Frog. Nag xob nagcua muab Frog nrawj tig tsi ncaj ke lawm ces yog li tam sim no David poob zoo rau tom hiavtxwv lawm. Nws tsi paub hais tias xyov yuav ua li cas nws thiaj yuav ciajsia taus. Nws pom ib lub menyuam nkoj kaspaj ua nws ntej. Cov tub tswjsaib lub kaspaj ntawd txawm pom nws. David caij Frog mus rau ntawm lub kaspaj. Tus thawj tswm lub kaspaj hais rau David kom tso lub nkoj tseg es cia li mus rau saum lub kaspaj. David tsi kam tso nws lub nkoj tseg, muab Frog tso tseg rau tom qab. Thaum ntawd David paub hais tias nws lub tsev tseem tshuav li ntawm 350 mais mam li mus txog. Txawm li ntawd los nws cia li txiav txim siab caij Frog los mus tsev li lawm. Cov tub tswjsaib lub nkoj kaspaj muab zaub mov thiab khoom siv rau David. David mam li pib nws txojkev uas deb kawg nkaus los mus tsev lawm.

VIETNAMESE

Câu chuyện này kể về David và con thuyền của cậu. Chiếc thuyền có tên *Frog*. Một cơn bão đẩy thuyền sang lệch hướng và giờ đây David bị lạc giữa biển khơi. Cậu không biết làm cách nào để sống sót. Cậu trông thấy một tàu nhỏ phía trước. David gây sự chú ý cho các thủy thủ trên tàu. David chèo thuyền *Frog* đến con tàu. Tàu trưởng bảo David rời bỏ thuyền để lên tàu. David không muốn rời bỏ thuyền *Frog*. David được biết là nhà cậu cách đây 350 dặm. Cuối cùng cậu quyết định chèo thuyền *Frog* về nhà. Thủy thủ đoàn biểu thức ăn và đồ dùng cho David. David bắt đầu cuộc hành trình dài về nhà.

CANTONESE

這個故事是關於大衛及他的小船. 小船名叫 *Frog*. 大風將小船吹離航線, 大衛現在迷失在海中. 他不知道如何生存下去. 他看到前面有一條船, 船上的船員也看到了他. 大衛將 *Frog* 駛向那條船. 船上的船長讓大衛登上大船, 放棄小船. 大衛不想離棄他的小船. 他知道離家有三百五十英哩後, 決定駕駛 *Frog* 航行回家. 船上的水手給了大衛一些食物和物資, 大衛便開始他漫長的回家航程.

CAMBODIAN

រឿងនេះនិយាយអំពី ដេវីដ និងទូកររបស់វា ទូកនេះ:ឈ្មោះា *Frog* ។ ខ្យល់ព្យុះមួយបោញ *Frog* ឱ្យសងដេញ្ញ ហើយឥឡូវនេះ: ដេវីដ វង្វេងនៅកណ្ដាលសមុទ្រ វាមិនដឹងថា ធ្វើវាយ៉ាងស។្សាសំវាយ៉ាងបណ្ដោយ វាឃើញកប៉ាល់ខ្ទះមួយនៅពីមុខវា វាធ្វើឱ្យក្រុមនាវិកកប៉ាល់ចាប់អារម្មណ៍ ដេវីដបើកដេវ *Frog* ទៅកកប៉ាល់។ នាយកកប៉ាល់ប្រាប់វាឱ្យកចោលទូកវា ហើយឱ្យឡើងមកលើកប៉ាល់ ដេវីដមិនចង់ចោលកចោលទូកវា, *Frog* ឡាងថៃ ៦ ១គ្រោះា។ ដេវីដ ដឹងថា ផ្ទះវានៅឆ្ងាយ ៣៥០ ម៉ាយ។ ប៉ុន្តេ:ជាទីបំផុតវាយ វាសម្រចថា បើកកប៉ាល់ ទូកនៅផ្ទះវិញ។ ក្រុមនាវិកកប៉ាល់ឱ្យអូបម៉ូរបស់បានទៅ ដេវីដ។ ដេវីដចាប់ផ្ដើមការធ្វើដំណើរ ដ៏ឆ្ងាយ របស់វា ទៅផ្ទះវិញ។

HAITIAN CREOLE

Istwa sa a pale konsènan David ak bato l lan. Bato an rele *Frog*. Yon tanpèt dezoryante *Frog* nan direksyon l ta prale a epi kounye a David vin pèdi sou lanmè. Li pa konn kijan li pral fè siviv. Li wè yon ti bato devan l. Li kapte atansyon ekipaj lan. David navige *Frog* nan direksyon bato an. Kapitèn bato an di David pou li kite bato pa l lan epi pou li monte abò bato an. David pa vle abandone bato l lan, *Frog*. David aprann lakay li a yon distans de 350 mil. Li deside pou li navige *Frog* nan direksyon lakay li kanmenm. Ekipaj bato an bay David manje ak kèk ekipman. David kòmanse vwayaj long li an pou l ale lakay li.

UNIT 2 • CHAPTER 3

To Risk or Not to Risk, by David Ropeik

ENGLISH

"To Risk or Not to Risk" is an informational text about being afraid. Most people are afraid of snake and spider bites, but these things don't happen to most people. Our early ancestors were scared of these types of things. This fear helped them survive in the caves and fields where they lived. This text explains that some fears are good. Sometimes, people are not scared if they like the activity, even if it is dangerous (risky). For example, skiing is dangerous but also fun. For some people, skiing is not too risky because it is fun. When it comes to our fears, our feelings often matter more than what we know is true.

SPANISH

"To Risk or Not to Risk" es un texto informativo acerca de los temores. La mayoría de las personas le tiene miedo a la picada de víboras y arañas, aunque eso no le sucede a mucha gente. Gracias a éste temor, nuestros antepasados vivían prevenidos, lo cual les ayudaba a sobrevivir en las cuevas y los campos donde vivían. El texto nos explica que algunos temores son beneficiosos. A veces, la gente no le teme a actividades que le gusta hacer, aun si esas actividades son peligrosas. Por ejemplo, el esquiar es peligroso, pero también es divertido. Pero para algunos, esquiar no es peligroso, precisamente por lo que es divertido. Cuando se trata de temores, nuestros sentimientos a veces son más importantes que la realidad.

HMONG

"To Risk or Not to Risk" yog ib zaj lus hais txog muaj qhov ntshai. Feem coob tib neeg ntshai nab thiab kablaug tsov tom, tiam sis cov neeg feem coob tsi raug tom. Peb pojkoob yawmkoob lawv ntshai tej yam zoo li no. Tej kev ntshai no pab ua rau lawv ciajsia tau nyob rau tej qhov zeb a thiab tej tiajnrag uas lawv nyob. Zaj no piav qhia tias ib txhia cov kev ntshai no kuj zoo thiab. Tej thaum, tej tib neeg tsi ntshai yog hais tias lawv nyiam yam ntawd, txawm yog hais tias nws txaus ntshai (muaj qhov raug mob taus). Ib qhov ua pivtxwv, caij ski yog ib qhov kasdas tiam sis kuj lomzem thiab. Rau ib txhia tib neeg, caij ski nws kuj tsi kasdas ua luaj twg vim rau qhov lomzem. Thaum nws los txog rau qhov uas peb ntshai lawm, zoo li qhov yus xav tau ntawd muaj qab hau tshaj qhov kev ntshai uas yus paub ntawd lawm.

VIETNAMESE

"To Risk or Not to Risk" là một bài viết mang tính chất tài liệu nói về nỗi lo sợ. Đa số người ta sợ bị rắn hoặc nhện cắn, nhưng ít người gặp chuyện này. Tổ tiên chúng ta sợ những điều như vậy. Nỗi lo sợ này giúp cho họ tồn tại được trong các hang động và cánh đồng là nơi sống của họ. Bài viết này giải thích rằng một số nỗi lo sợ có tác dụng tốt. Đôi khi, nếu thích một hoạt động nào đó thì con người không sợ, ngay cả khi hoạt động đó nguy hiểm (đầy rủi ro). Thí dụ, môn trượt tuyết nguy hiểm nhưng cũng vui. Một số người cho rằng môn trượt tuyết không nguy hiểm lắm vì họ cảm thấy vui. Khi nói về nỗi lo sợ, cảm giác của chúng ta thường đóng vai trò lớn hơn cả sự thật.

CANTONESE

To Risk or Not to Risk 是一篇關於恐懼感的知識性文章. 大部份人害怕被蛇及蜘蛛咬到, 但這些事不會出現在大部份人身上. 我們的祖先很害怕這樣的事, 這種恐懼感幫助他們在居住的洞穴或野外生存下來. 文章中說道, 有時懂得害怕是好事. 人們如果喜歡某種活動, 即使這種活動很危險, 他們有時候也不會感到害怕. 例如, 滑雪是危險的, 但卻很好玩. 對某些人來說, 就是因為好玩, 所以覺得滑雪並不太危險. 說到懼怕時, 我們的感覺往往會勝過我們的理智.

CAMBODIAN

"To Risk or Not to Risk" ជាសៀវភៅដ៏មានស្តីពីការភ័យខ្លាច។ មនុស្សជាច្រើនខ្លាចពស់ និងពីងពាងទៅ ក៏ការនេះវាមិនមែនយល់កើតឡើងចំពោះ មនុស្សភាគច្រើនឡើយ។ ដូនតាយើងពីដើម ខ្លាចនូវបណ្តាខ្លាប់ របៀ។ ការខ្លាចរឺឡូឃកគេសល្អស់នៅក្នុងស្បែងឬនៅព្រៃ ដែលគេសល់នៅ។ សៀវភៅនេះពន្យល់ ការខ្លាចនះ ជាការល្អ។ ពេលខ្លះ មនុស្សមិនខ្លាចឡ ប្រិកែលចិត្តសកម្មភាពនោះ ទោះជាវាមានគ្រោះក៏ដោយ។ ឧទាហរណ៍ ការលេងស្គីលើទឹកកកជាគ្រោះ ខ្លាក់ ទែវាសប្បាយឬ។ សំរាប់មនុស្ស ការលេងមិន ជាការប្រសប់ ទៅកាន ពីព្រោះវាសប្បាយ។ ពេលណាយើងខ្លាច ការ អារម្មណ៍យើងមែនធ្វើជា ស្តីដែលយើងស្គឺងនៅ ជាការពិត។

HAITIAN CREOLE

"To Risk or Not to Risk" se yon tèks enfòmasyonèl ki pale sou lè moun pè. Pifò moun pè pou koulèv oswa areye pa mòde yo, men se pa bagay ki janm rive pifò moun. Zansèt lontan nou yo te konn pè bagay sa yo tou. Laperèz sa a te konn pèmèt yo siviv nan twou gwòt ak chan kote yo te rete yo. Tèks sa eksplike gen kèk laperèz ki bon. Kèlkefwa, moun pa pè si yo renmen fè yon aktivite, menm si li danjre (riske). Pa egzanp, fè eski se yon bagay ki danjre men ki amizan tou. Pou kèk moun, fè eski pa twò danjre paske li amizan. Lè se kesyon laperèz nou yo, santiman nou yo souvan pi enpòtan pase sa nou konnen ki laverite a.

UNIT 2 • CHAPTER 4
Island of the Blue Dolphins, by Scott O'Dell

ENGLISH

In this reading, 12-year-old Karana is alone on an island. She must build a shelter where she can live. Karana uses rib bones from whales to make a fence. This fence protects her from wild dogs. Then she builds a house out of wood. There is a place for a fire in the middle of the house. Karana cooks fish on a flat rock. When she cooks seeds, she uses a basket that she made. To hide food from mice, Karana makes shelves in a large rock. By the time she is done, Karana has everything she needs to survive.

SPANISH

En esta lectura, Karana, una niña de 12 años de edad, está sola en una isla y tiene que construir un refugio donde pueda vivir. Karana usa huesos de las costillas de ballenas para hacer una cerca, la cual la protege de perros salvajes. Luego construye una casa de madera y deja un lugar en el centro para hacer fuego. Karana cocina pescado en una piedra lisa y usa una canasta que hizo para cocinar semillas. Para esconder los alimentos de los ratones, Karana hace estantes en una roca grande. Cuando termina de arreglar la casa, tiene todo lo que necesita para sobrevivir.

HMONG

Nyob rau zaj lus ntawm no, Karana uas muaj 12-xyoos ib leeg nyob rau thaj av muaj dej puagncig. Tus ntxhais no tsi muaj ib qhov chaw rau nws nyob li. Karana siv cov tav ntses whales coj los xov ua lajkab. Tus lajkab no thaiv tau nws tsi pub tej dev qus los tau. Ces nws mam li ua ib lub tsev uas yog siv ntoo. Nyob hauv plaws lub tsev nws muaj ib qhov chaw rau cub hluas taws. Karan ci ntses rau saum ib daim txiagzeb. Thaum nws ci cov noob, tus ntxhais ntawd siv ib lub pobtawb uas nws tau hiab. Karan tsim tau ib cov txee nyob rau hauv lub pob zeb cia tej zaub mov sub navtsuag thiaj nrhiav tsi tau. Thaum Karana ua tau tiav ces nws yuav muaj txhua yam uas xav kom muaj los cawm tau txojsia lawm.

Name ______________________________ Date ______________________

VIETNAMESE

Trong bài đọc này, cô bé Karana 12 tuổi sống một mình trên một hòn đảo. Cô phải xây một nơi trú ẩn. Karana dùng xương sườn của cá voi để làm hàng rào. Hàng rào này bảo vệ cô khỏi bị chó hoang tấn công. Sau đó cô dùng gỗ để xây nhà. Giữa nhà có chỗ để nhóm lửa. Karana nấu cá trên một hòn đá phẳng. Khi cô nấu hạt, cô dùng một cái rổ do cô tự làm. Để tránh cho chuột gặm thức ăn, Karana làm những cái kệ trong một hòn đá lớn. Khi làm xong tất cả, Karana có đủ mọi thứ cần thiết cho cuộc sống.

CANTONESE

在這篇文章中，十二歲的卡華娜單獨住在一小島上．她必須搭建一個可以居住的房舍．卡華娜用鯨魚的肋骨做成圍欄，這樣可以保護她免受野狗的攻擊．然後，她用木材建造房屋．在房子的中央預留了生火的地方．卡華娜在一塊石板上燒魚．當她煮種子時，她用自製的籃子．為了防止老鼠偷吃她的食物，卡華娜在一塊大石頭中做了食物架．當她完成所有工作時，卡華娜已擁有生存所需要的一切．

CAMBODIAN

នៅក្នុងការអាននេះ ការ៉ាណា អាយុ ១២ឆ្នាំ រស់នៅលើកោះមួយម្នាក់ឯង។ នាងត្រូវសង់ជម្រកមួយដែលនាងអាចរស់នៅបាន។ ការ៉ាណា ប្រើឆ្អឹងជំនីរបស់ត្រីបាឡែនធ្វើជារបងផ្ទះ។ របងនេះការពារនាងពីសត្វឆ្កែព្រៃ។ បន្ទាប់មកនាងសង់ផ្ទះពីឈើ។ មានកន្លែងសំរាប់ដុតភ្លើងនៅកណ្តាលផ្ទះ។ ការ៉ាណា ចំអិនត្រីនៅលើថ្មសំប៉ែតមួយ។ ពេលណានាងចំអិនគ្រាប់ធញ្ញជាតិ នាងប្រើកន្ត្រកដែលនាងធ្វើ។ ដើម្បីលាក់ម្ហូបពីសត្វកណ្តុរ ការ៉ាណា ធ្វើធ្នើនៅលើថ្មធំមួយ។ មុនពេលបញ្ចប់ការសង់នេះ ការ៉ាណា មានអ្វីៗដែលនាងត្រូវការសំរាប់ជីវិតរស់។

HAITIAN CREOLE

Nan lekti sa a, Karana ki gen 12 an poukont li sou yon zil. Tifi an dwe bati yon kote pou l ka rete. Karana itilize zo kòt balèn pou li fè yon kloti. Kloti sa a pwoteje l kont chyen souvaj yo. Aprè sa li bati yon kay an bwa. Gen yon plas pou limen dife nan mitan kay la. Karana kuit pwason sou yon moso wòch plat. Lè l ap kuit grenn, li itilize yon panye li te fè. Pou l ka sere manje pou sourit pa jwenn li, Karana fè etajè nan yon gwo wòch. Lè l fin fè tout bagay sa yo, Karana gen tout sa li bezwen pou l ka siviv.

UNIT 2 • CHAPTER 5

The Next Great Dying, by Karin Vergoth and Christopher Lampton

ENGLISH

"The Next Great Dying" is an informational text. It explains why plants and animals are disappearing from Earth. Mass extinction is when many species of plants and animals die in a short time. The disappearance of the dinosaurs is an example of a mass extinction. According to scientists, Earth is in the middle of a mass extinction now. Scientists think that about 30 different kinds of animals and plants (species) disappear each day. Humans cause extinction by destroying the places that animals and plants live. If this does not stop, many more species will die.

SPANISH

"The Next Great Dying" es un texto informativo que explica por qué están desapareciendo las plantas y los animales de nuestro planeta. La extinción en masa es cuando muchas especies de plantas y animales mueren en un espacio corto de tiempo. La desaparición de los dinosaurios es un ejemplo de una extinción en masa. Según los científicos, la Tierra está en este momento en medio de una extinción en masa. Los científicos piensan que cerca de unas 30 especies diferentes de animales y plantas desaparecen cada día. Los seres humanos causan la extinción al destruir los lugares en los cuales viven las plantas y los animales. Si eso no deja de suceder, muchas más especies morirán.

HMONG

"The Next Great Dying" yog ib zaj qhia kom yus paub. Nws piav qhia txog tias yog vim li cas tej nroj thiab tej tsiaj pheej ploj hauv daim Av mus lawm. Tu noob thoob yog ib lub sib hawm luv uas tej tshiaj thiab nrojtsuag tau tuag. Qhov uas cov tsiaj dinosaurs ploj tag kuj yog ib qhov pivtxwv zoo heev rau lo lus tu noob thoob. Raws li cov kws tshawb nrhiav los sis scientists tau hais mas tam sim no lub Ntiajteb tabtom nyob rau hauv nruabnrab caij uas tu noob thoob. Cov kws tshawb nrhiav xav hais tias nyob rau ib hnub twg tejzaum yuav muj li ntawm 30 yam tsiaj thiab nrojtsuag tau ploj. Tej tib neeg ua rau tu noob los ntawm kev rhuav tsiaj txhu thiab nrojtsuag tej chaw nyob. Yog hais tias tsi tso tseg , tseem yuav muaj ntau hom tuag ntxiv thiab.

VIETNAMESE

"The Next Great Dying" là một bài viết mang tính chất tài liệu. Bài viết giải thích tại sao cây cối và động vật đang biến dần khỏi Trái Đất. Sự tuyệt chủng hàng loạt xảy ra khi nhiều loài cây cỏ và động vật bị chết trong vòng một thời gian ngắn. Sự biến mất của loài khủng long là một thí dụ cho sự tuyệt chủng hàng loạt. Theo các nhà khoa học, Trái Đất giờ đây đang trải qua một giai đoạn tuyệt chủng hàng loạt. Các nhà khoa học cho rằng mỗi ngày có khoảng 30 loài động vật và cây cỏ khác nhau bị mất đi. Con người gây nên sự tuyệt chủng hàng loạt qua việc phá hủy nơi sinh sống của động vật và cây cỏ. Nếu không chấm dứt, sẽ có thêm nhiều loài sinh vật bị tuyệt chủng.

CANTONESE

The Next Great Dying 是一篇知識性文章，解釋為什麼植物和動物正從地球上消失。集體滅絕是指很多品種的植物和動物在短時間內滅亡。恐龍的消失便是集體滅絕的一個例子。科學家說，地球目前正處在一場集體滅絕中。科學家認為每天約有三十種不同的動物和植物消失。人類破壞動、植物的生存環境，是導致滅絕的原因。如果不能制止人類的破壞行為，更多的物種將會滅亡。

CAMBODIAN

"The Next Great Dying" ជារឿ]រ៉ាវៃដ៏មាន ឮយ៉ា។ រឿ]រ៉ាវៃ៖ ព្យល់ពីហេតុផ្លី៣៣ជារឹក្ខជាតិ
និងសត្វចាន៊ូ]បាងពីៃផែ្ដី៖។ ការ សុទ្ធឌ៌ជមួយសាំ៣ត៌ំ៉ំកីៃ៖ឡ៉ែង នៅៃ៤ល ណៃឌរុក្ខជាតិនិ៍និងសត្វជាៃ្រើ៖ស្ល៉ាប៊
នៅក្តុងៃ៤ល ឌិ្ជ៌្ទីឮយ៉ា។ ការ ៣ថ់បង់សត្វឆ្យោយណាស៍, គឺជាឧ ទាហរណ៍មួយៃៃ ការ សុទ្ធឌ៌ជ៌ីៃ្ំ៉៖។ ៃៅ៣ៃៃៃ៣ម
អ្នកវិៃ្ញាសាស្ត្រ ៃៃ៖ដី៧៣ៃ៖៖ៃ៖រ៉ី៌រណាល ៧៣ៃ ៃៃា៖ការ សុទ្ធឌ៌ជ៌ី៌ំ៉ៃ៖។ អ្នកវិៃ្ញាសាស្ត្រកិ៊ៃ៣, រុក្ខជារឹ
និងសត្វ្រៃប្៉ៃៃ ៃ ៣០ មុ៖(៣ៃ)៣ថ់បង់មួយៃៃ្ត៉៖។ មនុ៖ុៃ្តអ្នកបណ្ណាល៌៛ មានការ សុទ្ធឌ៌ជៃ៖ៃ្ំ៉ែ៖ ៃៅឧ
ការ បំផ្លាញៃ៣ៃៃង់៉ៃ៖លសន្ថ៌ិសុក្ខជា ៃ៊ស៍នៅ៧។ បៃៃៃ្ញាៃ៖ មៃៃល ប៉៖ ៧៣ជាៃ្រៃ៖ៃ៉ិ៌ៃ៏ៃស្ល៉ាប៊។

HAITIAN CREOLE

"The Next Great Dying" se yon tèks enfòmasyonèl. Li eksplike pouki rezon plant ak bèt yo ap disparèt sou Latè. Gen yon ekstenksyon an mas se lè anpil espès plant ak bèt mouri nan yon ti kras tan. Disparisyon dinozò yo se yon egzanp ekstenksyon an mas, Selon syantifik yo, Latè nan mitan yon peryòd ektenksyon an mas kounye a. Syantifik yo panse apeprè 30 kalite plant ak bèt diferan (espès yo) ap disparèt chak jou. Se lèzòm ki lakòz ekstenksyon an lè yo detwi kote bèt ak plant yo abitye viv. Si sa pa sispann, anpil lòt espès pral disparèt.

UNIT 3 • CHAPTER 1
I Have No Address, by Hamza El Din

ENGLISH

In the poem "I Have No Address," the speaker is a sparrow. The sparrow flies around Earth. It sings for peace everywhere. It smiles and cries. The sparrow does not live in one place. It travels. It washes away pain everywhere with its tears. People are like boats on rough waves. The sparrow is like a peaceful shore. The sparrow says that when people join hands, the world will be full of hope and love. In the last stanza, the happy sparrow is sleeping on a branch. It is dreaming that it is flying everywhere.

SPANISH

En el poema "I Have No Address", el narrador es un gorrión. El gorrión vuela alrededor del planeta y canta por la paz. También ríe y llora. Él no vive en ningún lugar en especial. Viaja y borra la pena con sus lágrimas a donde quiera que va, ya que dice que la gente vive como los botes en aguas bravas. El gorrión es como una playa pacífica. También dice que cuando la gente se una de las manos, el mundo se llenará de esperanza y amor. En la última estrofa, el gorrión duerme feliz en una rama y sueña que vuela por todos lados.

HMONG

Nyob rau hauv zaj lus paivyi uas "I Have No Address," tus hais cov lus no yog ib tug noog dawbtxia. Tus noog dawbtxia no ya ncig lub ntiajteb. Nws hu nkauj kom muaj txojkev thajyeeb rau txhua qhov chaw. Nws quaj thiab luag ntxhi. Tus noog dawbtxia no nws tsi yog nyob rau ib qhov chaw xwb. Nws ncig mus rau txhua qhov. Nws cov kua muag ntxuav txhua yam mob tawm mus. Tej tib neeg nyiam caij nkoj mus rau tej qhov dej ntas muajceem. Tiam sis tus noog dawbtxia zoo li tus dej uas tusyees tsi txawj ntas. Tus noog dawbtxia hais tias thaum twg yog tib neeg los tuavtes ua ke ces yuav ua rau lub ntiajteb puv npo rau txojkev ciasiab thiab kev hlub. Nyob rau lwm nqi lus paivyi, tus noog dawbtxia muaj kev zoo siab thiab pw tsaugzog nyob rau saum ib tus ceg ntoo. Nws tabtom ua npausuav txog ya mus rau txhua qhov chaw.

VIETNAMESE

Trong bài thơ "I Have No Address," nhân vật chính là một con chim sẻ. Chim sẻ bay vòng quanh Trái Đất. Chim hót cho hòa bình khắp nơi. Chim cười và khóc. Chim sẻ không sống ở cùng một chỗ. Chim bay từ nơi này sang nơi khác. Bằng những giọt nước mắt của mình, chim làm trôi đi nỗi đau ở mọi nơi. Con người tựa như những con thuyền trên sóng động. Chim sẻ như một bờ cát thanh bình. Chim nói rằng khi con người nắm chặt tay nhau, thế giới sẽ tràn đầy hy vọng và tình yêu. Trong khổ thơ cuối, con chim sẻ hạnh phúc đang ngủ trên một cành cây. Chim mơ rằng chim bay khắp đó đây.

CANTONESE

在這篇 I Have No Address 的詩中，朗誦者是一隻麻雀。麻雀飛過全世界，到處為和平歌唱。他會歡笑，也會哭泣。麻雀並不住在一個固定地方，他四處周遊。他用眼淚洗去四周的痛苦。人們好像在巨浪中的小船，麻雀好像一處平靜的海岸。麻雀說當人們手拉手時，世界將充滿希望和愛。在最後一節中，快樂的麻雀正在樹枝上睡覺。他夢見自己正在四處飛翔呢。

CAMBODIAN

នៅក្នុងកំណាព្យ "I Have No Address," អ្នកនិយាយគឺជាសត្វចាបមួយ។ សត្វចាបនេះហោះហើរ ជុំវិញផែនដី។ វាច្រៀងសម្រាប់សន្តិភាពគ្រប់ទីកន្លែង។ វាញញឹម ហើយវាស្រែកយំ។ សត្វចាបនេះ មិននៅមួយកន្លែង ទេ។ វាធ្វើដំណើរ។ វាលប់លាងចេញនូវការឈឺចាប់គ្រប់កន្លែង ដោយទឹកភ្នែករបស់វា។ មនុស្សប្រៀបដូចជាទូកនៅលើលោក ទឹកភ្លោតក្រក។ សត្វចាបប្រៀបដូចជ្រោយសន្តិភាពមួយ។ សត្វចាបនិយាយថា ពេលណាមនុស្សចាប់ដៃគ្នា ពិភពលោកនឹង ពោរពេញទៅដោយក្ដីសង្ឃឹម និងសេចក្ដីស្រឡាញ់។ នៅក្នុងឃ្លាចុងក្រោយ សត្វចាបដ៏សាទរនេ កំពុងដេកនៅលើ មែកឈើ មួយ។ វាយល់សប្ដិថា វានិយាយហើរគ្រប់ទីកន្លែង។

HAITIAN CREOLE

Nan powèm "I Have No Address," oratè a se yon ti zwazo yo rele mwano. Mwano a vole sou tout tè a. Li chanje pou lapè tout kote. Li souri epi li kriye. Mwano an pa rete yon sèl kote. Li vwayaje. Li lave doulè toupatou avèk dlo ki sot nan je l. Moun se tankou bato ki sou dlo ajite. Mwano an tankou yon rivaj pezib. Mwano an di lè moun mete men yo ansanm, lemonn pral ranpli ak lespwa ak lanmou. Nan dènye estwòf lan, mwano an kouche sou yon branch ak kè kontan. Li ap reve l ap vole toupatou.

UNIT 3 • CHAPTER 2
The Voyage of the Lucky Dragon, by Jack Bennett

ENGLISH

This story takes place around 1970, after the Vietnam War. The new government is taking control of all businesses in Vietnam. A man from the new government comes to Phan Thi Chi's shop. He tells Phan Thi Chi that the shop belongs to the government now. The man says Phan Thi Chi and his family must move to government camps. The family will learn to be farmers there. The man leaves. Phan Thi Chi tells his family that they should run away to a small village. There, they will fish on his father's boat. Phan Thi Chi's son says he will. Aunt Binh is not sure. In the end, everyone decides to go.

SPANISH

Esta historia se lleva a cabo a finales de la década de 1970, después de haberse terminado la Guerra de Vietnám. El nuevo gobierno de Vietnám toma control de todos los negocios del país y un representante del nuevo gobierno llega a la tienda de Phan Thi Chi. El representante le dice a Phan Thi Chi que ahora la tienda le pertenece al gobierno y que él y su familia se tienen que ir a vivir a un campamento del gobierno. También le dice que allí tendrán que aprender a trabajar en el campo. Cuando el representate se va, Phan Thi Chi le dice a su familia que se deberían escapar a un pueblo pequeño y que allí podrán pescar tranquilos en el bote de su padre. El hijo de Phan Thi Chi dice que está de acuerdo con él, pero la tía Binh no está segura. Sin embargo, al final todos deciden ir.

HMONG

Zaj dab neeg ntawm no muaj tshwm sim nyob rau cheeb tsam ntawm xyoo 1970, tsi ntev tom qab tsov rog Nyablaj. Tsoomfwv tshiab tau los tswj kav tagnrho txhua yam kev lagluam nyob rau tebchaw Nyablaj. Muaj ib tug txivneej sawv cev rau tsoomfwv tshiab txawm tuaj rau ntawm Phan Thi Chi lub khw. Nws hais rau Phan Thi Chi tias tam sim no lub khw yog tsoomfwv li lawm. Tus txivneej hais tias Phan Thi Chi thiab nws tsev neeg yuav tsum tau tawm mus nyob rau hauv tsoomfwv tej vajloog los sis camps. Tsev neeg yuav mus kawm txog kev ua liaj ua teb nyob rau tod. Ces tus txivneej txawm mus lawm. Phan Thi Chi hais rau nws tsev neeg hais tias ntshai lawv yuav tau khiav mus rau ib lub zos me. Nyob rau tod, lawv mam li siv nws txiv lub nkoj mus cuab ntses. Phan Thi Chi tus tub hais tias nws yuav ua li ntawd. Phauj Binh tseem tsi tau paub zoo hais tias xyov nws yuav mus los tsi mus. Thaum kawg txhua leej txhua tus puav leej txiav txim siab mus huv tibsi.

VISIONS **READING SUMMARIES** Unit 3

VIETNAMESE

Truyện xảy ra vào cuối thập niên 1970, sau Chiến Tranh Việt Nam-Mỹ. Chính quyền mới giành lấy quyền kiểm soát tất cả các cơ sở kinh doanh ở Việt Nam. Một viên chức của chính quyền mới tới cửa hàng của Phan Thi Chi. Ông nói với Phan Thi Chi rằng giờ đây cửa hàng thuộc về chính phủ. Ông nói rằng Phan Thi Chi và gia đình phải dọn đến trại của chính phủ. Ở đó cả gia đình sẽ học làm nông dân. Ông bỏ đi. Phan Thi Chi bảo gia đình nên chạy trốn tới một ngôi làng nhỏ. Ở đó, họ sẽ đánh cá trên thuyền của người cha. Con trai của Phan Thi Chi đồng ý. Dì Binh còn phân vân. Cuối cùng, mọi người đồng ý ra đi.

CANTONESE

這個故事發生在越戰之後的一九七零年代後期。新政府控制了越南所有的商業。一個新政府的官員去到潘氏志的店裏。他告訴潘氏志，商店現在已經屬於政府了。那人說，潘氏志及他的家人必須搬到政府的營地去。他們將在那裏學習耕種。那人離開後，潘氏志告訴家人，他們應該逃往一個小鄉村。在那裏，他們可以用他父親的船打魚。潘氏志的兒子說他願意去，平嬸母卻拿不定主意。但最後，所有人決定一同離去。

CAMBODIAN

រឿងនេះ១កើតឡើងនៅចុងទសវត្ស ១៩៧០ ក្រោយសង្គ្រាមវៀតណាម។ រដ្ឋាភិបាលថ្មីប្រមូលយកគ្រប់ស្ថានដ្ឋ ទាំងអស់នៅវៀតណាម។ បុរសម្នាក់ពីរដ្ឋាភិបាលថ្មីនេះ មកកាន់ហាងរបស់ ផាន់ ធី ជី។ គាត់ប្រាប់ ផាន់ ធី ជី ថាឥឡូវហាងនេះ ជារបស់រដ្ឋាភិបាលហើយ។ បុរសនេះនិយាយនា ផាន់ ធី ជី និងគ្រួសារ ត្រូវតែទៅរស់ នៅ ក្នុង របស់រដ្ឋាភិបាល។ គ្រួសារត្រូវរៀនធ្វើស្រែនៅទីនោះ។ បុរសនេះ ធាកចេញទៅ។ ផាន់ ធី ជី ប្រាប់គ្រួសារ ឲ្យ រត់គេច ទៅឯភូមិតូចមួយ។ នៅទីនោះ ពួកគេ អាចនេសាទឆ្លើលើទូករបស់ឪពុកគេ។ កូនប្រុស ផាន់ ធី ជី និយាយថា គាត់ឯកតៅ។ អ្នកមីងប៊ិញ ពុំ ទាន់សម្រេចចិត្ត នៅឡើយ។ ប៉ុន្តែ ម៉ងក្រោយមកអ្នកទាំងអស់គ្នាសម្រេចចិត្ត នៅតែចាកចេញ ម្នាក់ៗសុទ្ធតែ នៅទីនោះ។

HAITIAN CREOLE

Istwa sa a rive nan fen lane 1970 yo, aprè lagè Vyetnam lan. Nouvo gouvènman an pran kontwòl tout biznis nan Vyetnam. Yon mesye nan nouvo gouvènman an vin nan magazen Phan Thi Chi lan. Li di Phan Thi Chi magazen an se pou gouvènman an li ye kounye a. Mesye a di Phan Thi Chi ansanm ak fanmi l yo dwe al viv nan kan gouvènman an. Fanmi an pral aprann pou yo vin fèmye la. Mesye a pati. Phan Thi Chi di fanmi l yo dwe sove ale nan yon ti vilaj. Nan kote sa a, yo pral fè lapèch sou bato papa l lan. Tigason Phan Thi Chi an di li pral fè sa. Matant Binh pa fin si. Alafen, tout moun deside ale.

UNIT 3 • CHAPTER 3
The Time Bike, by Jane Langton

ENGLISH

In this science fiction story, Eddy has a new bike that he does not like. He hides it in a dark place, and it glows there. Sparks flash when Eddy touches it. When Eddy looks at it, he sees two dials. One dial says "Days," and the other says "Years." He sees a tag that says "TIME BIKE." Eddy hears Eleanor and Aunt Alex talking in the kitchen. He wonders if the bike can travel back in time to December. He turns one of the dials. The bike shakes and the bell rings. Eddy looks outside, but it does not look like it is December. He thinks the bike does not travel in time. Then Eddy hears his aunt and Eleanor saying the same words he heard earlier. He traveled back in time.

SPANISH

En esta historia de ciencia ficción, Eddy tiene una bicicleta que no le gusta. Cuando Eddy trata de guardar la bicicleta en un lugar oscuro, se da cuenta de que la bicicleta se ilumina sola. Cuando se acerca y toca la bicicleta, salen chispas de ella. Entonces se da cuenta de que la bicicleta tiene dos botones: uno que dice "Días" y el otro que dice "Años" , y que también tiene un rótulo que dice "BICICLETA DE TIEMPO". Eddy oye a Eleanor y la tía Alex hablando en la cocina. Eddy se pregunta si la bicicleta podrá regresar al pasado diciembre y mueve uno de los botones. Al moverlo, la bicicleta se mueve agitadamanete de un lado a otro y le suena la campana. Eddy mira hacia afuera, pero no parece ser diciembre, así que concluye que la bicicleta no puede viajar por el tiempo. Luego Eddy oye a Eleanor y a su tía decir las mismas palabras que habían dicho antes, así que él sí viajó por el tiempo.

HMONG

Nyob rau zaj dab neeg cuav ntawm no, Eddy muaj ib lub luvthij tshiab uas nws tsi nyiam li. Nws muab lub luvthij zais rau ib qhov chaw uas tsau ntuj ces nws txawm ci rau qhov chaw ntawd. Thaum Eddy kov nws txawm cia li tawg ci pivplev tuaj. Thaum Eddy ua zoo saib, nws pom muaj ob lub ntswjtig. Muaj ib lub ntswjtig hais tias "Hnub," hos muaj ib lub hais tias "Xyoo." Nws txawm pom ib daim ntawv tiv qhia hais tias "MOOS LUVTHIJ." Ces Eddy txawm hnov Eleanor thiab Phauj Alex nkawv hais lus nyob rau tom chav ua noj tuaj. Thaum ntawd nws xav rau hauv nruabsiab hais tias lub luvthij puas yuav nkag ncig rov qab mus tau rau lub sib kaum ob hlis ntuj dhau los lawd. Ces nws txawm tig ib lub ntswj ntawd. Lub luvthij txawj tshee thiab cov tswb txawm cia li nrov. Eddy saib rau sab nraum zoov, tiam sis nws tsi zoo li yog lub sib hawm kaum ob hlis ntuj li. Nws xav hais tias lub luvthij rov qab tsi tau rau sib hawm yav dhau los lawd. Ces Eddy txawm hnov tib cov lus uas nws phauj thiab Eleanor nkawv tau hais dhau tag puas ta lawm. Nws tau rov qab mus rau sib hawm dhau los lawm.

VIETNAMESE

Trong truyện khoa học viễn tưởng này, Eddy có một chiếc xe đạp mới mà cậu không thích. Khi cậu giấu ở một nơi tối, xe đạp tự nhiên chiếu sáng lên. Ánh sáng lóe lên khi Eddy chạm vào xe. Khi Eddy nhìn xe đạp, cậu thấy hai mặt chữ. Một mặt có chữ "Ngày," và mặt kia có chữ "Năm." Cậu thấy một cái nhãn đề chữ "XE ĐẠP THỜI GIAN." Eddy nghe Eleanor và Dì Alex nói chuyện trong nhà bếp. Cậu thắc mắc là không biết chiếc xe đạp có dẫn cậu ngược thời gian đến Tháng Mười Hai được hay không. Cậu xoay một trong hai mặt chữ. Chiếc xe rung và chuông reng lên. Eddy nhìn ra ngoài, nhưng trời không trông giống như Tháng Mười Hai. Cậu nghĩ rằng xe đạp không du lịch xuyên thời gian được. Rồi Eddy nghe dì và Eleanor nói cùng các câu với nhau mà lúc nãy cậu đã nghe. Cậu đã đi ngược thời gian.

CANTONESE

在這篇科幻小說中，艾迪有一輛他不喜歡的新自行車．他把自行車藏在黑暗的地方，可它卻會發光．當艾迪觸摸它時，還會閃出火花．艾迪注視著自行車，他看到兩個圓盤，一個圓盤叫「日期」，另一個叫「年份」．他還看到一個「時間自行車」的標簽．艾迪聽到艾蓮娜及愛羅斯嫲每在廚房中說話．他想知道這輛自行車能否將時間帶回十二月．他轉動其中一個圓盤．自行車發出震動，車鈴大響．艾迪向外張望，但並不像是十二月的日子．他認為自行車不會將時光倒流．接著，艾迪聽到他的嫲每與艾蓮娜說著他曾經聽過的話．他真的回到以前的時光了．

CAMBODIAN

នៅក្នុងរឿងវិទ្យាសាស្ត្រនេះ អេឌី មានកង់ថ្មីមួយដែលវាមិនចូលចិត្តសោះ។ វាលាក់កង់នេះ នៅកៃន្លែង ងងឹតមួយ ប៉ុន្តែកង់នេះ បែ ញ ពន្លឺ នៅពេលណា អេឌី ៈ ពាល់ វា ។ កាលណា អេឌី សម្លឹងមើល វា អេឌី ឃើញ ថ្រងមូលពីរ។ ថ្រង មួយ សរសេរ ថាក់ថា "ខែ" ហើយ មួយ ទៀត សរសេរ ថាក់ថា "ឆ្នាំ"។ វា ឃើញ ស្លាក សរសេរ ថាក់ថា "កង់ ពេល វេលា"។ អេឌី ឮ លឺ ស្ត្រី អេ ឡាណ័រ និង មិង ភាម្ត្រីក និយាយ គ្នា នៅ ក្នុង ផ្ទះ បាយ។ វាឆ្ងល់ ថា តើ កង់ នេះ អាច នឹង នាំ ពេល វេលា ត្រលប់ ទៅ ខែ ធ្នូ វិញ បានទេ ។ វា បង្វិល ថ្រង មួយ ក្នុង ចំណោម ថ្រង ទាំង ពីរ។ កង់ញ័រ ហើយ កណ្ដឹង បាន ឮ ឮ ។ អេឌី មើល ទៅ ក្រៅ ទៅ មើ មិន ឃើញ ថ្ងៃ ខែ ធ្នូ សោះ ។ វា គិត ថា កង់ នេះ មិន ផ្លើ ដំណើរ ឆ្លង កាត់ ពេល វេលា។ បន្ទាប់ មក វា ឮ ព្រ ឪ ស្ត្រី អេ ឡា ណ័រ និង ភាម្ត្រីក ទ ្រុ៣សស្ត្រី ដែល វា ធ្លាប់ ឮ ។ វាពិត ជា ត្រលប់ ទៅ ក្រោយ ថ ្ងៃ ខែ ត្រលប់ ទៅ ពេលវេលា។

HAITIAN CREOLE

Nan istwa syans fiksyon sa a, Eddy genyen yon nouvo bisiklèt li pa renmen. Li sere l yon kote ki fè nwa, epi li reyone nan fè nwa a. Lè Eddy touche l etensèl klere. Lè Eddy gade l, li wè de kadran. Yon kadran di "Jou," epi lòt kadran an di "Ane." Li wè yon etikèt ki di "BISIKLÈT POU EKSPLORE TAN." Eddy tande Eleanor ak matant Alex ap pale nan kuizin nan. Li mande tèt li si bisiklèt lan ka vwayaje nan le tan pou l tounen nan mwa desanm. Li tounen youn nan kadran yo. Bisiklèt lan souke epi klwòch sonnen. Eddy gade deyò a, men li pa sanble se mwa desanm. Li pa panse bisiklèt lan vwayaje nan le tan. Epi Eddy tande matant li ak Eleanor ap di menm mo li te tande yo anvan sa. Li te vwayaje nan le tan.

Name _____ Date _____

Why We Can't Get There From Here, by Neil de Grasse Tyson

ENGLISH

This informational text explains how hard it is to travel long distances in space. If we travel at 7 miles (11.3 km) per second, it takes 100,000 years to get to the nearest star. *Helios B* is the fastest space probe. It travels at a speed of 42 miles (67.6 km) per second. At that speed, travel to the closest star takes 15,000 years. To get very far in space, people need to travel as fast as light. Light travels at 186,000 miles (300,000 km) per second. It takes a lot of energy to travel this fast. Traveling to other stars will probably never happen because the distances in space are so large.

SPANISH

Este texto informativo explica lo difícil que es viajar largas distancias en el espacio. Si viajamos a 7 millas (11.3 km) por segundo, nos tomaría 100,000 años llegar a la estrella más cercana. *Helios B* es la nave más rápida que tenemos y viaja a una velocidad de 42 millas (67.6 km) por segundo. A esa velocidad, le tomaría 15,000 años llegar a la estrella más cercana. Para recorrer largas distancias en el espacio, hay que poder viajar a la velocidad de la luz, que es 186,000 millas (300,000 km) por segundo. Pero se requiere mucha energía para poder viajar a esa velocidad. Viajes interestelares probablemente nunca se llevarán a cabo, porque las distancias en el espacio son tan grandes.

HMONG

Cov lus qhia ntawm no piav txog tias txoj kev mus saum ntuj deb thiab nyuaj mus npaum li cas. Yog hais tias peb siv sib hawm mus li ntawm 7 mais (11.3 kislus mev) tauj ib xeesnkoos, nws yuav siv li 100,000 xyoo mam li yuav mus ze rau cov hnub qub. Helios B yog ib lub mus nrhiav xyuas uas ya ceev tshaj plaws. Nws ya ceev li ntawm 42 mais (67.6 kislus mev) tauj ib xeesnkoos. Qhov khiav tau ceev li ntawd, yuav siv sib hawm li 15,000 xyoo thiaj yuav mus txog rau lub hnub qub uas ze tshaj plaws. Kom mus tau deb tshaj plaws rau saum ntuj, tib neeg yuav tsum mus kom tau ceev npaum li qhov pom kev. Qhov pom kev mus ceev li ntawm 186,000 phav mais (300,000 kislus mev) tauj ib xeesnkoos. Nws yuav tsum tau muaj lub zog loj heev thiaj mus tau ceev li no. Qhov yuav mus rau lwm cov hnub qub ntshai yuav muaj tsi taus vim tias nyob rau saum ntuj nws loj dav heev.

VIETNAMESE

Bài viết mang tính chất tài liệu này giải thích xem việc du hành một khoảng cách dài trong không trung khó đến mức nào. Giả sử chúng ta đi 7 dặm (11.3 km) mỗi giây, thì phải đến 100,000 năm sau mới đến được ngôi sao gần nhất. *Helios B* là tàu thăm dò vũ trụ nhanh nhất. Tàu bay với vận tốc 42 dặm (67.6 km) mỗi giây. Với vận tốc này, phải mất 15,000 năm mới đến được ngôi sao gần nhất. Muốn đi đâu ở ngoài vũ trụ, con người cần phải du hành với vận tốc của ánh sáng. Ánh sáng truyền 186,000 dặm (300,000 km) mỗi giây. Phải tốn nhiều năng lượng mới đi nhanh được như vậy. Có lẽ ta sẽ không bao giờ đến được những ngôi sao khác bởi vì khoảng cách ngoài vũ trụ quá lớn.

CANTONESE

這篇知識性文章說明了在太空中長途旅行的困難．如果我們以每秒7英哩的速度（11.3公里）飛行，需要十萬年才能到達最近的星球。*Helios B* 是最快的太空船，每秒可飛行42英哩（67.6公里）．以這個速度，前往最近的星球需要一萬五千年．要前往太空的遠處，人類要以光速飛行．光以每秒18萬6千英哩（30萬公里）的速度飛行．需要極大的能量才能達到這一飛行速度．前往其他星球似乎不可能實現，因為太空的距離實在太遠了．

CAMBODIAN

សៀវភៅដៃទំមាន១៖ឆ្ល្យល់អំពីការលំបាកក្នុងការធ្វើដំណើរឆ្ងាយនៅក្នុងលំហរអាកាស។ បើសើនធ្វើដំណើរនៅក្នុងល្បឿន ៧ ម៉ាយ (១១.៣ គីឡូម៉ែត្រ) ក្នុងមួយវិនាទី រាប់ដំណោលពេល ១០០,០០០ ឆ្នាំដើម្បីទៅកាន់ផ្កាយដែលនិងជាងគេ។ *Helios B* ជាសានអវកាសដែលល្បឿនជាងគេ។ រាប់ដំណើរក្នុងល្បឿន ៤២ ម៉ាយ (៣៧.៧ គីឡូម៉ែត្រ) ក្នុងមួយវិនាទី។ នៅក្នុងល្បឿននេះ ការធ្វើដំណើរទៅផ្កាយដោយ ជិច ត្រូវចំណោលពេល ១៥,០០០ ឆ្នាំ។ ដើម្បីធ្វើដំណើរ ឡាល្បឿននៅក្នុងលំហរអាកាស មនុស្សត្រូវធ្វើដំណើរ ឡាល្បឿនមួរជាពន្លឺ។ ពន្លឺធ្វើដំណើរក្នុងល្បឿន ១០៦,០០០ ម៉ាយ (៣០០,០០០ គីឡូម៉ែត្រ) ក្នុងមួយវិនាទី។ រាប់ដំណោលសន មណលច្រើន ណស់សរាប់ធ្វើដំណើរ ឡាល្បឿនបែបនេះ។ ការធ្វើដំណើរទៅផ្កាយបប្រើបាន ជា មិនភាគកើតទៅឡើងទេ ដ៏ព្រោះថ ម្ចាស់ ទៅក្នុងលំហរអាកាសធំៗដំណោល់។

HAITIAN CREOLE

Tèks enfòmasyonèl sa a eksplike kouman li difisil pou vwayaje long distans nan lespas. Si nou vwayaje a yon vitès 7 mil (11.3 km) pa segonn, li pran 100 000 an pou rive nan etwal ki pi pre a. *Helios B* se sond espasyal ki pi rapid. Li vwayaje a yon vitès 42 mil (67.6 km) pa segonn. Nan vitès sa a, vwayaj pou rive nan etwal ki pi pre a pran 15 000 an. Pou rive lwen nan espas, moun bezwen vwayaje nan menm vitès ak limyè. Limyè vwayaje a yon vitès 186 000 mil (300 000 km) pa segonn. Sa pran anpil enèji pou vwayaje rapid konsa. Vwayaje pou al nan lòt etwal petèt pap janm rive paske distans yo nan lespas twò gran.

UNIT 3 • CHAPTER 5

The California Gold Rush, by Pam Zollman, & Dame Shirley and the Gold Rush, by Jim Rawls

ENGLISH

"The California Gold Rush" is an informational text. In 1849, people go to California to look for gold. Newspapers call them forty-niners. Most of the forty-niners are not ready for life in California. They live in tents or wagons. Some sleep in holes in the ground. The forty-niners work long days. Often they do not find any gold.

"Dame Shirley and the Gold Rush" is a story about a woman who goes to a mining camp during the Gold Rush. Friends tell Dame Shirley that the camp is not safe for women. This does not stop her from going. Dame Shirley falls off her mule. Dust covers her. Dame Shirley wants to go on anyway. Nothing will stop her on her great adventure.

SPANISH

"The California Gold Rush" es un texto informativo. En 1849, mucha gente va a California en busca de oro. Los diarios llaman a esta gente los *forty-niners* (los del año cuarenta y nueve). La mayoría de ellos no están listos para vivir en California, y tienen que dormir en carpas o vagones, o hasta en huecos en el suelo. Trabajan muchas horas y pocos hayan oro.

"Dame Shirley and the Gold Rush" es una historia corta acerca de una mujer que va a un campo de minas durante la Fiebre del Oro. La mujer se llama Dama Shirley y sus amigos le dicen que vivir en el campamento no es seguro para una mujer, pero eso no la detiene. En una ocasión, la Dama Shirley se cae de una mula y se llena de polvo al caerse, pero ella continúa, ya que nada se interpondrá a su gran aventura.

HMONG

"The California Gold Rush" yog ib zaj lus qhia kom paub txog. Nyob rau xyoo 1849, tej tib neeg mus rau lub xeev California mus nrhiav kub. Tej ntawv navxeem pheev hu lawv ua cov plaubcaug-cuaj vim rau qhov lub caij neeg tuaj mus siblaub siblug no yog xyoo ib txhiab cuaj pua plaubcaug cuaj. Feem coob ntawm cov plaubcaug cuaj no lawv npaj tsi txhij rau txoj kev ua lub neej nyob rau hauv lub xeev California. Lawv nyob rau cov tsev pheebsuab los yog xamlaub tej xwb. Ib txhia lawv pwv hauv tej qhov uas nyob hauv pegteb. Cov plaubcaug-cuaj no lawv ua haujlwm tsheej hnub txog tsaus ntuj li. Ntau zaug lawv kuj nrhiav tsi tau kub.

"Dame Shirley and the Gold Rush" yog ib zaj dab neeg hais txog ib tug pojniam uas nws mus rau tom ib qhov chaw khawb kub nyob rau lub caij sib xeem mus nrhiav kub los sis hu ua Gold Rush. Tej phoojwg hais rau Dame Shirley tias lub chaw ntawd lawv tsi tso siab rau pojniam mus nyob. Txawm muaj li ntawd los qhov no cheem tsi tau nws nyob li. Dame Shirley poob saum nws tus nees zag los rau pemteb. Txawm npaum ntawd los Dame Shirley tseem xav mus li thiab. Yuav tsi muaj ib yam dabtsi uas yuav cheem tau nws txoj hauvkev pheej moo no hlo li.

VIETNAMESE

"The California Gold Rush" là một bài viết mang tính chất tài liệu. Vào năm 1849, nhiều người đi đến California để tìm vàng. Báo chí gọi họ là người "forty-niners" tức là người "năm bốn mươi chín". Phần lớn những người này không lường trước được cuộc sống ở California. Họ sống trong các túp lều hay xe ngựa. Một số người ngủ trong các hang lỗ dưới mặt đất. Họ làm việc cả ngày dài. Nhiều khi họ không tìm được vàng.

"Dame Shirley and the Gold Rush" là truyện kể về một người đàn bà đi đến trại đào vàng trong thời Đổ Xô Đi Tìm Vàng. Bạn bè nói với Dame Shirley rằng trại này không an toàn cho phụ nữ. Điều này không làm cô lùi bước. Dame Shirley té xuống khỏi con la. Bụi đất phủ đầy người cô. Dù sao đi nữa Dame Shirley vẫn muốn tiếp tục cuộc hành trình. Không có gì có thể ngăn cản được cô trong cuộc mạo hiểm vĩ đại này.

CANTONESE

The California Gold Rush 是一篇知識性文件．一八四九年，人們前往加尼福尼亞州尋找黃金．報章稱這些人為 forty-niners（四九人）．大部份「四九人」並不適應加州的生活．他們住在帳篷或馬車內，一些人睡在地面的洞穴中．「四九人」長時間工作，但通常卻找不到任何黃金．

Dame Shirley and the Gold Rush 講述一個女子在淘金熱時期前往礦場的故事．達米・莎莉的朋友告訴她，礦場對女子來說並不安全．但這無法阻止她前往．達米・莎莉從驢背上跌下來，塵埃沾涌全身．達米・莎莉一往無前，沒有任何東西可以阻止她的偉大歷程．

CAMBODIAN

"The California Gold Rush" ជាសេ]វិភៅដ៏មានអ្ថយ។ ក្នុងឆ្នាំ ១៨៤៩ មនុស្សនាគ្នានៅកាន់កាលីហ្វ័រញ៉ា ដើម្បីរកមាស។ សារពទមាន ឲ្យឈ្មោះ ថា forty-niners (មនុស្សន្នៃសិបប្រាំបួន)។ មនុស្សន្នៃសិបប្រាំបួនភាគច្រើនមិនទាន់ស្គាល់នៅក្នុងដ៏កដីកាលីហ្វ័រញ៉ានៅឡើយទេ។ ពួកគេសុំនៅក្នុងខ្ទមសំ៣ ឬក្នុងរទេះ។ ខ្លះ៖គេនៅក្នុងរូងក្នុងដីឯ។ មនុស្សន្នៃសិបប្រាំបួននៃការស្វ៉ារ៉ាងក្នុងមួយខ្ងៃ ជាញ៉ឹកញាប់តែគ មាស មិនបានឡើយ។

"Dame Shirley and the Gold Rush" ជារ៉ឿងមួយអំពីស្រ្ដីម្នាក់ដែលនៅកាន់ជំរុំរ៉ែ ក្នុងឪ៊ខាន់សំរសកមាស។ មិត្តភក្ដិប្រាបនៅ ថែម សេ៉លី ថាជំរុំ៖ មិន មានសុវត្ថិភាពសំ្មាបស្រ្ដីទេ។ បញ្ហា៖មិនខាច បញ្ឈប់នាងមិនឲ្យនៅឡើយទេ។ ថែល សេ៉លី ធ្លាក់ពីលើរ៉េះនាង។ លំងង់ធូ្លគ្របបលើនាង។ នោះ៖ម៉ាងណា ថែម សេ៉លី នៅរ៉ឹងនិងបន្ដដំណើរនៅ មុនឡើ]ៗ។ គ្មានអ្វីនឹងបញ្ឈប់នាងក្នុងការ ស្វ៉ងព្រងដ៏ដ៏ល បស់នាងឡើយ។

HAITIAN CREOLE

"The California Gold Rush" se yon tèks enfòmasyonèl. An 1849, moun ale nan Kalifòni pou jwenn lò. Jounal yo rele yo "forty-niners" (mesye lane 49 yo). Pifò "mesye lane 49 yo" pat prè pou lavi nan Kalifòni. Yo abite sou tant oswa karavàn. Kèk dòmi nan twou nan tè a. "Mesye lane 49 yo" travay long jounen. Souvan yo pa jwenn ankenn lò.

"Dame Shirley and the Gold Rush" se yon istwa konsènan yon fanm ki ale nan yon kan minyè pandan "Presipitasyon pou Lò" an. Zanmi yo di Dame Shirley kan an pa an sekirite pou fanm. Sa pa anpeche l ale. Dame Shirley tonbe sou cheval li an. Pousyè kouvri l. Dame Shirley vle kontinye ale kanmenm. Anyen pap kanpe l nan gran avanti li an.

UNIT 4 • CHAPTER 1

Water Dance, by Thomas Locker

ENGLISH

The poem "Water Dance" shows that water is many things. Water is the rain falling from the sky. Water is a stream running over forest rocks. In the mountains, water falls from a stone cliff. Water fills a lake. Water flows in rivers in the middle of valleys. High above the earth, water is in the clouds. The wind and the dark sky contain the water of a powerful storm. The drops of water in the air after a storm reflect the colors of the rainbow. Water takes many forms as it dances through the world.

SPANISH

El poema "Water Dance" dice que el agua es muchas cosas. El agua es la lluvia que cae del cielo, y un arroyo que corre sobre las rocas del bosque. En las montañas, el agua cae de un peñasco rocoso. El agua llena un lago y el agua fluye en los ríos y en medio de los valles. Encima de nosotros, hay agua en las nubes. El viento y el cielo oscuro contienen el agua de una tormenta poderosa. Las gotas de agua en el aire después de una tormenta reflejan los colores del arco iris. El agua toma muchas formas mientras danza por el mundo.

HMONG

Zaj lus paivyi "Water Dance" qhia tau tias dej yog ntau yam. Dej yog cov nag poob saum ntuj los. Dej yog ib tug dej ntwg los saum tej pobzeb los. Nyob rau saum tej roob, dej poob saum ib lub pobzeb ib ntaj rua los. Dej puj nkaus ib lub pag. Dej ntwg nrias ua havdej nyob rau tej plaws tiajnrag. Siab tshaj puag saum cov av, dej nyob rau hauv tej fuab. Tej cua thiab lub ntuj tsaus nciab ntim dej muaj nag xob nagcua uas muaj zog kawg nkaus.Tom qab nag xob nag cua los dhau lawm dej poob saum ib ntaj ntuj zoo li zaj sawv. Dej hloov mus ua ntau yam lub sib hawm nws seevcev mus thoob lub ntiajteb.

VIETNAMESE

Bài thơ "Water Dance" cho thấy nước có nhiều dạng. Nước là mưa rơi từ trên trời. Nước là dòng suối chảy qua các phiến đá trong rừng. Trên núi, nước chảy xuống từ vách đá. Nước chứa đầy hồ. Nước chảy trong các con sông ở giữa thung lũng. Phía trên Trái Đất, nước ở trong mây. Gió và bầu trời tối chứa nước ở dạng một cơn bão mạnh. Các giọt nước trong không khí sau một trận bão phản chiếu các màu của cầu vồng. Nước biến thành nhiều dạng do quá trình chuyển hóa vòng quanh thế giới.

CANTONESE

Water Dance 這首詩顯示了水的多樣性．水是從天上掉下的雨．水是沖過林中岩石的溪流．在群山中，水從石崖上落下．水注涌湖泊．水在山谷中匯成河流．在高高的天上，水存在於雲層之中．疾風和黑暗的天空中蘊藏著暴風雨的降水．風暴過後，空氣中的水珠折射出彩虹的顏色．水以不同的形式，跳躍在世界每個角落．

CAMBODIAN

កំណាព្យ "Water Dance" បង្ហាញថា ទឹកជារវត្ថុច្រើនបែបៗ។ ទឹកជាភ្លៀងដែលធ្លាក់ពីលើមេឃ។ ទឹកជាស្ទឹងមួយដែលហូរកាត់ថ្មក្រៀម នៅក្នុងព្រៃ។ នៅតាមភ្នំ ទឹកធ្លាក់ពីលើលក្ខណ្ឌមួយ។ ទឹកបំពេញបឹងមួយៗ។ ទឹកហូរក្នុងស្ទឹងនៅកណ្តាលជ្រលងភ្នំ។ នៅខ្ពស់លើមេឃ ទឹកជាពពក។ ខ្យល់និងមេឃងងឹតមានផ្ទុកទឹកនៃព្យុះភ្លៀងដ៏ខ្លាំងមួយ។ ដំណក់ទឹកនៅក្នុងខ្យល់ ក្រោយពីភ្លៀងហើយ បញ្ចាំងពណ៌ជាឥន្ទនូ។ ទឹកមានសណ្ឋានច្រើនបែប មុនដែលវារាំរាំជុំវិញពិភពលោក។

HAITIAN CREOLE

Powèm "Water Dance" lan montre dlo se anpil bagay. Dlo se lapli ki tonbe sot nan syèl. Dlo se wiso ki koule sou wòch nan forè yo. Nan mòn yo, dlo tonbe soti nan yon falèz wòch. Dlo ranpli yon lak. Dlo koule nan mitan vale yo. Byen wo depase latè, dlo a nan nyaj yo. Van an ak syèl nwa a genyen dlo pou yon tanpèt pisan. Gout dlo nan lè a aprè yon tanpèt reflete koulè akansyèl lan. Dlo pran anpil fòm pandan l ap danse atravè lemonn.

UNIT 4 • CHAPTER 2

Persephone and the Seasons, by Heather Amery

ENGLISH

In this myth, Demeter is the goddess of plants. Persephone is her daughter. Pluto, the god of the Underworld, loves Persephone. He takes her to the Underworld. Demeter is sad about losing her daughter. The plants begin to die because Demeter no longer takes care of them. People and animals are starving. The gods ask Pluto to let Persephone return. Pluto says she can go back home if she has not eaten any food from the Underworld. Persephone only ate a few seeds. Pluto lets her go home for half the year. Demeter is happy when her daughter comes home in the spring. Plants grow and there is plenty of food. Demeter is sad when her daughter goes back to the Underworld in the fall. The weather gets cold, and plants stop growing.

SPANISH

En este mito, Demeter es la diosa de las plantas y Persephone es su hija. Pluto, el dios del Ultramundo, ama a Persephone y se la lleva al Ultramundo. Demeter se entristece por perder a su hija y las plantas se comienzan a morir porque Demeter las deja de cuidar. Las personas y los animales comienzan a sufrir hambre, así que los dioses le piden a Pluto que permita que regrese Persephone a casa. Pluto responde que ella podrá regresar si no ha comido nada del Ultramundo. Como Persephone sólo ha comido unas pocas semillas, Pluto permite que regrese a casa por medio año. Demeter se pone contenta cuando su hija regresa en la primavera. Entonces las plantas vuelven a crecer y hay bastante comida. Pero Demeter se vuelve a poner triste cuando su hija regresa al Ultramundo en el otoño. Caundo ella se va, el clima se enfría y las plantas dejan de crecer.

HMONG

Nyob rau zaj dab neeg no, Demeter yog ib tug niam vaj ntxwv pojdab rau tej nroj tsuag. Persephone yog nws tus ntxhais. Pluto, yog tug vajntxwv dab rau hauv Nruab Av thiab nws nyiam Persephone heev. Tus vaj ntxwv dab no coj tus hluas nkauj no mus rau hauv Nruab Av. Demeter tu siab heev vim tias nws tus ntxhais tsi nrog nws nyob ntxiv lawm. Tej nroj tsuag pib tuag vim rau qhov Demeter tsi tu lawv lawm. Tej tib neeg thiab tej tsiajtxhu tshaib plab heev. Cov vaj ntxwv dab tau thov kom Pluto cia li tso Persephone rov qab. Pluto hais tias nws rov qab los yeej tau yog hais tias nws tsi tau noj ib yam zaub mov nyob rau Nruab Av. Persephone rua yog tau noj ob peb lub noob xwb. Pluto cia nws rov qab mus tsev tau ib nrab xyoo. Demeter tus ntxhais rov qab los tsev lub caij paj mab paj ntoos hlav thiab tawg mas ua rau nws zoo siab heev. Tej nroj tsuag los loj hlob thiab zaub mov los kuj muaj puj npo txaus noj txaus haus. Thaum lub caij ntuj tsaug nws tus ntxhais yuav rov qab mus rau hauv Nruab Av, Demeter yuav tu siab heev. Tej fuabcua yuav no heev tuaj, thiab tej nroj tsuag los yuav tso tseg tsi hlav ntxiv lawm.

VIETNAMESE

Trong truyện huyền thoại này, Demeter là bà chúa của các loài cây. Persephone là con gái bà. Pluto, là Diêm Vương, có lòng yêu Persephone. Ông mang cô tới Âm Phủ. Demeter buồn bã vì mất đứa con gái yêu. Cây cỏ bắt đầu chết vì Demeter không còn chăm sóc cho chúng nữa. Con người và động vật chết đói. Các vị thần yêu cầu Pluto cho Persephone về nhà. Pluto nói rằng cô chỉ được về nhà nếu cô chưa ăn thứ gì từ Âm Phủ. Persephone chỉ ăn có vài hạt giống mà thôi. Pluto cho phép cô về nhà trong vòng nửa năm. Demeter rất sung sướng khi con gái về lại nhà vào mùa xuân. Cây cỏ phát triển và do đó có rất nhiều thức ăn. Demeter buồn bã khi con gái mình phải trở lại Âm Phủ vào mùa thu. Thời tiết trở nên lạnh lẽo, và cây cỏ ngừng phát triển.

CANTONESE

在這個神話中，狄美達是穀神，晉惜封是她的女兒。冥神培度愛上了晉惜封。他把她帶去地下世界。狄美達對失去女兒十分傷心。穀物開始死亡，因為狄美達不再照料它們。人們及動物開始捱餓，眾神要求培度讓晉惜封回去。培度說只要她沒有吃地下世界的食物，她可以回家。晉惜封只吃了少許種子。培度容許她回家半年。狄美達在春天看到女兒回來，十分高興。穀物生長，又有了很多食物。當她的女兒在秋天返回地下世界時，狄美達感到很傷心。天氣轉涼，穀物也停止生長。

CAMBODIAN

នៅក្នុងរឿងព្រេងបុរាណនេះ ទីម៉ីត័រ ជាក្បួនវេវា។ ផេសើហ្វូន ជាកូនបស់នាង។ ព្លូ ជាទេវរាជនៃឋា នរក។ គាត់ស្រឡាញ់ ផេសើហ្វូន។ គាត់យកនាងទៅកាន់ឋានក្រោម។ ទីម៉ីត័រ ក្រៀមក្រំដែលបាត់កូនស្រីៗ។ កូ ជាតិចាប់ផ្ដើមស្លាប់ ព្រោះទីម៉ីត័រ មិនបានថែទាំវាតទៀត។ មនុស្សនិងសត្វកំពុងឃ្លាន។ ពួកទេវតាសុំ ពូ ខ្លួនឱ្យ ផេសើហ្វូន មកវិញ។ ពូ និយាយថា នាងអាចត្រឡប់ទៅវិញបាន បើនាងមិនបរិភោគស្ដ្បីកឬចានៅ ឋានក្រោម។ ផេសើហ្វូន បរិភោគតែគ្រាប់ណ៍ដ៏ ប៉ុន្មានៗ។ ពូ ឱ្យនាងត្រឡប់ផ្ទះកន្លះឆ្នាំៗ ទីម៉ីត័រ រីករាយ ពេលឃើញកូនស្រី មកគ្រប់វិញក្នុងពេលរដូវៗ។ ក្រូជាច្រើនដុះ ហើយមានអាហារ ជាច្រើនៗ ទីម៉ីត័រ ក្រៀមក្រំ កាលណាកូនស្រី ត្រឡប់ទៅឋានក្រោមវិញនៅរដូវស្លឹកឈើជ្រុះ។ អាកាសសប្រជាក់ ហើយកូនជាបិល បណ្តោះណៗ

HAITIAN CREOLE

Nan mit sa a, Demeter se deyès plant yo. Persephone se pitit fi li. Pluto, dye souteren an, renmen Persephone. Li mennen l nan monn souteren an. Demeter tris paske li pèdi pitit li an. Plant yo kòmanse mouri paske Demeter pa pran swen yo ankò. Moun ak zannimo yo grangou. Dye yo mande Pluto pou l kite Persephone tounen. Pluto di li ka retounen lakay li si li pat manje ankenn manje nan monn souteren an. Persephone te sèlman manje kèk grenn. Pluto kite l ale lakay li pou mwatye ane a. Demeter kontan lè pitit li retounen lakay li nan prentan. Plant yo grandi epi gen ase manje. Demeter tris lè pitit li retounen nan monn souteren an nan otòn. Tanperati a fè frèt, epi plant yo sispann grandi.

VISIONS **READING SUMMARIES** Unit 4

UNIT 4 • CHAPTER 3

The Circuit, by Francisco Jiménez

ENGLISH

In this short story, a teenager and his family are moving. They are going to look for work. The family finds work picking grapes. When the grape season is over, the boy goes to school. His teacher asks him to read, but he does not know many of the words. During recess, the boy asks his teacher for help with the words he does not understand. He spends the rest of the month working with his teacher. One day, the teacher asks if he would like to learn to play the trumpet. The boy is excited. When he gets home, he sees that his family has packed their things. They are going to move again.

SPANISH

En esta historia corta, un joven y su familia se trastean en busca de trabajo. La familia encuentra trabajo cosechando uvas. Cuando la temporada de cosecha de uvas se acaba, el joven va a la escuela. En la escuela, su maestro le pide que lea, pero él no conoce muchas de la palabras. Durante el descanso, el joven le pide al maestro que le ayude a entender las palabras que no reconoció. Él dura el resto del mes trabajando con su maestro. Un día, su maestro le pregunta si le gustaría aprender a tocar la trompeta y él se pone muy contento. Cuando regresa a casa, se da cuenta de que la familia ha empacado todo, porque se tienen que volver a trastear.

HMONG

Nyob rau hauv zaj dab neeg no, ib tug tub hluas thiab nws tsev neeg tabtom khiav mus. Yog lawv khiav mus nrhiav haujlwm. Tsev neeg nrhiav haujlwm hlais txiv mabxwv. Thaum lub caij txiv mabxwv dhau mus lawm, tus menyuam tub ntawd rov qab mus kawm ntawv. Nws tus xib hwb hais kom nws twm ntawv, tiam sis feem ntau nws tsi paub cov ntawv sau ntawd. Thaum txog lub sib hawm tawm mus ua si, tug menyuam tub ntawd thov nws tus xib hwb pab qhia tej tug ntawv uas nws tsi paub twm rau nws. Nws siv tagnrho lub hlis ntawd kawm ntawv nrog nws tug xib hwb. Muaj ib hnub, tus xib hwb nug saib nws puas xav tshuab lub rajxyu. Tug menyuam tub ntawd kub siab lug tos tsi taus li. Thaum nws mus txog tsev, nws pom tias nws tsev neeg twb sau lawv tej khoom tiav tag ntim zoo tos lawm. Lawv twb npaj txhij yuav rov qab khiav dua thiab.

VIETNAMESE

Trong truyện ngắn này, một thiếu niên và gia đình phải dọn nhà sang nơi khác. Họ đi tìm việc làm. Gia đình tìm được công việc hái nho. Khi đến hết mùa nho, cậu đi học trường. Thầy giáo bảo cậu đọc một đoạn văn, nhưng có nhiều từ cậu không biết. Vào giờ giải lao, cậu nhờ thầy hướng dẫn các từ cậu không hiểu. Cậu học với thầy này cho đến cuối tháng. Một ngày nọ, thầy hỏi cậu có muốn học thổi kèn trumpet hay không. Cậu rất háo hức. Khi về nhà, cậu thấy gia đình đã thu dọn mọi thứ. Họ lại phải dời nhà lần nữa.

CANTONESE

在這個小故事中，一個少年與他的家人一同搬家．他們在尋找工作．一家人找到採葡萄的工作．當葡萄季節過後，男孩上學去．老師要他朗讀，但他不認識太多的字．在課間休息時，男孩請求老師教他生字．他利用這個月餘下的時間跟著老師學習．一天，老師問他是否願意學吹喇叭，男孩十分興奮．當他回家時，發現家人正在收拾行裝．他們又要搬家了．

CAMBODIAN

រឿងខ្លីនេះនិយាយអំពីក្មេងជំទង់ម្នាក់និងគ្រួសារវាកំពុងផ្លាស់ទីលំនៅ។ ពួកគេទៅរកការងារធ្វើ។ គ្រួសារ រកបានការងារបេះផ្លែទំពាំងបាយជូរ។ ពេលអស់រដូវទំពាំងបាយជូរ អូចាទៅ ក្មេងនេះទៅសាលារៀន។ គ្រូវាញវាឧាត ឲ វាមើលសៀវភៅ ក្សារាជ្របើ។ នៅពេលរេឡារេង ក្មេងនេះស្ម្ងរ គ្រូឲ្យឧួយសណ្តល់ពាក្សាដែលវាមិនយល់។ វាខំណាយ ពេល អូចាវៃនេះ រៀនជា អូលយគ្រូវា ខែអូយគ្រូស្មៀ ៣ បើវាឧានរៀងផ្ទៃផ្ទុំថ្វៃ។ ក្មេងនេះរំភើបបិត្តៗ។ ពេលទៅដល់ ផ្ទះ វាឃើញគ្រួសារវារៀបតីឥវ៉ាន់ៗ។ ពួកគេនឹងផ្លាស់ទីកន្លែងទៀត។

HAITIAN CREOLE

Nan istwa kout sa a, yon adolesan ak fanmi l ap demenaje. Yo pral chèche travay. Fanmi an jwenn travay pou ranmase rezen. Lè sezon rezen an fini, tigason an al lekòl. Pwofesè l mande l pou l li, men li pa konnen anpil mo. Pandan rekreyasyon, tigason an mande pwofesè l pou l ede l avèk mo li pa konprann yo. Li pase rès mwa yo ap travay avèk pwofesè l an. Yon jou, pwofesè a mande l si li ta renmen aprann jwe twonpèt. Tigason an kontan anpil. Lè l rive lakay li, li wè fanmi l fè pakèt yo. Yo pral demenaje ankò.

Name _____ Date _____

The Elements of Life, by Paul Bennett

ENGLISH

This informational reading is about the elements. All things are made up of elements. Long ago, people thought earth, air, fire, and water were the only elements. Today, we know about 109 elements. Some elements are metal, such as gold and silver. Some elements are in our bodies. Hydrogen and oxygen are elements that make water. The elements move through cycles in our natural world. When something dies, its elements go into the soil. The soil feeds new plants. People and animals eat the plants, and the cycle starts over. Humans must be careful to help keep this delicate cycle.

SPANISH

Esta lectura informativa es acerca de los elementos naturales. Todo está formado de elementos. Hace mucho tiempo, algunos creían que la tierra, el aire, el fuego y el agua eran los únicos elementos. Hoy en día, conocemos cerca de 109 elementos. Algunos son metales, como el oro y la plata. Nuestro cuerpo contiene elementos. El hidrógeno y el oxígeno son los elementos que conforman el agua. Los elementos pasan por ciclos en el mundo natural: cuando algo muere, los elementos que lo formaban regresan al suelo, el suelo alimenta a nuevas plantas y las personas y los animales se comen las plantas. Luego el ciclo se repite. A los seres humanos nos corresponde asegurarnos de proteger este delicado ciclo de vida.

HMONG

Zaj lus tshaj tawm no yog qhia txog ntau yam khoom tseem ceeb (elements) uas sib sau los ua ke. Tagnrho txhua tsav txhua yam puav leej yog peem tsheej los ntawm muaj ntau yam khoom los sib sau. Puag thaum ub, tej tib neeg xav hais tias lub ntiajteb, fuabcua, hluav taws, thiab dej yog cov ntau yam uas tseem ceeb ntawd. Niaj hnub nim no, peb paub txog muaj 109 yam diam. Ib txhia ntawm cov khoom tseem ceeb no yog hlau, los mus rau kub thiab nyiab hob. Ib txhia cov tseem ceeb no nws nyob rau hauv peb lub nrog cev. Hydrogen (rojcua) thiab oxygen (pa) yog cov khoom tseem ceeb uas ua tau dej. Cov khoom tseem ceeb no ncig mus los nyob rau hauv lub ntiajteb no. Thaum muaj tej yam uas nws tuag mus lawd, nws cov khoom tseem ceeb ntawd mus rau hauv cov av lawm. Cov av yug tej nroj tsuag. Tej tib neeg thiab tej tsiajtxhu noj cov nroj tsuag ntawd, ces nws rov qab muaj tshiab ncig mus los dua ntxiv.

VIETNAMESE

Bài đọc mang tính chất tài liệu này nói về các nguyên tố. Mọi vật được cấu tạo bởi các nguyên tố. Hồi xưa, người ta tưởng rằng các nguyên tố duy nhất là đất, không khí, lửa, và nước. Ngày nay, chúng ta biết rằng có 109 nguyên tố. Một số nguyên tố là kim loại, chẳng hạn như vàng và bạc. Một số nguyên tố khác có trong cơ thể chúng ta. Hydrô và oxy là các nguyên tố tạo thành nước. Các nguyên tố tuần hoàn theo chu kỳ trong thế giới tự nhiên của chúng ta. Khi một vật chết đi, các nguyên tố trong cơ thể biến thành đất. Đất nuôi cây cỏ mới. Con người và động vật ăn cây cỏ, và chu trình bắt đầu lại từ đầu. Con người phải cẩn thận để giúp bảo vệ chu trình mỏng manh này.

CANTONESE

這篇知識性讀物講的是關於元素．所有物件都由元素組成．很久以前，人們認為泥土、空氣、火和水是唯一的元素．現在，我們知道總共約有109種元素．部份元素是金屬，例如金和銀．部份元素存在於我們體內．氫和氧是組成水的元素．元素在大自然中循環轉換．當生物死亡，它的元素進入土壤．土壤滋養新的植物．人及動物吃下植物，循環又重新開始．人類必須小心保護這個脆弱的循環過程．

CAMBODIAN

ការអានបទចំមាងនេះ ស្ដីអំពីសារ ធាតុ។ រឿៗទាំងអស់កើតឡើងពីសារ ធាតុ។ កាលពីឡូរលង់ មនុស្សគិតថា មានដៃ ដី, ខ្យល់, ភ្លើង និងទឹក ប៉ុណ្ណោះដែលជាសារ ធាតុ។ សព្វថ្ងៃយើង ដឹងថាមានសារ ធាតុ ១០៩មុខ។ សារ ធាតុ ខ្លះជាលោហធាតុ មួចជាមាសនិងប្រាក់ជាដើម។ សារ ធាតុខ្លះនៅក្នុងខ្លួនយើង។ ហ៊ីដ្រូជែននិង អុកស៊ីជែន ជាសារធាតុដែលបង្កើតជាទឹក។ សារ ធាតុផ្ទេរ ទីលំនៅរបស់វាល់ៗ ឡើងនៅក្នុងពិភពធម្មជាតិយើង នេះ។ ពេលណាអ្វីមួយ ស្លាប់ទៅ សារ ធាតុបស់វាក្លាយទៅជាដី។ ដីចិញ្ចឹមុក្ខជាតិថ្មីៗ។ មនុស្សនិងសត្វបរិភាគុក្ខជាតិ ហើយការវិលវល់ តាប់ផ្ដើមជាថ្មី។ មនុស្សត្រូវប្រយ័ត្ន ដើម្បីស្ការការវិលវល់ដ៏ប្រណាំងនេះ។

HAITIAN CREOLE

Lekti enfòmasyonèl sa a se konsènan eleman yo. Tout bagay fèt ak eleman. Lontan, moun te panse latè, lè, dife, ak dlo se eleman sa yo sèlman ki te genyen. Jodi a, nou konnen apeprè 109 eleman. Kèk eleman yo se metal, tankou lò ak lajan. Kèk eleman se nan kò nou yo ye. Idwojèn ak oksijèn se eleman ki fè dlo. Eleman yo deplase selon yon sik nan monn natirèl nou an. Lè yon bagay mouri, eleman li yo ale nan tè a. Tè a nouri nouvo plant yo. Moun ak zannimo manje plant yo, epi sik lan rekòmanse ankò. Lèzòm dwe fè atansyon pou yo ede sik delika sa a.

UNIT 5 • CHAPTER 1
Rosa Parks, by Andrea Davis Pinkney

ENGLISH

This biography is about Rosa Parks. Rosa Parks is famous because she did not give up her bus seat to a white man. At the time, the law said that African Americans had to give up their seats to white people on crowded buses. Parks was working with a group to end these unfair laws. She wanted to make a change. On December 1, 1955, she did. Parks got on a bus and sat in the back. A white man entered the bus and could not find an empty seat. Parks did not give up her seat for the white man. The police arrested her. Parks's act on the bus started the Montgomery bus boycott. African Americans refused to ride the buses. This helped change unfair laws.

SPANISH

Esta biografía es acerca de Rosa Parks, quien es famosa por no haber cedido su puesto a un hombre blanco en un autobús. En ese entonces, la ley decía que los afroamericanos tenían que ceder sus puestos a los blancos en autobuses con los puestos llenos. Park trabajaba con un grupo para acabar con esas leyes injustas. Ella quería hacer algo significativo para esa causa, y el 1º de diciembre de 1955 lo logró. Parks se subió en un autobús y se sentó en la parte de atrás. Luego, un hombre blanco entró al autobús y no encontró un asiento desocupado, pero Parks no le cedió el puesto al hombre blanco y la policía la arrestó. Con la acción de Parks en ese autobús, comenzó una huelga de autobuses en Montgomery, en la que los afroamericanos se rehusaron a montar en ellos. Esas acciones ayudaron a hacer que se cambiaran esa leyes injustas.

HMONG

Zaj lus hais no yog piav qhia txog Rosa Parks. Rosa Parks lub npe nrov nto moo kawg li vim tias nws tsi kam muab nws lub rooj caij tsheb npav tso tseg rau ib tug txiv neej dawb. Nyob rau lub sib hawm ntawd, txojcai teev tseg hais tias cov tib neeg Asfiliskas Asmesliskas yuav tsum tau zam chaw nyob tseg rau cov neeg tawv dawb yog thaum rooj tog tsi txaus zaum lawm. Parks tau koomtes nrog ib pab neeg sawv tawm tsam txojcai uas tsi ncaj ncees no. Nws xav kom txojcai hloov. Nyob rau lub kaum ob hlis ntuj tim 1, 1955, nws tau nqi tes kiag. Parks nkag rau ib lub tsheb npav thiab zaum nyob rau tom qab. Ces mam muaj ib tug txiv neej tawv dawb nkag los tiam sis nws nrhiav tsi tau rooj zaum lawm. Parks tsi kam zam lub rooj rau tus txiv neej dawb ntawd zaum. Tub ceevxwm txawm ntes nws. Qhov tub ceevxwm ntes Parks li no thiaj tau muaj kev tsa paib tsi txaus siab nyob rau Montgomery txog ntawm txojcai rau cov tsheb npav. Cov Asfliskas Asmesliskas tsi kam caij tsheb npav ntxiv. Qhov lawv ua li no pab hloov tau txojcai tsi ncaj ncees.

VIETNAMESE

Cuốn tiểu sử này nói về Rosa Parks. Rosa Parks nổi tiếng vì cô không nhường chỗ ngồi trên xe buýt cho một người đàn ông da trắng. Vào thời đó, luật pháp quy định người Mỹ gốc Châu Phi phải nhường chỗ cho người da trắng nếu xe buýt chật. Parks lúc đó đang hợp tác với một nhóm người nhằm chấm dứt các đạo luật bất công này. Cô muốn góp phần vào việc thay đổi xã hội. Vào ngày 1 tháng Mười Hai, 1955, cô làm đúng như vậy. Parks bước lên xe buýt và ngồi ở hàng ghế sau. Một người đàn ông da trắng lên xe và không tìm được ghế trống. Parks không nhường chỗ cho ông. Cảnh sát bắt cô. Hành động của Parks trên xe buýt đã khởi động một cuộc tẩy chay xe buýt tại Montgomery. Người Mỹ gốc Châu Phi từ chối đi xe buýt. Sự việc này giúp thay đổi bộ luật bất công.

CANTONESE

這是一篇關於羅莎·柏嘉斯的傳記。羅莎·柏嘉斯因為不肯讓位給一個白人而出名。當時，法律規定非洲裔美國人在擠擁的巴士內要讓位給白人。柏嘉斯與一組人共同努力，要終止這些不公平的法律。她希望進行改變。一九五五年十二月一日，她做到了。柏嘉斯登上一輛公車，坐在後排。一個白人上了車，找不到空位。柏嘉斯沒有把她的坐位讓給那白人。警察拘捕了她。柏嘉斯在巴士上的行動觸發了「蒙哥馬利」拒乘巴士運動。非洲裔美國人拒絕乘搭巴士。這場運動促成了不公平法律的改變。

CAMBODIAN

ប្រវត្តិរបនេះស្ដីពី រ៉ូសា ផាក។ រ៉ូសា ផាក ជាមនុស្សល្បីម្នាក់ ព្រោះនាងមិនព្រមឲ្យកន្លែងអង្គុយនៅ លើរថយន្តប៊ុស នៅដែរស្បែកសម្បុរស្បែកឃើយ។ នៅពេលនោះ ច្បាប់បានចែងថា ជនស្បែកខ្មៅត្រូវឲ្យរថយន្តកន្លែងនៅ ដែរស្បែកសនៅពេលរថយន្តប៊ុសចង្អៀត។ ផាក ធ្វើកិច្ចការ ជាមួយមនុស្សមួយក្រុមដើម្បីបញ្ចប់ច្បាប់មិនសុច្ឆិតនេះ។ នាងចង់ធ្វើឲ្យមានការផ្លាស់ប្ដូរ។ នៅថ្ងៃទី១ ខែធ្នូ ឆ្នាំ១៩៥៥ នាងកំពុងតែធ្វើ ផាកឡើងរថយន្តប៊ុស ហើយនាងអង្គុយនៅ ខាងក្រោយ។ ជនស្បែកសម្បុរឡើងរថយន្តប៊ុស ហើយគាត់រកមិនឃើញកន្លែងទេ។ ផាក មិនព្រមឲ្យកន្លែងអង្គុយនៅដែរ ស្បែកនោះទេ។ ប៉ូលីសបានចាប់នាង។ សកម្មភាពផាកនៅលើរថយន្តប៊ុសបានចាប់ផ្ដើមឲ្យ មានការដក ឃ្លាំមនុស្សមន្ទីលក្រុងហ្គោម្ការី ប៊ុស មិនគ្រាមើរ។ ជនជាតិស្បែកខ្មៅប្រតិសាធមិន ជិះប៊ុស។ ការនេះ ជួយឲ្យផ្លាស់ប្ដូរ ច្បាប់មិនសុច្ឆិតនេះ។

HAITIAN CREOLE

Byografi sa a se konsènan Rosa Parks. Rosa Parks selèb paske li pat vle bay yon mesye blan plas li nan yon otobis. Nan lè sa a, lalwa te di Afriken ameriken te dwe bay moun blan plas yo nan otobis ki twò chaje. Parks t ap travay ak yon gwoup pou mete fen a lwa sa yo ki pa jis. Li te vle fè yon chanjman. Le 1e desanm 1955, li te fè sa. Parks monte nan yon otobis epi li chita dèyè. Yon mesye blan monte nan otobis lan epi li pat ka jwenn yon plas vid. Parks pat bay plas li a pou mesye blan an te ka chita. Lapolis te arete l. Aksyon Parks nan otobis lan te kòmanse bòykot otobis Montgomery an. Afriken Ameriken te refize monte otobis yo. Sa te ede chanje lwa enjis sa yo.

UNIT 5 • CHAPTER 2

The Gettysburg Address, by Kenneth Richards and Abraham Lincoln

ENGLISH

This historical narrative includes a speech given by President Abraham Lincoln in 1863. Lincoln goes to speak at a special event. The event is to honor Civil War soldiers who died at the Battle of Gettysburg. Lincoln wants everyone to know how he feels about these soldiers. He works carefully on his speech. It is only two pages long, but every word is very important to him. Lincoln reads his speech. He talks about the people who started the United States and their idea that all men are equal. The Civil War is going on at the time. The war is about this idea. Lincoln says everyone should remember the men who died. He tells the group to continue the work of these men. Everyone claps and sings when he finishes the speech.

SPANISH

Esta narración histórica incluye un discurso dado por el Presidente Abraham Lincoln en 1863. Lincoln fue a un evento para honorar a los soldados de la Guerra Civil que murieron en la Batalla de Gettysburg. Él quiere que todos sepan lo que siente por esos soldados y trabaja cuidadosamente en su discurso. Aunque el discurso es de tan sólo dos páginas de largo, cada palabra para Lincoln es muy importante. En el discurso, habla acerca de quienes comenzaron este país y sus ideales, y del concepto de que todas las personas son iguales. La Guerra Civil todavía se estaba peleando en ese entonces, y él dice que esa Guerra era para mantener vivos esos ideales. Lincoln dice que todos deberían recordar a los hombres que han muerto en la Guerra y que deberían continuar el trabajo que ellos comenzaron. Cuando acaba de dar el discurso, los miembros de la audiencia aplauden y comienzan a cantar.

HMONG

Zaj dab neeg piav tseg ntawm no nws muaj cov lus uas nom Abraham Lincoln tau hais nyob rau xyoo 1863. Lincoln mus hais lus nyob rau ib lub chaw sawv daws tuaj mus sib koom phijxej. Qhov kev tuaj mus sib koom no yog mus hawm thiab qhuas txog cov tub rog uas tau raug tuag lub sib hawm lub tebchaw rov sib tua (Civil War) nyob rau nplua tsov rog nyob rau Gettysburg (Battle of Gettysburg). Lincoln xav kom sawv daws paub txog hais tias nws xav li cas txog cov tub rog no. Nyob rau cov lus hais ntawd nws ua tib zoo piav. Nws tham txog cov neeg uas tau pib tsim muaj lub tebchaws United States thiab piav txog lawv tej tswvyim uas tias txhua tus neeg yeej muaj vajhuam sib luag. Lub sib hawm ntawd lub teb chaw tseem niaj hnub sib tua. Kev sib tua no twb yog vim txog lub tswvyi no xwb. Lincoln hais tias txhua leej txhua tug yuav tsum tau nco txog cov txiv neej uas lawv tau tuag ntawd tej txiaj ntsim. Nws hais rau pab tib neeg tuaj mloog ntawd kom yuav tsum ua cov txiv neej tau tuag ntawd tegnum tauj. Thaum nws hais lus tag lawd, lawv npuajtes thiab hu nkauj zoo siab ua ke.

VIETNAMESE

Bài tường thuật lịch sử này bao gồm bài diễn văn của Tổng Thống Abraham Lincoln vào năm 1863. Lincoln đến diễn thuyết tại một buổi tưởng niệm đặc biệt được tổ chức nhằm ca ngợi những chiến sĩ đã hy sinh tại Chiến Trường Gettysburg trong cuộc Nội Chiến. Lincoln muốn mọi người hiểu cảm xúc của ông về những người lính này. Ông chuẩn bị rất kỹ cho bài diễn văn. Bài diễn văn chỉ dài có hai trang, nhưng từng từ ngữ đều có ý nghĩa rất quan trọng đối với ông. Lincoln đọc bài diễn văn. Ông nói về những người có công lập quốc Hoa Kỳ và lý tưởng của họ là mọi người đều bình đẳng. Cuộc Nội Chiến lúc ấy vẫn đang tiếp diễn, cũng chỉ vì lý tưởng này. Lincoln nói rằng mọi người nên tưởng nhớ đến những chiến sĩ đã nằm xuống. Ông có lời nhắn gởi đến khán giả là phải tiếp tục sự nghiệp của các vị này. Mọi người vỗ tay và hát sau khi ông kết thúc bài diễn văn.

CANTONESE

這篇歷史記敘文中包括了阿伯拉罕‧林肯總統在一八六三年的演講辭。林肯在一次特別活動中發表了演講。這次活動是為了記念南北戰爭時在吉他堡戰役中犧牲的士兵。林肯希望每個人都能了解他對這些士兵的感受。他細心準備了演講辭。雖然只有兩頁，但每一個字對他都很重要。林肯宣讀他的演講辭，他提及美國的開國元勳以及他們關於人人平等的理念。當時南北戰爭正在進行中，而戰爭正是為了實現這一理念。林肯說，每個人都應記住這些陣亡者。他告訴大家，要繼續這些人未盡的工作。當他演講完畢，每個人都拍手唱和。

CAMBODIAN

ការរៀបរាប់ពីប្រវត្តិសាស្ត្រនេះ រាប់បញ្ចូលទាំងសុន្ទរកថារបស់ប្រធានាធិបតេយ្យ អេប្រាហាំ លីនកុន នៅ ឆ្នាំ ១៨៣។ លីនកុន នៅទីនោះនិយាយនៅក្នុងព្រឹត្តិការណ៍សម្ពោធ កម្មវិធីនេះ គឺដើម្បីគោរពទាហានដែលស្លាប់នៅក្នុង សង្រ្គាមក្នុងស្រុកនៅសមរភូមិ ។ ហ្គេតធីស្ព័រ។ លីនកុន ចង់ឲ្យគ្រប់គ្នាស្គាល់អារម្មណ៍ផ្ទាល់ខ្លួនពោះ៖ ទាហានទាំងនេះ។ គាត់សរសេរសុន្ទរកថាដ៏ប្រសើរ។ វាមានប្រវែងពីរទំព័រ ប៉ុន្តែគ្រប់ពាក្យមានសារៈសំខាន ណាស់ចំពោះគាត់។ លីនកុន អានសុន្ទរកថារបស់គាត់។ គាត់និយាយអំពីមនុស្សដែល ចាប់ផ្តើមសហរដ្ឋនេះ ហើយ គំនិតរបស់ទាំងនោះគឺឲ្យមនុស្សទាំងអស់ស្មើភាពគ្នា។ សង្រ្គាមក្នុងស្រុកមាននៅពេលនោះ។ សង្រ្គាមស្តីពីគំនិត នេះ។ លីនកុន និយាយថា គ្រប់គ្នាគួរបណ្ដុះដែលស្លាប់។ គាត់ប្រាប់នៅក្នុងក្រុមឲ្យបន្តកិច្ចការរបស់អ្នកទាំងនោះ។ ទាន់ៗខ្លួនៗ គ្រប់ៗគ្នាៈផៃ ហើយច្រៀងនៅពេលគាត់បញ្ចប់សុន្ទរកថា។

HAITIAN CREOLE

Narasyon istorik sa a enkli yon diskou prezidan Abraham Lincoln te fè an 1863. Lincoln al pale nan yon evenman espesyal. Evenman an se pou onore sòlda lagè sivil yo ki te mouri nan batay Gettysburg lan. Lincoln te vle pou tout moun konnen ki santiman li te genyen pou sòlda sa yo. Li te pran anpil tan pou l travay sou diskou li an. Li gen sèlman de paj men chak mo enpòtan pou li anpil. Lincoln li diskou li an. Li pale konsènan moun ki te kòmanse Etazini epi lide yo te genyen kote tout moun egal ego. Lagè Sivil la t ap fè ravaj lè sa a. Lagè a se konsènan lide sa a. Lincoln di tout moun dwe sonje moun ki te mouri yo. Li di gwoup lan pou li kontinye travay mesye sa yo. Tout moun bat bravo epi chante lè l te fini ak diskou li an.

UNIT 5 • CHAPTER 3
So Far from the Bamboo Grove, by Yoko Kawashima Watkins

ENGLISH

"So Far from the Bamboo Grove" is a story about a Japanese boy named Hideyo. Hideyo lives with the Kim family in northern Korea. He is trying to escape from the Communists in northern Korea. He is going to southern Korea. Hideyo swims across a river that is guarded by Communist soldiers. He swims under the water to get out of the guard's light. Hideyo hears gunshots. He is not sure if the guards are shooting at him. Bullets hit the water around him. He reaches the other side of the river. Hideyo hopes the Kim family knows that he made it safely to freedom.

SPANISH

"So Far from the Bamboo Grove" es una historia acerca de un niño japonés llamado Hideyo, quien vive con una familia de apellido Kim en Corea del Norte. Hideyo está tratando de ir hacia el sur de Corea para escapar de los comunistas del norte. Hideyo nada a través de un río que está vigilado por soldados comunistas. Hideyo nada bajo el agua para que no lo delaten las luces. De pronto, escucha disparos y no está seguro si los guardias le disparan a él. Los disparos caen a su alrededor, pero Hideyo finalmente alcanza a llegar al otro lado del río. Hideyo espera que la familia Kim sepa que llegó sano y salvo al otro lado.

HMONG

"So Far from the Bamboo Grove" yog ib zaj dab neeg txog ib tug menyuam tub Yeebpooj npe hu ua Hideyo. Hideyo nyob nrog tsev neeg Kim hauv qaumteb Kauslim. Nws nrhiav kev khiav tawm Koos Sam Kauslim qaumteb. Nws yuav mus rau Kauslim qabteb. Hideyo ua luam dej hla ib tug dej uas cov tub rog Koos Sam tau zov. Nws ua luam dej nkag hauv qab thu kom cov tub rog zov ntawd lub teeb rom pom tsi txog. Hideyo hnov phom nrov ntau teg. Nws paub tsi zoo hais tias xyov puas yog cov tub rog zov ntawd tua nws los tsi yog. Cov mostxwv raug dej ib puagncig nws. Nws luam mus txog rau sab ntug dej tid lawm. Hideyo cia siab hais tias nyaj tsev neeg Kim yuav paub lawm tias nws tau khiav dhau txojkev ntxhovsiab mus rau txojkev ywjpheej lawm.

VIETNAMESE

"So Far from the Bamboo Grove" là một câu chuyện kể về một cậu bé Nhật Bản tên Hideyo. Hideyo sống với gia đình họ Kim ở Bắc Hàn. Cậu cố gắng trốn thoát khỏi quân Cộng Sản ở Bắc Hàn. Cậu muốn đến Nam Hàn. Hideyo bơi qua một con sông có lính Cộng Sản trấn thủ. Cậu bơi ở dưới mặt nước để tránh ánh sáng của lính gác. Hedeyo nghe tiếng súng bắn. Cậu thắc mắc không biết có phải lính gác đang bắn cậu hay không. Đạn dược bắn vào vùng nước xung quanh cậu. Cậu bơi được đến bờ bên kia. Hedeyo hy vọng gia đình họ Kim biết rằng cậu đã đến vùng tự do an toàn.

CANTONESE

So Far from the Bamboo Grove 講述一個名叫英世的日本小孩的故事．英世住在北韓的金姓家庭中．他想逃離北韓的共產統治，前往南韓．英世游過一條由共產黨士兵守衛的河流．為了躲避守衛的燈光，他在水下潛游．英世聽到槍聲，他不確定守衛是否向他射擊．子彈擊中他周圍的河水．他游到了河的對岸．英世希望金家的人知道他平安地獲得了自由．

CAMBODIAN

"So Far from the Bamboo Grove" ជារឿង មួយនិយាយអំពីក្មេងប្រុស ជប៉ុន ម្នាក់ឈ្មោះ៖ ហ៊ីដេយ៉ា។ ហ៊ីដេយ៉ា រស់នៅជាមួយគ្រួសារ គីម នៅប្រទេសកូរ៉េខាងជើង។ វាសាកល្បងរត់គេចពីក្មេងមួយនិងកូប៉ារខាងជើង។ វាទៅ កូរ៉េខាងត្បូង។ ហ៊ីដេយ៉ា ហែលឆ្លងមួយនៃលមយាយឈ្មោះ៖ ... ...

HAITIAN CREOLE

"So Far from the Bamboo Grove" se yon istwa konsènan yon tigason japonè ki rele Hideyo. Hideyo abite avèk fanmi Kim nan Kore dinò. L ap eseye chape pou l li anba men kominis yo nan Kore dinò. Li pral nan Kore disid. Hideyo naje nan yon rivyè sòlda kominis yo ap siveye. Li naje anba dlo a pou l ka pase anba limyè gad lan. Hideyo tande kout zam. Li pa sèten si se sou li gad yo ap tire. Bal yo rive nan dlo kote li ye a. Li ateri nan lòt bò rivyè a . Hideyo espere fanmi Kim lan konnen li rive jwenn lalibète l san danje.

UNIT 5 • CHAPTER 4

Alone, by Samantha Abeel, & Samantha's Story, by Samantha Abeel

ENGLISH

In the poem "Alone," the poet writes that there is a place we go when we are alone. In this place, birds fly freely. There is a fog in this place that protects us. When we are in this place, we are free to do what we choose.

"Samantha's Story" is an autobiography about Samantha Abeel. She has a learning problem at school. Seventh grade is a bad year for Samantha. One thing that helps her feel better is her writing class. Writing helps her do what she does well. In eighth grade, people at the school place her in special classes. This changes her life. She is comfortable in class now. Samantha says that if you have a learning problem, you must find something you are good at.

SPANISH

En el poema "Alone", la poeta escribe que hay un lugar al que vamos cuando estamos solos. En ese lugar, las aves vuelan con completa libertad y hay una neblina que nos protege. Cuando estamos allí, podemos hacer lo que queramos.

"Samantha's Story" es una autobiografía de Samantha Abeel, quien tiene un problema de aprendizaje en la escuela. El séptimo grado es un año difícil para Samantha, pero algo que la hace sentir bien es su clase de escritura. La clase de escritura le ayuda, porque es algo que ella puede hacer bien. Cuando llega al octavo grado, en la escula la ponen en clases con ayuda especial. Eso le cambia la vida, ya que por fin se siente cómoda en una clase. Samantha dice que si alguien tiene un problema de aprendizaje, debe hallar algo que pueda hacer bien.

HMONG

Nyob rau hauv zaj lus paivyi "Alone," tus tshwm lub tswvyim no sau hais tias muaj ib qhov chaw rau peb mus thaum peb nyob ib leeg lawm xwb. Nyob rau qhov chaw no, peb nyob ywjsiab xav ua dabtsi los nyob ntawm peb xaiv li xwb.

"Samantha's Story" yog ib phau ntawv qhia txog Samantha Abeel. Tus ntxhais no nws muaj teeb meem rau txojkev kawm nyob rau tom tsev kawm ntawv. Qib xya yog ib xyoos uas tsi zoo rau Samantha hlo li. Ib qho uas zoo zog rau nws ces yog hoob kawm sau ntawv. Sau ntawv yog ib qho uas pab tau nws rau yam uas nws ua tau zoo. Nyob rau qib yim, ces cov tib neeg tom tsev kawm ntawv muab nws tso kawm rau cov hoob phijxej lawm. Qhov ntawm no cia li hloov hlo nws lub neej. Nyob hauv hoob nws tso siab plhuav lawm. Samantha hais tias yog koj muaj teeb meem rau txojkev kawm, koj yuav tsum tau nrhiav ib yam uas koj ua tau zoo.

VIETNAMESE

Trong bài thơ "Alone," nhà thơ viết rằng mỗi khi cô đơn chúng ta có thể tìm đến một nơi. Nơi này có chim bay tự do. Chúng ta được một màn sương mù bao bọc và che chở. Ở nơi này, chúng ta có thể tự do làm bất cứ điều gì mình muốn.

"Samantha's Story" là một cuốn tự truyện kể về Samantha Abeel. Cô mắc phải tình trạng khó tiếp thu bài học. Năm học lớp bảy là một năm đặc biệt khó khăn đối với Samantha. Có một lớp giúp cô cảm thấy tự tin hơn là lớp viết văn. Việc viết lách tạo điều kiện cho cô tập trung vào năng khiếu của mình. Lên lớp tám, cô được xếp vào các lớp đặc biệt. Điều này làm thay đổi hẳn cuộc sống của cô. Giờ đây cô học tốt ở trường. Samantha nói rằng nếu mắc phải tình trạng khó tiếp thu bài học, ta cần phải tập trung vào môn nào hợp với năng khiếu của mình.

CANTONESE

在 Alone 一詩中，詩人寫出當我們孤單時可以去的一個地方。在那裡，鳥兒自由地飛翔。那裡有一層霧氣掩護著我們。在那個地方，我們可以自由地做我們想做的事情。

Samantha's Story 是撒瑪花‧阿比的一篇自傳。她在學校裏學習有困難。對撒瑪花來說，七年級是很糟的一年。令她感到較為開心的是寫作課。寫作可以發揮她的特長。在八年級時，學校把她編進了特別班，這改變了她的生活。現在，她在班中感覺很自在。撒瑪花說，如果你有學習困難，你一定要找出一些你的特長。

CAMBODIAN

នៅក្នុងកំណាព្យ "Alone," អ្នកនិពន្ធកាព្យសរសេរថា មានកន្លែងដែលយើងទៅ កាលណាយើងឯកោ។ នៅកែន្លងនេះ សត្វបក្សីហោះហើរសេរី។ មានកែន្ថុបនៅទីនេះ ដែលការពារយើង។ ពេលណាយើងនៅទីនេះ យើងមានសេរីភាពធ្វើអ្វីៗដែលយើងចង់ធ្វើ។

"Samantha's Story" ជាប្រវត្តិរូបរបស់ សាម៉ែនថា អាបែល។ នាងមានបញ្ហារៀនសូត្រនៅសាលា។ ថ្នាក់ទី៧ជាឆ្នាំដ៏ក្រក់របស់ សាម៉ែនថា។ រៀនមួយដែលជួយឲ្យនាងមានความ មុ៉ន្លៃ្មើង គឺថ្នាក់រៀនសរសេរ។ ការសរសេរជួយឲ្យនាងបន្លួញ្ជរអ្វីៗដែលនាងពូកែ។ នៅថ្នាក់ទី៨ អ្នកសាលាបានក្នុងឲ្យនៅថ្នាក់ដ៏ពិសេស។ ការនេះ ធ្វើឲ្យជីវិតនាងស្រស្រួយ។ នាងនៅក្នុងថ្នាក់បានស្រលដ៏ស្រួលរា, សាម៉ែនថា និយាយថា បើអ្នកមានបញ្ហាក្នុងការរៀនសូត្រ អ្នកត្រូវរកអ្វីមួយដែលអ្នកពូកែ។

HAITIAN CREOLE

Nan powèm "Alone," powèt la ekri genyen yon kote nou ale lè nou sèl. Nan kote sa a, zwazo yo vole san pwoblèm. Genyen yon bwouya nan kote sa a ki pwoteje nou. Lè nou nan kote sa a, nou lib pou nou fè sa nou vle.

"Samantha's Story" se yon otobyografi sou Samantha Abeel. Li gen yon pwoblèm pou l aprann lekòl. Setyèm klas se yon move ane pou Samantha. Yon bagay ki ede l santi l miyò se klas ekriti li an. Lè l ekri sa ede l fè sa li fè byen. Nan uityèm klas, moun nan lekòl lan mete l nan klas espesyal. Sa chanje lavi l. Li alèz nan klas li kounye a. Samantha di si w genyen yon pwoblèm pou aprann, ou dwe chèche yon bagay ou fè byen.

UNIT 6 • CHAPTER 1

Mr. Scrooge Finds Christmas, Adapted by Aileen Fisher

ENGLISH

The first scene of this play takes place in Ebenezer Scrooge's office. Mr. Scrooge is a mean man who does nothing to help others. In Scene 2, Mr. Scrooge and Bob Cratchit are at work. A man visits the office and asks for money to help poor people. Mr. Scrooge has money to help, but he says no. Marley's ghost and three spirits watch all of this happen. Marley is Mr. Scrooge's dead business partner. Marley wants to warn Mr. Scrooge that he thinks too much about work and making money. Marley wants Mr. Scrooge to think more about helping other people. The three other spirits agree to help Marley with his plans. As the scene ends, young boys sing Christmas songs.

SPANISH

La primera escena de esta obra de teatro se lleva a cabo en la oficina de Ebenezer Scrooge. El señor Scrooge es un hombre rudo que no hace nada para ayudar a nadie. En la segunda escena, El señor Scrooge y Bob Cratchit están trabajando. Un hombre visita la oficina y les pide dinero para ayudar a los pobres. Aunque el señor Scrooge tiene dinero, él dice que no va a colaborar. El fantasma de Marley y tres espíritus observan lo sucedido. Marley es el difunto compañero de negocios del señor Scrooge. Marley quiere advertirle al señor Scrooge que él piensa demasiado en el trabajo y en hacer dinero. Marley quiere que el señor Scrooge piense más en ayudar a otros. Los otros tres espíritus se ponen de acuerdo para ayudar a Marley a llevar a cabo sus planes. Al final de la escena, niños cantan canciones navideñas.

HMONG

Thawj zaj txog qhov yeeb yam no yog pib nyob rau hauv Ebenezer Scrooge lub loo kam. Tus Mr. Srooge yog ib tug txiv neej phem heev nws yeej tsi kam ua ib yam dabtsi pab rau lwm tug li. Nyob rau zaj ob, Mr. Srooge thiab Bob Cratchit nyob rau tom haujlwm. Ib tug txiv neej tuaj thov nyiaj ntawm nkawv loo kam mus pab rau cov neeg pluag. Mr. Srooge yeej muaj nyiaj pab, tiam sis nws teb hais tias tsi muaj. Marley tus mojzeeg thiab peb tug ntsujplig saib ntsoov txhua yam no tshwm sim. Marley yog Mr. Srooge ib tug uas tau koomtes nrog nws ua lagluam dhau los lawd tiam sis nws tau tuag lawm. Marley xav ceebtoom rau Mr. Srooge paub tias nws muab xav heev txog qhov ua haujlwm thiab nrhiav kom muaj nyiaj hwv lawm. Marley xav kom Mr. Srooge yuav tsum tau xav txog pab lwm tug tib neeg ntau tshaj. Peb tug ntsujplig nrog nws pom zoo koomtes pab nws rau lub tswvyim uas nws muaj no. Thaum zaj yeeb yam no yuav los xaus, ib co tub hluas pib hu cov nkauj txog hnub Yesxus los xyus.

VIETNAMESE

Màn mở đầu của vở kịch này diễn ra tại văn phòng của Ebenezer Scrooge. Ông Scrooge là một người đàn ông xấu tính không bao giờ làm gì để giúp người khác. Trong Màn 2, Ông Scrooge và Bob Cratchit đang ở sở làm. Một người đàn ông đến văn phòng và hỏi xin tiền để giúp người nghèo. Ông Scrooge có tiền, nhưng lại từ chối. Hồn ma của Marley và ba con ma khác quan sát và thấy tất cả. Marley trước khi chết là cộng sự viên của Ông Scrooge. Marley muốn cảnh báo Ông Scrooge rằng ông lo nghĩ quá nhiều đến công việc và việc kiếm tiền. Marley muốn Ông Scrooge để ý hơn đến việc giúp đỡ người khác. Ba hồn ma kia đồng ý giúp Marley thực hiện kế hoạch này. Vào phần cuối của màn này, các cậu bé hát những bài hát Giáng Sinh.

CANTONESE

活劇的第一幕發生在依班尼沙‧士谷的辦公室．士谷先生是一個吝嗇鬼，他不會做任何事去幫助別人．在第二幕中，士谷先生及波比‧格莈正在工作．有人走進辦公室，請求捐款來幫助貧窮的人．士谷先生有錢可以幫助別人，但他卻說沒有．馬利的靈魂和三個幽靈目睹整個過程．馬利是士谷先生已去世的生意合伙人．馬利想警告士谷先生，他太關注工作和賺錢．馬利希望士谷先生能多幫助別人．那三個幽靈同意幫助馬利實行他的計劃．當該幕結束時，男孩們在頌唱聖誕歌．

CAMBODIAN

ភាគទី១នៃឈុតនេះ៖ កើតឡើងនៅក្នុងការិយាល័យរបស់ អេប៊ីនីសឺ ស្ក្រូច ជាមនុស្សកាចម្នាក់ ដែលមិនធ្វើអ្វីជួយអ្នកដទៃឡើយ។ ក្នុងភាគទី២ លោក ស្ក្រូច និង បប ក្រាចឆិ នៅកំឡុងធ្វើការ។ បុរសម្នាក់មកពេលការិយាល័យ ហើយសុំលុយដើម្បីជួយអ្នកក្រីក្រ។ លោក ស្ក្រូច មានលុយសំរាប់ជួយ ទែគាត់មិនយាយ ១។ ខ្មោចម៉ាលី និងព្រលឹងបី មើលឃើញភ្នែកដែលកើតឡើងនៅពីអំពស់នេះ។ ម៉ាលី ជាដៃគូជំនួញ របស់លោក ស្ក្រូច ដែលស្លាប់ទៅ។ ម៉ាលី ចង់ហាមលោក ស្ក្រូច នាគាត់ហួសហេតុពេកពីការការងនិងលុយ។ ម៉ាលី ចង់ឲ្យលោក ស្ក្រូច គិតដែរទោម៉ាច់ពើការជួយមនុស្សដទៃ។ ព្រលឹងបីឲ្យសល់ព្រមឲ្យស ម៉ាលី តាម គំនាងរបស់គាត់។ ក្នុងនាំកបញ្ចប់ ក្មេងប្រុស១ត្រៀងច៉ំរ៉ៀងបុណ្យឈ្នុបកំណើខ្រេ១យល្ង។

HAITIAN CREOLE

Premye sèn teyat sa ap pase nan biwo Ebenezer Scrooge. Mesye Scrooge se yon nonm mechan ki pa renmen fè anyen pou ede lòt moun. Nan Sèn 2, mesye Scrooge ak Bob Cratchit ap travay. Yon mesye vin vizite biwo an pou l mande lajan pou ka ede moun ki pòv. Mesye Scrooge gen ase kòb pou l ta ka bay yon kout men, men li refize. Fantom Marley ak twa lespri ap gade tout sa k ap pase a. Marley se defen patnè biznis mesye Scrooge. Marley vle avèti mesye Scrooge li panse twòp ak zafè travay epi fè lajan. Marley vle pou mesye Scrooge panse plis pou l ede lòt moun. Twa lòt lespri yo dakò pou ede Marley ak plan l yo. Lè sèn lan pral fini, plizyè jèn tigason ap chante chante Nwèl.

UNIT 6 • CHAPTER 2

The House on Mango Street, by Sandra Cisneros

ENGLISH

This selection is from the novel "The House on Mango Street." For many years, the author's parents always say they will own a house someday. They say the house will have running water and three bathrooms. It will be white with a big yard. They move many times. The author and her family now own a house. The house is on Mango Street. This house is not like the house in the parents' stories. It is small and red. There is no front yard, and the backyard is very small. Everyone shares one bathroom and one bedroom. This is not the house the author wants. Her parents say this will be their house for only a short time. This is what they always say.

SPANISH

Esta es una selección de la novela "The House on Mango Street". Por muchos años, los padres de la autora han dicho que algún día van a tener su propia casa. Ellos dicen que la casa tendrá plomería y tres baños, que será blanca y tendrá un jardín grande. La familia se muda muchas veces y por fin un día tienen su propia casa. La casa es en la Calle Mango. La casa no es exactamente como la describían sus padres en sus relatos. La casa es pequeña y roja, no hay jardín al frente y el patio de atrás es pequeñito. Todos comparten un baño y una habitación. Esta no es la casa que quiere la autora. Sus padres le dicen que ésta sera su casa sólo por un corto tiempo. Eso es lo que ellos siempre dicen.

HMONG

Zaj dab neeg no yog los ntawm phau ntawv "The House on Mango Street." Tau ntau xyoo los mas tus sau zaj no nws niam thiab nws txiv ib txwm hais tias nkawv yuav muaj ib lub tsev uas yog nkawv li kiag. Nkawv hais tias lub tsev ntawd nws yuav muaj kais dej thiab hoob nab huvsi. Lub tsev ntawd nws yuav yog xim dawb thiab muaj lub vaj loj heev. Nkawv khiav ntau zaug lawm. Tus sau zaj no thiab nws tsev neeg lawv muaj lawv ib lub tsev uas yog lawv li lawm. Lub tsev no yog nyob rau txojkev Mango. Lub tsev no nws tsi zoo li zaj dab neeg txog niam thiab txiv nkawv lub tsev. Nws me thiab yog xim liab. Ntawm qab khav nws tsi muaj av li, thiab tom qaum tsev los nqaim heev. Txhua leej txhua tug siv tib lub hoob nab thiab tib chav pw xwb. Lub tsev no tsi yog ib lub uas tus sau zaj dab neeg no xav tau. Tus ntxhais no niam thiab txiv hais tias lawv yuav nyob lub tsev no tsi ntev. Nkawv yeej ib txwm hais li no los tau ntev lawm.

VIETNAMESE

Bài này được trích từ cuốn tiểu thuyết "The House on Mango Street." Đã nhiều năm rồi, cha mẹ của tác giả luôn luôn nói rằng một ngày nào đó họ sẽ mua nhà. Họ nói rằng căn nhà này sẽ có nước máy và ba phòng tắm. Căn nhà sẽ được sơn màu trắng và có sân rộng. Họ dọn nhà nhiều lần rồi. Giờ đây tác giả và gia đình đã có một căn nhà trên đường Mango. Căn nhà không giống như căn nhà mà cha mẹ cô đã tả. Căn nhà này nhỏ và được sơn màu đỏ. Không có sân trước, và sân sau lại rất nhỏ. Mọi người dùng chung một phòng tắm và phòng ngủ. Đây không phải là căn nhà mà tác giả đã từng mong muốn. Cha mẹ cô nói rằng họ chỉ tạm ở đây thôi. Lúc nào họ cũng nói câu này.

CANTONESE

這篇選自一本名叫 The House on Mango Street 的小說．多年以來，作者的父母經常說，總有一天他們會擁有一所房子．他們說房子會有自來水和三套浴室．房子會是白色的，還有大花園．他們搬了很多次家．作者及她的家人現在擁有一所房子．房子在芒果街，但並不像她父母故事中的房子．房子很小，而且是紅色的．沒有前花園，後花園也很小．所有人共用一套浴室和一個睡房．這不是作者想要的房子．她父母說，這只是他們暫時的房子．他們老是這樣說．

CAMBODIAN

ការកម្រង់នេះរើញ មកអំពីប្រលោមលោក "The House on Mango Street." ។ ជាច្រើនឆ្នាំ ឪពុកម្ដាយអ្នកនិពន្ធ ថែងថែងនិយាយថាគាបង់មាន ថ្ងៃណាមួយៗ គេនិងសោយផ្ទះ ម្ដងណោះ និងមានប្រេបង់ទឹក រើយនិងបង្គន់បីកន្លែង។ វាមានពណ៌ស ជាមួយនិងច្បារដ៏ធំមួយៗ គេផ្លាស់ផ្ទះ ជាច្រើនឧឆ្លង អ្នកនិពន្ធនិងគ្រួសារ ឥឡូវនេះ មានផ្ទះ មួយៗ ផ្ទះនៅលើផ្លូវម៉ាងហ្គោ ម៉ែសហ្គោ ផ្ទះនេះ មិនមុនគេនៅក្នុងរឿង របស់ឪពុកម្ដាយនាងៗ វាតូច រើយមានពណ៌ក្រហមៗ គ្មានច្បារនៅមុខៗ រើយច្បារនៅក្រោយតូចណាស់ៗ គ្រប់គ្នាប្រើបង្គន់ មួយនិងបន្ទប់គេង មួយដូចគ្នាៗ ផ្ទះនេះ មិនមែនជាផ្ទះ ដែលអ្នកនិពន្ធចង់បានទេៗ ឪពុកម្ដាយនាងនិយាយថា នេះគឺ ជារបស់ពួកគាត់ សម្រាប់រស់នេះពេលមួយ ថ្ងៃៗ នេះគឺជាអ្វី ដែលពួកគាត់តែងតែនិយាយៗ

HAITIAN CREOLE

Seleksyon sa a soti nan woman "The House on Mango Street." Pandan plizyè ane, paran otè a toujou ap di yon jou yo va posede yon kay. Yo di kay lan pral gen dlo potab ak twa twalèt. Kay la ap gen pou l pentire an blan epi l ap gen yon gran lakou. Yo demenaje plizyè fwa. Otè a ak fanmi l kounye a gen yon kay. Kay la nan Mango Street. Kay sa pa sanble ak kay paran yo te konn ap rakonte a. Kay la kwense epi li pentire an wouj. Pa gen lakou devan kay lan, epi lakou dèyè kay lan piti anpil. Tout moun pataje yon sèl twalèt ak yon sèl chanm akouche. Sa se pa kay otè a te vle a. Paran l yo di kay sa a y ap gen pou rete ladan l pou yon ti kras tan sèlman. Se sa yo toujou di.

UNIT 6 • CHAPTER 3

The Pearl, by John Steinbeck

ENGLISH

Kino and Juana are a poor couple with a sick baby. To earn money, Kino dives for pearl oysters. An oyster may contain a pearl, but this is not common. While he is underwater, Kino knows that Juana is praying in the boat. She prays for something to heal their baby Coyotito. Kino sees a large oyster lying by itself. He picks this oyster. Kino thinks it may have a pearl inside. In the boat, Kino opens the oyster. Inside, he finds a large pearl. Kino and Juana are excited. They look at Coyotito. The baby is already getting better.

SPANISH

Kino y Juana son una pareja pobre con un bebé enfermo. Para ganar dinero, Kino se zambulle en el agua en busca de madreperlas. Aunque puede haber una perla en una ostra, eso no es muy común que ocurra. Kino sabe que Juana ora en el bote mientras el nada. Ella ora y pide que algo suceda para que se sane su bebé, llamado Coyotito. De repente, Kino ve una ostra grande y la recoge, pensando que de pronto tiene una perla por dentro. En el bote, Kino abre la ostra y encuentra una perla grande. Kino y Juana están dichosos. Miran tiernamente a su bebé y ven que ya se está mejorando.

HMONG

Kino thiab Juana nkawv muaj ib tug menyuam mos thiab pluag heev. Kom tau nyiaj los siv ces Kino ploj mus qab thu dej mus nrhiav cov hlaws qwj. Ib lub qwj pliasdeg twg tejzaum nws kuj muaj li ib lub hlaws, tiam sis qhov muaj li no tsawg heev. Thaum nws tseem nyob rau hauv qab dej thu, Kino paub hais tias Juana nws tabtom thov ntuj nyob rau saum lub nkoj. Yog nws thov pab kom ib yam dabtsi yuav los kho nkawv tus menyuam Coyotito. Kino pom ib lub qwj pliasdeg nyob ib leeg. Nws khaws lub qwj pliasdeg no. Kino xav hais tias tejzaum yuav muaj ib lub hlaws nyob rau sab hauv lub nrogcev. Thaum nyob hauv lub nkoj lawm, Kino muab lub qwj pliasdeg cem qhib. Nyob rau sab hauv nruab nrog, nws pom muaj ib lub hlaws loj heev. Kino thiab Juana zoo siab heev. Nkawv tig mus saib rau Coyotito. Tus mos ab twb zoo lawm.

Name ______________________________ Date ____________________

VIETNAMESE

Kino và Juana là một cặp vợ chồng nghèo có con nhỏ bị bệnh. Để kiếm tiền, Kino lặn xuống biển để tìm trai ngọc. Một con trai có thể chứa một hòn ngọc, nhưng điều này ít khi xảy ra. Lúc ở dưới nước, Kino biết rằng Juana đang cầu nguyện ở trên thuyền. Cô cầu nguyện cho con mình, là Coyotito, được lành bệnh. Kino trông thấy một con trai lớn đang nằm một mình. Ông nhặt con trai lên. Kino nghĩ rằng có thể có một hòn ngọc ở bên trong. Trên thuyền, Kino mở con trai ra. Trong đó có một hòn ngọc lớn. Kino và Juana rất phấn khởi. Họ nhìn Coyotito. Đứa bé giờ đây đã có vẻ khỏe mạnh hơn rồi.

CANTONESE

堅奴及祖娜是一對貧窮夫婦，他們有一個患病的嬰孩．為了賺錢，堅奴潛水採捕珍珠蠔．一個蠔內或許有珍珠，但並不常有．當堅奴在水下工作時，他知道祖娜正在船上祈禱．她祈求能有醫治他們孩子高沃鐵圖的良藥．堅奴看到一隻獨臥水底的大蠔．他摘了這隻蠔．堅奴想這隻蠔內可能會有珍珠．回到船上，堅奴打開那隻蠔．在裏面他找到一顆大珍珠．堅奴和祖娜十分高興，他們看著高沃鐵圖，孩子已經漸漸好起來了．

CAMBODIAN

គីណូ និង ជូអាណា ជាប្តីប្រពន្ធក្រម្នាក់ ដែលមានកូនតូចឈឺម្នាក់។ ដើម្បីរកលុយ គីណូ មុជទឹករកគុជ គ្រុំសមុទ្រ។ គ្រុំមួយអាចមានគុជមួយក្នុងខ្លួនវា តែទេះ មិនមែនជាការធម្មតាទេ។ ពេលដែលគាត់ចុះទៅនៅក្នុងទឹក គីណូ ដឹងថា ជូអាណាបន់ស្រន់នៅលើទូក។ នាងបន់ឲ្យមានថ្នាំសំរាប់ព្យាបាលកូនឈ្មោះ កូយ៉ូទីតូ។ គីណូ ឃើញ គ្រុំធំមួយនៅតែឯង។ គាត់រើសគ្រុំនេះ។ គីណូ គិតថាវាប្រហែលជាមានគុជនៅខាងក្នុងហើយ។ នៅលើទូក គីណូ បើកគ្រុំ។ នៅខាងក្នុង គាត់រកឃើញគុជធំមួយ។ គីណូនិងជូអាណា រីករាយចិត្ត។ ពួកគេសម្លឹងមើលទៅ កូយ៉ូទីតូ។ ទារកក៏ជារួចទៅហើយ។

HAITIAN CREOLE

Kino ak Juana se yon koup pòv ki gen yon tibebe malad. Pou fè lajan, Kino oblije plonje dèyè zuit pou jwenn pèl. Yon zuit ka gen yon pèl ladan l, men sa pa rive souvan. Pandan l anba dlo an, Kino konnen Juana ap priye nan bato an. Li konn priye pou tibebe yo an, Coyotito, ka jwenn gerizon. Kino wè yon gwo zuit ki poukont li. Li ranmase zuit lan. Kino panse li ka byen gen yon pèl anndan l. Nan bato an, Kino louvri zuit lan. Li jwenn anndan l yon gwo pèl. Kino ak Juana kontan anpil. Yo gade Coyotito. Tibebe an deja kòmanse refè.

UNIT 6 • CHAPTER 4

What Will Our Towns Look Like?, by Martha Pickerill

ENGLISH

This World Wide Web article describes towns in the future. Today many inventions make life easy, but they are harmful to Earth. Cars use gas and move people quickly, but they make the air dirty. Electric heat and light burn up coal and oil. This also pollutes the air. Towns of the future will get better. Many people will work at home. They will talk with co-workers by computer. Cars will run on clean fuels. Food will be grown close to home. Power will come from windmills and solar panels. Finally, waste will empty into enclosed swamps. Special plants and fish will clean the waste water.

SPANISH

Este artículo del Internet describe ciudades del futuro. Hoy en día, muchos inventos hacen que la vida sea más fácil que antes, pero muchos son dañinos para el planeta. Por ejemplo, los automóbiles transportan a la gente rápidamente, pero usan gasolina y contaminan el aire. Los calentadores eléctricos y la electricidad queman carbón y gasolina, y eso también contamina el aire. Las ciudades del futuro no producirán tanta polución, porque más gente trabajará desde sus casas y se comunicarán con sus compañeros de trabajo por medio de computadores. Los automóbiles usarán energía que no contamine el medio ambiente. Los alimentos se producirán localmente y el poder para generar energía se obtendrá de molinos de viento y de paneles solares. Además, los desperdicios irán directamente a gigantes cisternas cerradas en las que plantas y peces especiales limpiarán los residuos.

HMONG

Tsab xov xwm World Wide Web no piav txog tej zos nyob rau yav pemsuab. Niaj hnub tam sim no muaj tsim tawm ntau yam ua rau lub neej yoojyim lawm, tiam sis tej no nws tsi zoo rau lub Ntiajteb. Tej tsheb nws siv roj thiab xa tib neeg mus tau ceev heev, tiam sis lawv kuj ua rau cov fuabcua qias tuaj. Faisfab ntaiv thiab hluavtaws yog siv tej ncaisthee (coal) thiab roj (oil) hlawv ua. Qhov ntawm no puav leej ua rau cov fuabcua qias tuaj. Tej zos yav pemsuab yuav zoo ntxiv. Coob tus neeg yuav ua haujlwm nyob tom tsev. Lawv yuav siv tej cuab yeej computers los nrog lawv tej khub ua haujlwm sib tham lawm xwb. Tsheb yuav siv tej roj uas huv lawm. Tej khoom noj los yuav cog nyob ze tsev. Tej faisfab yuav tsim los ntawm kivcua zom tawm thiab los ntawm lub hnub lawm xwb. Thaum kawg, yuav khawb qhov faus tej khibnyawb lawm. Tej dej uas qias yuav muaj tej nroj tsuag phijxej thiab ntses pab tu rau kom huv lawm thiab.

VIETNAMESE

Bài viết trên mạng này mô tả các thành phố trong tương lai. Ngày nay có nhiều phát minh giúp cho cuộc sống tiện nghi hơn, nhưng lại gây hại cho Trái Đất. Xe hơi sử dụng xăng và giúp con người vận chuyển nhanh chóng, nhưng lại làm không khí dơ bẩn. Các lò sưởi và bóng đèn chạy bằng điện đòi hỏi phải đốt than và dầu, cũng làm ô nhiễm không khí. Các thành phố trong tương lai sẽ đỡ hơn. Nhiều người sẽ làm việc tại gia. Họ nói chuyện với đồng nghiệp qua máy vi tính. Xe hơi chạy bằng nhiên liệu sạch sẽ. Thức ăn được nuôi trồng gần nhà. Năng lượng được tạo ra từ cối xay gió và pin mặt trời. Cuối cùng, rác sẽ được đổ vào các đầm lầy có rào bọc. Các loài cá và cây cỏ đặc biệt sẽ làm sạch nước thải.

CANTONESE

這篇網頁上的文章描述了未來的都市。現在的很多發明令人類生活變得輕鬆，但卻對地球造成傷害。汽車使用汽油，使人類交通快捷，但卻污染空氣。電熱和電燈要燃燒煤及油，同樣污染空氣。未來的都市將會變得更好。很多人在家中工作，他們通過電腦與同事溝通。汽車將採用清潔燃料。食物將在家中附近種植。能源將來自風力及太陽能。最後，廢物將在密封的沼澤內處理。特殊的植物和魚類將會淨化污水。

CAMBODIAN

អត្ថបទនៅលើអ៊ីនធឺណិត៖ បរិយាយពីទីក្រុងនៅពេលអនាគត។ សព្វថ្ងៃ ការបង្កើតរបស់ថ្មីៗផ្សេងៗវិញធ្វើការស្រួល ថែរវាថ្មីៗមានៗគ្រោះ៖ ឡាក់មេឡានៃសនីៗ ឡានៗប្រើសាំង រើយសក្តិកនៅមនុស្សៗបានឆាប់ជាងឈើៗ ថែរវាថ្មីៗធ្វើឡានៗ ដួលថយៗ ក្រុងក្នុងៗ មាស់ក៏នៅ ឱិ ក៏ឯៗសត្តិសៗ សុខ្យស្រុកៗ ឱៗក៏ធ្វើឡានៗ ដួលៗ នៅ ថែៗ នីក្រុងៗ ថ្មីៗ ប្រសើរ ជាងៗ ៖ មនុស្សៗ ច្រើនៗ ន ធ្វើការ នៅ ផ្ទះៗ ៖ គេ នឹង ឆ្លាយ ជា អ្នកៗ ធ្វើការ ជា មួយគ្នា ម៉ាស៊ីនៗ ឡានៗ នឹង ឈើៗ រៀ ការ ប្រស្រុលៗ ព័ណ៌នឹងៗ នៅ ថែ ឲ្យៗ ៖ នា មណ្ឌល នឹងៗ ក៏ ឯ យក ភ័ង្គ ន ការៗ ស្រុល នឹងៗ ផ្ទះ ភ័ង្គ ឲ្យៗ នឹ បញ្ចប់ សំរាម នឹងៗ នាក់ បញ្ចូល នៅៗ ក្នុងៗ បឹងៗ មួយៗ ថែល បិទៗ ជិតៗ ៖ នឹ មុចៗ ជា ថ្ងៃ នឹងៗ ធ្វើៗ ព័ណ៌ស្រោៗ នឹ សំ ភ័ង្គ នឹ សំ អាត នឹ ក៏ ភ័ង្គ លៗ ៖

HAITIAN CREOLE

Atik sou Entènèt sa dekri kouman vil yo pral ye nan lavni. Jodi a gen anpil envansyon ki rann lavi pi fasil, men yo koze domaj pou Latè. Otomobil yo itilize gazolin epi yo deplase moun rapidman, men yo sal lè moun ap respire a. Chofaj elektrik ak limyè itilize chabon ak luil. Sa polye lè a tou. Vil yo nan lavni pral amelyore. Anpil moun ap gen pou travay lakay yo. Yo pral pale ak konpayon travay yo pa òdinatè. Otomobil yo pral itilize kabiran ki pwòp. Manje yo ap pral fèt pi pre kay moun. Se moulen a van ak pano solè ki pral founi enèji. Finalman, yo pral dechaje dechè yo nan marekaj ki fèmen. Ap gen plant ak pwason espesyal ki pral netwaye dlo sal.

Name _____

Date _____

Dear Family,

In class, we learned about mysteries. _____ (student's name) would like to share with you the stories we read.

The Loch Ness Monster, by Malcolm Yorke Tourists and scientists all over the world try to prove that there is a creature like a dinosaur living in a lake in Scotland.

Mystery of the Cliff Dwellers The ruins of an ancient society remain high in the cliffs of Mesa Verde, Colorado. Nobody knows what happened to the people who lived there.

Yawning, by Haleh V. Samiei Scientists have never discovered exactly why people yawn. This reading describes some theories and research.

The Sneak Thief, by Falcon Travis A police inspector uses clues to solve a crime.

The Legend of Sleepy Hollow, by Washington Irving In the small town of Sleepy Hollow, a headless horseman rides through the streets at night.

We would also like you to take a few moments to participate in an activity about mysteries to share with the class. Thank you for your support.

Sincerely,

_____ (Teacher)

Talk with someone at home about an unsolved mystery. Choose one from the box, or think of another one you know.

1. Explain what the mystery is. _____

   _____

   _____

2. What is one theory that you know that explains the mystery?

   _____

   _____

3. What does your family member think is the explanation?

   _____

   _____

4. What do you think explains the mystery? _____

   _____

   _____

Unsolved Mysteries
The Cliff Dwellers
Extinction of Dinosaurs
UFOs
Crop circles
The Bermuda Triangle
Stonehenge
Big Foot/Sasquatch
The Great Pyramids
Atlantis
Roswell/Area 51
The Loch Ness Monster

Nombre _____

Fecha _____

Estimada familia:

En nuestra clase, aprendimos acerca de misterios. A _____
(nombre del estudiante) le gustaría compartir con usted las historias que leímos.

The Loch Ness Monster, por Malcolm Yorke Turistas y científicos de todo el mundo tratan de comprobar que hay una criatura parecida a un dinosaurio, que vive en un lago de Escocia.

Mystery of the Cliff Dwellers Las ruinas de una sociedad antigua permanecen en las alturas de Mesa Verde, Colorado. Nadie sabe lo que sucedió con sus habitantes.

Yawning, por Haleh V. Samiei Los científicos nunca han logrado descubrir por qué bostezamos. Esta lectura describe algunas teorías e investigaciones.

The Sneak Thief, por Falcon Travis Un inspector de policía usa claves para resolver un misterio.

The Legend of Sleepy Hollow, por Washington Irving En el pueblo de Sleepy Hollow, un cabalgante sin cabeza monta su caballo de noche por las calles.

Ahora nos gustaría que participara en una actividad acerca de misterios, para luego compartirla con el resto de la clase. Muchas gracias por su apoyo.

Cordialmente,

_____ *[Maestra(o)]*

Habla con alguien en casa acerca de un misterio que no haya sido resuelto. Escoge entre los misterios en la caja a la derecha o piensa en otro misterio que te interese.

1. Explica en qué consiste el misterio. _____

_____

_____

2. ¿Qué teoría que conoces explica el misterio?

_____

_____

3. ¿Qué piensa el miembro de tú familia que explica el misterio?

_____

_____

4. ¿Qué piensas tú que explica el misterio? _____

_____

_____

Misterios sin resolver
Los moradores de los barrancos
La extinción de los dinosaurios
Los OVNIS
Los círculos en los sembrados
El Triángulo de las Bermudas
Stonehenge
Big Foot/Sasquatch
Las pirámides de Egipto
Atlantis
Roswell/Área 51
El Monstruo de Loch Ness

Tên _____

Ngày _____

Kính Gởi Phụ Huynh,

Trong lớp, chúng tôi đã tìm hiểu về những điều bí ẩn. _____ *(tên học sinh)* muốn chia xẻ với quý vị những câu chuyện chúng tôi đã đọc.

The Loch Ness Monster, tác gia Malcolm Yorke Khách du lịch và các nhà khoa học trên khắp thế giới cố chứng minh rằng có một con vật trông giống khủng long sống dưới hồ ở Scotland.

Mystery of the Cliff Dwellers Tàn tích của một xã hội cổ xưa còn đọng lại trên các vách đá ở Mesa Verde, Colorado. Không ai biết điều gì đã xảy ra cho những người đã từng sống ở đó.

Yawning, tác gia Haleh V. Samiei Cho đến nay, các nhà khoa học chưa khám phá ra được chính xác lý do khiến con người ngáp. Bài này mô tả một số giả thuyết và nghiên cứu.

The Sneak Thief, tác gia Falcon Travers Một thanh tra viên cảnh sát sử dụng các manh mối để phá một vụ án.

The Legend of Sleepy Hollow, tác gia Washington Irving Tại một thị trấn nhỏ có tên Sleepy Hollow, một ky sĩ không đầu cưỡi ngựa vòng quanh đường phố vào ban đêm.

Chúng tôi cũng xin quý vị dành một ít thời giờ để tham dự một hoạt động về những điều bí ẩn nhằm trình bày với lớp học. Xin cám ơn sự hỗ trợ của quý vị.

Trân trọng,

_____ *(Giáo viên)*

Hãy thảo luận với một người thân trong nhà về một điều bí ẩn chưa được giải đáp. Chọn một bí ẩn từ ô dưới đây, hoặc nghĩ ra một bí ẩn khác mà em biết.

1. Giải thích điều bí ẩn đó là gì. _____

_____

_____

2. Hãy nêu một giả thuyết mà em biết nhằm giải thích cho bí ẩn này.

_____

_____

3. Người thân của em nghĩ điều gì giải thích cho bí ẩn này?

_____

_____

4. Em nghĩ điều gì giải thích được cho bí ẩn này? _____

_____

_____

Những Bí Ẩn Chưa Được Giải Đáp
Người Sống Trên Vách Đá
Sự Tuyệt Chủng Của Loài Khủng Long
Đĩa Bay
Khoảnh Hình Tròn Ở Đồng Lúa
Vùng Tam Giác Quỷ
Kiến Trúc Stonehenge
Khỉ Chân Lớn/Sasquatch
Kim Tự Tháp Ai Cập
Vương Quốc Atlantis
Roswell/Khu 51
Quái Vật Hồ Loch Ness

Npe _____

Vasthib _____

Dear Family,

Nyob rau hauv hoob, peb tau kawm txog tej yam uas tseem nkagsiab tsi tau zoo txog. _____ *(Menyuam npe)* xav muab cov dabneeg uas peb tau kawm tag no coj los qhia rau nej sub nej thiaj tau kawm nrog peb ua ke.

The Loch Ness Monster, los ntawm Malcolm Yorke Cov neeg ncig ua si thiab cov scientists uas nyob rau txhua lub tebchaws sim saib puas nrhiav tau povthawj qhia tias nws tseem muaj ib hom tsiaj zoo li dinosaur nyob rau ib lub pas dej tuag hauv tebchaws Scotland.

Mystery of the Cliff Dwellers Lub zos txheej thaus uas puamtsuaj lawd tseem muaj nyob rau puag saum ib nta tsag av Mesa Verde, Colorado.

Yawning, los ntawm Haleh V. Samiei Cov scientists yeej tseem tsi tau nrhiav tau hais tias yog vim li cas tib neeg ho rua lo. Cov lus qhia ntawm no piav txog ib txhia raws kev xav thiab kev tshawb nrhiav.

The Sneak Thief, los ntawm Falcon Travis Ib tug kws xwj uas yog tug tub ceevxwm siv tej yam uas nrhiav pom coj los ua chaw taug yam kevtxhaum uas tshwm muaj.

The Legend of Sleepy Hollow, los ntawm Washington Irving Nyob rau hauv lub menyuam zos uas hu ua Sleepy Hollow, nws muaj ib tug txiv neej tsi muaj taub hau pheej caij nees taug tej kev rau yav raus ntuj.

Ntxiv ntawm no peb xav thov nej siv sib hawm ib pliag los koom tes pab teb cov lus nug uas hais txog yam tseem nkagsiab tsi tau zoo nram qab no pub rau cov menyuam lubxiv tau kawm nyob rau hauv hoob. Ua tsaug rau nej txojkev txhawb nqa no.

Xee npe,

_____ *(Xib hwb)*

Nrog ib tug hauv tsev tham txog tej yam uas tseem tsi tau nkagsiab tias yog tim licas ntawd. Koj xaiv ib yam tawm los ntawm lub npov sab xis tom no los yog koj mam nrhiav ib yam uas txawv cov no los yeej tau thiab.

1. Piav saib qhov tseem tsi tau nkagsiab zoo no yog dabtsi?

   _____

   _____

2. Yam tseem tsi tau nkagsiab zoo no yog tim licas thiab nej lub tswvyim raws nej xav ho yog pom li cas?

   _____

3. Koj tsevneeg xav licas txog yam tseem tsi tau nkagsiab zoo no; puas muaj los lus teb qhia tias yog tim li cas?

   _____

4. Txog ntawm qhov tseem tsi tau nkagsiab zoo no yog li cas tiag?

   _____

Yog Tim Licas Ntwad

Cov nyobsaum ib nta zeb a

Dinosaurs tu noob

Cov UFOs

Qoob loo luam pⁱiablua ua vajvoos

The Bermuda Triangle

Pawg pobzeb Stonehenge

Tus taw loj/Sasquatch

The Great Pyramids

Thooj Av nyob plawvdej hiavtxwv Atlantic uas plojlawm

Roswell/Cheebtsam 51

Tus dab Loch Ness

姓名:_____

日期:_____

各位尊敬的家庭成員:

　　在課堂上,我們學習了有關懸疑的內容。_____ (學生名字)想與各位分享我們上課時讀過的故事。

The Loch Ness Monster, by Malcolm Yorke 全世界的觀光客和科學家都想證明,在蘇格蘭的湖中生活著一種長得像恐龍的生物。

Mystery of the Cliff Dwellers 古代社會的遺跡保留在科羅拉多州梅莎爾地的懸崖上。無人知道當時住在那裡的人們曾經有過甚麼經歷。

Yawning, by Haleh V. Samiei 科學家從未發現人們打呵欠的真正原因。這篇文章講述了某些理論及研究。

The Sneak Thief, by Falcon Travis 一名警官利用各種跡象來偵破一宗罪案。

The Legend of Sleepy Hollow, by Washington Irving 在一個名叫 Sleepy Hollow 的小鎮上,無頭騎士騎馬踏過深夜的街道。

　　我們還希望各位能抽出時間參與一項有關懸疑的活動,與全班同學一起分享。感謝各位的支持。

順祝安康,

_____ (教師)

與一位家人討論一項未解決的懸疑。可以從框內選擇一項,也可以討論你所知道的其他懸疑。

1. 說明此項懸疑的由來。_____
_____
_____

2. 你知道有哪一種理論可以解釋此項懸疑?_____
_____

3. 你的家人以為哪種說法可以解開此項懸疑?_____
_____
_____

4. 你以為哪種說法可以解開此項懸疑?_____
_____
_____

未解決的懸疑
懸崖居民
恐龍的滅絕
UFO
麥田怪圈
百慕大三角區
古石柱群
大腳怪/大腳印
大金字塔
亞特蘭提斯

School-Home Connection
Sharing Visions
ជំពូក ១ ការប្រើងប្រក្ខុតប្រជែង

ជូនចំពោះគ្រួសារ.

នៅក្នុងថ្នាក់ យើងរៀនអំពីការអាថ៌ក្នុងប្រាំង។ _____ (ឈ្មោះសិស្ស)
ឈ្មោះសិស្ស ចង់និយាយប្រាប់អ្នកពីរឿង ដែលយើងបានអាន។

The Loch Ness Monster, by Malcolm Yorke ព្ចេកទេសចរណៈនិងព្ចេកវិទ្យាសាស្ត្រ
នៅពេលពេញពិភពលោក សាកល្បងរកភស្ត_តាំងឲ្យឃើញថា មានសត្វចម្លែកដ៏ធំចម
ជាយណាស័រ រស់នៅក្នុងបឹងមួយនាប្រទេស ស៊ុតម៉្លែន។

Mystery of the Cliff Dwellers ភ្នាព្ជហិនហ្ជោតនៃសង្គមបុរាណាមួយ
ន្ជៅមានស្ថល់ថ្លាង់ខ្លស់នៅល្ជាក់ភ្នំ ម៉ិសា ផ្ជូឱ ក្នុងរូដ_ កាឡ្ជរ៉ាដូ។ គ្មាននរណាម្នាក់ដឹងថា
អ្នកដែលកេតឡ្ជឹងចំពោះមនុស្សដែលរស់នៅទិនៅ៩ឡ្ជេយ។

Yawning, by Haleh V. Samiei អ្នកវិទ្យាសាស្ត្រមិនទាន់ដែលរកឃើញឲ្យច្បាស់ថា
ហេតុអ្ជ៊បានជាមនុស្សស្ជាប។ ការ អានន្ជេរៀបរាប់ពីការរ្ជុបមន_ខ្លះនិងការរសារវ្ជ៉ារ៉ៈខ្ជ។

The Sneak Thief, by Falcon Travis ប៉ូលិសម្នាក់ប្រើប្រស្នារដើម្បីដោះស្រាយអំពីឧក្រិដ_
កម្ម៉ៈ។

The Legend of Sleepy Hollow, by Washington Irving នៅក្ជុងទីក្រុងភ្ចួចមួយនៃស្រុក
រូបរធេយ ៈឲ្យលឡ្ជូ អ្នកជិៈស្ជេះគ្មានក្បាលម្នាក់ ជិៈស្ជេះតាមផ្ជូវ៉ថ្លល់នៅពេលយប៉ប៉។

យើងក៏ចង់ឲ្យអ្នកចំណាយពេលមួយភ្លេត ចូលរួមសកម្ជភាពអំពីការអាថ៌កចាំង
ដើម្បីប្រាប់សិស្សក្នុងថ្នាក់។ សូមអរគុណដល់ការ គាំទ្ររបស់អ្នក។

ដោយសេចាៈស៉ុគ្រ

_____ (គ្រូបង្រៀន)

និយាយជាមួយនរណាម្នាក់នៅ៩ៈ អំពីអាថ៌កចាំងណាមួយដែលមិនទាន់រកឃើញការពិត។
ជ្រើសរើសមួយពីប្រទប់ខាងក្រោមនេះ ឫ គិតរកមួយផ្ជេ៉ងដែលអ្នកដឹង។

	អាថ៌កចាំងដែលរកមិនទាន់រ
១, ពន្យល់ តើអាថ៌កចាំងនេះជាអ្វី។ _____	ឃ្លាក
_____	ការផុតព្ជជ៍នៃជាយណាស័រ
_____	ចាសហោរ
	វង្ងក់ក្នុងចំការ
២, អ្វីដែលជារូបមន_មួយ ដែលអ្នកដឹងថារ៉ាពន្យល់ពីអាថ៌កំចាំងនេះបាន?	ត្រីកោណ
_____	ច៦ល្ជរ
_____	ជីងធ
_____	ក្រុងអាថ្ជេនទីស
៣, តើសមាជិកគ្រួសារអ្នកគិតថា ការពន្យល់ក្នុងអាថ៌កំចាំងនេះជាអ្វីទៅ?	វៃលានតិស
_____	ឡ្ជូស៉ិលេល?ៈរក ៥១
_____	សត្វចម្លែក
_____	
៤, អ្វីដែលអ្នកគិតថារ៉ាពន្យល់អំពីអាថ៌កំចាំងនេះ បាន? _____	
_____	

Non _____

Dat _____

Chè Fanmi,

Nan klas, nou te aprann konsènan mistè yo. _____ *(non elèv lan)* ta renmen pataje avèk ou kèk nan istwa nou te li yo.

The Loch Ness Monster, ekri pa Malcolm Yorke Touris ak syantifik yo patou nan lemonn eseye pwouve genyen yon kreyati tankou yon dinozò k ap viv nan yon lak nan Scotland.

Mystery of the Cliff Dwellers Win ansyen sosyete sa a rete byen wo nan falèz Mesa Verde, Colorado. Pèsonn moun pa konnen kisa ki te rive moun ki te abite la yo.

Yawning, ekri pa Haleh V. Samiei Syantifik yo pa janm te dekouvri poukisa moun baye. Lekti sa a dekri kèk teyori ak rechèch.

The Sneak Thief, ekri pa Falcon Travis Yon enspektè lapolis itilize endis pou rezoud yon krim..

The Legend of Sleepy Hollow, ekri pa Washington Irving Nan ti vil yo rele Sleepy Hollow, yon chevalye san tèt ap galope nan lari yo aswè.

Nou ta renmen pou ou pran yon ti moman pou patisipe nan yon aktivite osijè mistè ou ka pataje ak klas lan. Mèsi pou sipò w.

Sensèman,

_____ *(Pwofesè)*

Pale ak yon moun lakay ou sou yon mistè ki pa rezoud. Chwazi youn nan bwat la, oswa panse sou yon lòt ou konnen.

1. Eksplike kisa mistè a ye. _____
_____
_____

2. Ki teyori ou konnen ki eksplike mistè an?
_____
_____

3. Kisa manm fanmi w panse eksplikasyon an ye?
_____
_____

4. Kisa ou panse ki eksplike mistè an? _____
_____
_____

Mistè ki pa Rezoud
Moun ki te abite sou Falèz yo
Ekstenksyon Dinozò yo
OVNI yo
Sèk nan Chan yo
Triyang Bèmid
Stonehenge
Lòm Sovaj/Lòm Nèj
Gran Piramid yo
Atlantis
Roswell/Zòn 51
The Loch Ness Monster

Name _____

Date _____

Dear Family,

In class, we learned about survival. _____ *(student's name)* would like to share with you the stories we read.

How I Survived My Summer Vacation, by Robin Friedman A teenage boy wants to write a novel during the summer. However, he keeps running into problems.

The Voyage of the *Frog*, by Gary Paulsen A teenage boy is lost alone in a small boat at sea.

To Risk or Not to Risk, by David Ropeik This article discusses human fears and why we have them.

Island of the Blue Dolphins, by Scott O'Dell A young girl survives alone on a small island in the Pacific Ocean.

The Next Great Dying, by K. Vergoth and C. Lampton This article discusses the large number of species that are becoming extinct every day.

We would also like you to take a few moments to participate in an activity about survival to share with the class. Thank you for your support.

Sincerely,

_____ *(Teacher)*

Talk with someone at home. Imagine that you have been accidentally left behind in one of these places:

a. **a deserted island in the Pacific Ocean**

b. **the middle of the Gobi Desert**

c. **the cold wilderness of Alaska**

Choose an area: _____

With your family member, create an imaginary Survival Kit.

1. Think about what you will need to survive in this area for two weeks, until you are rescued.

2. Make a list of 10 items.

3. Rank the items according to how important they are to your survival. Item #1 is the most important item. Item #10 is the least important.

4. Talk about why each item is important.

Survival Kit

1. _____

2. _____

3. _____

4. _____

5. _____

6. _____

7. _____

8. _____

9. _____

10. _____

Nombre _____

Fecha _____

Estimada familia:

En nuestra clase, aprendimos acerca de la supervivencia. A _____
(nombre del estudiante) le gustaría compartir con usted las historias que leímos.

How I Survived My Summer Vacation, por Robin Friedman Un joven quiere escribir una novela durante el verano. Sin embargo, se le presentan problemas.

The Voyage of the *Frog*, por Gary Paulsen Un joven está perdido y solo en altamar en un bote pequeño.

To Risk or Not to Risk, por David Ropeik Este artículo trata acerca de los temores humanos y del por qué los sentimos.

Island of the Blue Dolphins, por Scott O'Dell Una niña sobrevive sola en una isla del Océano Pacífico.

The Next Great Dying, por K. Vergoth and C. Lampton Este artículo trata acerca del gran número de especies que están desapareciendo a diario.

Ahora nos gustaría que participara en una actividad acerca de la supervivencia, para luego compartirla con el resto de la clase. Muchas gracias por su apoyo.

Cordialmente,

_____ *[Maestra(o)]*

Habla con alguien en casa. Imagínate que te ha tocado quedarte solo en uno de los siguientes lugares:

a. **en una isla desierta del Océano Pacífico**

b. **en medio del Desierto de Gobi**

c. **en los friolentos bosques de Alaska**

Escoge una de las áreas: _____

Haz un botiquín de supervivencia imaginario con el miembro de la familia que hayas escogido.

1. Piensen en lo que necesitarían para sobrevivir en esa área por dos semanas, hasta que los rescaten.

2. Hagan una lista de diez cosas.

3. Organicen las cosas de acuerdo a lo importante que sean para su supervivencia. El artículo #1 es el más importante. El artículo #10 es el menos importante.

4. Hablen del por qué cada artículo es importante.

Botiquín de supervivencia

1. _____

2. _____

3. _____

4. _____

5. _____

6. _____

7. _____

8. _____

9. _____

10. _____

Tên _____

Ngày _____

Kính Gởi Phụ Huynh,

Trong lớp, chúng tôi đã tìm hiểu về sự sinh tồn. _____ (tên học sinh) muốn chia xẻ với quý vị những câu chuyện chúng tôi đã đọc.

How I Survived My Summer Vacation, tác gia Robin Friedman Một cậu thiếu niên muốn viết tiểu thuyết vào mùa hè. Tuy nhiên, cậu cứ bị trục trặc liên tục.

The Voyage of the *Frog*, tác gia Gary Paulsen Một cậu thiếu niên một mình bị lạc trên một chiếc thuyền nhỏ giữa đại dương.

To Risk or Not to Risk, tác gia David Ropeik Bài viết này thảo luận về các nỗi lo sợ của con người và lý do gây nên nỗi lo sợ

Island of the Blue Dolphins, tác gia Scott O'Dell Một cô bé sống một mình trên một hòn đảo nhỏ ở Thái Bình Dương.

The Next Great Dying, tác gia K. Vergoth va C. Lampton Bài viết bàn về việc mỗi ngày có một số lượng lớn các loài sinh vật bị tuyệt chủng.

Chúng tôi cũng muốn xin quý vị dành một ít thời giờ tham gia một hoạt động về sự sinh tồn nhằm trình bày với lớp học. Xin cám ơn sự hỗ trợ của quý vị.

Trân trọng,

_____ (Giáo viên)

Hãy thảo luận với một người thân trong nhà. Tưởng tượng rằng tình cờ em bị bỏ lại ở một trong những nơi sau đây:

   a.   một hòn đảo hoang ở Thái Bình Dương

   b.   giữa Sa Mạc Gobi

   c.   vùng hoang vắng lạnh lẽo ở Alaska

Chọn một nơi: _____

Cùng với người thân, hãy tưởng tượng ra một Bộ Dụng Cụ Sinh Tồn.

1. Nghĩ ra những thứ em cần để sống qua ngày trong nơi này trong vòng hai tuần cho đến em được cứu thoát.

2. Lập một danh sách gồm 10 thứ.

3. Xếp các thứ đồ theo thứ tự quan trọng đối với sự sinh tồn. Vật #1 quan trọng nhất. Vật #10 kém quan trọng nhất.

4. Thảo luận tại sao mỗi thứ lại quan trọng.

Bộ Dụng Cụ Sinh Tồn

1. _____
2. _____
3. _____
4. _____
5. _____
6. _____
7. _____
8. _____
9. _____
10. _____

Npe _____

Vasthib _____

Nyob zoo,

Nyob rau hauv hoob, peb tau kawm txog tias yuav ua cas thiaj ciaj tau sia _____ *(Menyuam npe)*xav muab cov dab neeg uas peb kawm lawd coj los qhia rau nej sub nej thiaj tau nrog peb kawm ua ke.

How I Survived My Summer Vacation, los ntawm Robin Friedman Ib tug tub hluas xav sau ib phau ntawv nyob rau lub caij ntujso. Tiamsi, nws pheej ntsib teebmeem li.

The Voyage of the *Frog*, los ntawm Gary Paulsen Ib tug tub hluas nyob ib leeg hauv lub menyuam nkoj poobzoo tom dej hiavtxwv.

To Risk or Not to Risk, los ntawm David Ropeik Tsab ntawv ntawm no tham txog tib neeg tej kev ntshai thiab qhia tias yog vim li cas peb ho muaj tej ntawd..

Island of the Blue Dolphins, los ntawm Scott O'Dell Ib tug menyuam ntxhais ciajsia taus ib leeg hauv thaj menyuam av uas muaj dej puagncig nyob rau tom tus dej hiavtxwv Pacific Ocean.

The Next Great Dying, los ntawm K. Vergoth & C. Lampton Tsab ntawv no tham txog ntau hom tsiaj txhu uas tab tom yuav tu noob mus.

Ntxiv ntawm no mus peb xav thov koj siv sib hawm ib pliag los koom tes pab teb cov lus nug txog tias yuav ua cas thiaj cawm tau txojsia nyob rau nram qab no pub rau cov menyuam nyob hauv hoob tau kawm. Ua tsaug ntau rau qhov nej pab txhawb nqa no.

Xee npe,

_____ *(Xib hwb)*

Nrog ib tug nyob hauv tsev tham. Xav txog tias leejtwg hnov qab koj tseg rau ib qhov chaw nram qab no lawm:

a. ib thaj av nyob hauv plawv dej tom Pacific Ocean

b. tom plawv hav mojsab qhua Gobi Desert

c. nyob rau ntujtxias teb no hauv tebchaws Alaska

Xaiv ib qho chaw: _____

Nrog rau ib tug hauv koj tsev neeg tham, ua zoo xav saib tej khoom yuav cawm tau txojsia dim yog yam twg.

1. Xav saib yam uas koj yuav tsum tau muaj los pab cawm txojsia rau ob asthiv txog thaum muaj neeg tuaj cawm koj saib yog yam twg.

2. Sau kom muaj 10 yam khoom siv

3. Tso yam khoom tseem ceeb tshaj uas yuav cawm tau txojsia ua ntej. Yam #1 yog yam tseem ceeb tshaj plaws. Yam #10 yog yam uas tsis tshua tseem ceeb pes tsawg.

4. Sib tham txog ib yam zuj zug saib yog vim li cas nws ho tseem ceeb.

Cov Khoom Cawmsiav

1. _____

2. _____

3. _____

4. _____

5. _____

6. _____

7. _____

8. _____

9. _____

10. _____

姓名:_____

日期:_____

各位尊敬的家庭成員:

在課堂上,我們學習了有關生存的內容。_____ *(學生名字)* 想與各位分享我們上課時讀過的故事。

How I Survived My Summer Vacation, by Robin Friedman 一位少年想在暑假中寫小說,但卻連連遇上問題。

The Voyage of the Frog, by Gary Paulsen 一位少年駕著小船,獨自迷失在大海上。

To Risk or Not to Risk, by David Ropeik 這篇文章探討了人的恐懼感以及我們為何會感到懼怕。

Island of the Blue Dolphins, by Scott O'Dell 一位少女獨自在太平洋中的一個小島上生存。

The Next Great Dying, by K. Vergoth and C. Lampton 這篇文章討論了每天正瀕臨滅絕的大批物種。

我們還希望各位能抽出時間參與一項有關生存的活動,與全班同學一起分享。感謝各位的支持。

順祝安康,

_____ *(教師)*

與一位家人討論。假設你被人無意中遺留在以下一處地方:

    a. 太平洋中的一個荒島
    b. 戈壁沙漠的中央
    c. 阿拉斯加寒冷的荒野

選擇一個地方:_____

與家人一起,設想出一套救生包。

1. 想一想在被營救前,你需要有哪些物品才能在該地區生存兩個星期。
2. 列出十項物品。
3. 依據對於生存的重要性,依次排列各項物品。第一項最重要,第十項最不重要。
4. 談談每項物品的重要性何在。

救生包
1. _____
2. _____
3. _____
4. _____
5. _____
6. _____
7. _____
8. _____
9. _____
10. _____

ឈ្មោះ _____

កាលបរិច្ឆេទ _____

ជូនចំពោះគ្រួសារ.

នៅក្នុងថ្នាក់ យើងរៀនអំពីការផ្សាស់ប_រ។ _____ (ឈ្មោះសិស្ស)
ចង់ប្រាប់អ្នកអំពីរឿង ដែលយើងបានអាន។

How I Survived My Summer Vacation, by Robin Friedman
កេ◌ងប្រុសជំទង់ម្នាក់ចង់សរសេរប្រលោម លោកនៅក្នុងរដូវកេ_ វ។ ប៉ុន្ដែ_វាចេះតែជួបបញ្ហា។

The Voyage of the *Frog*, by Gary Paulsen កេ◌ងប្រុសជំទង់ម្នាក់វង្វេងនៅកណ_លសមុទ្រ
ក្នុងទូកតូចមួយ តែម្នាក់ឯង។

To Risk or Not to Risk, by David Ropeik
អត្ថបទនេះវិភាគអំពីការភ័យខ្លាចរបស់មនុស្សនិងហេតុអ្វីយើងខ្លាច។

Island of the Blue Dolphins, by Scott O'Dell
កេ◌ងស្រីជំទង់ម្នាក់តស៊ូរស់ម្នាក់ឯងនៅលើកោះតូចមួយក្នុងមហា សមុទ្រប៉ាស៊ីហ្វិក។

The Next Great Dying, by K. Vergoth and C. Lampton
អត្ថបទនេះវិភាគអំពីពូជសត្វជាច្រើនដែលកំពុងផុត ពូជរៀងរាល់ថ្ងៃ។

យើងក៏ចង់ឲ្យអ្នកចំណាយពេលមួយភ្លេត ចូលរួមសកម្មភាពអំពីការតស៊ូរស់
ដើម្បីប្រាប់សិស្សក្នុងថ្នាក់។ សូមអរគុណដល់ការ គាំទ្ររបស់អ្នក។

ដោយសេចក្ដីគោរព

_____ (គ្រូបង្រៀន)

និយាយជាមួយអរណាម្នាក់ទៅថ_៖។
ស្រមើថាអ្នកត្រូវគេទៅតម្បោលដោយឲ្យ៉ូ◌ចងឲ្យតែម្នា
កំងនៅកន្លែងណាម្នាក់នៃកន្លែងទាំងនេះ ;

ក, កោះខ្វាច់មួយក្នុងមហាសមុទ្រប៉ាស៊ីហ្វិក

ខ, កណ_លវាលខ្សាច់ គូប៊ី

គ, ទីរហោចថានគ្រជាក់ស៍នៃ អាឡាស្កា

រីសកកន្លែងមួយ _____

ជាមួយសមាជិកគ្រួសារ បង្កើតឲ្យមានប្រដាប់ប្រដា
សំរាប់តស៊ូរស់ដោយការស្រៃ៍ម៉។

១, ក្បិតពីអ្វីដែលអ្នកត្រូវការដើម្បីរស់នៅតំបន់នោះចំនួន
ព័រសថា_ហា_ រ៉ូតដល់អ្នកត្រូវគេទៅសង្គ្រោះ

២, ធ្វើបញ្ជីដែលមានរបស់របរ ១០មុខ។

៣, ដាក់របស់តាមលំដាប់
ទៅតួម្រមៃ៎◌ការសខាន្របស់វាសំរាប់ការតស៊ូរស់របស់អ្នក។
របស់ទី ១ ជារួបស់ដែលសខាន់ជាងគេបំផុត។ របស់ទី
១០ ជារបស់សខាន់តិចជាគេបំផុត។

៤, និយាយពីហេតុអ្វីបានជារបស់មួយៗវាមានសារៈសំខាន់។

ប្រដាប់ប្រដាសំរាប់តស៊ូរស់

1. _____

2. _____

3. _____

4. _____

5. _____

6. _____

7. _____

8. _____

9. _____

10. _____

Non _____

Dat _____

Chè Fanmi,

Nan klas, nou te aprann konsènan siviv. _____ *(non elèv lan)* ta renmen pataje avèk ou kèk nan istwa nou te li yo.

How I Survived My Summer Vacation, ekri pa Robin Friedman Yon tigason adolesan vle ekri yon woman pandan sezon ete a. Men, l ap plede tonbe nan pwoblèm.

The Voyage of the *Frog*, ekri pa Gary Paulsen Yon tigason adolesan poukont li nan yon ti bato nan lanmè.

To Risk or Not to Risk, ekri pa David Ropeik Atik sa a diskite laperèz lèzòm epi poukisa nou genyen yo.

Island of the Blue Dolphins, ekri pa Scott O'Dell Yon jèn fi siviv sou yon ti zil nan Oseyan Pasifik lan.

The Next Great Dying, ekri pa K. Vergoth ak C. Lampton Atik sa a diskite sou pakèt kantite espès k ap vin ekstenk chak jou.

Nou ta renmen pou ou pran yon ti moman pou patisipe nan yon aktivite osijè siviv ou ka pataje ak klas lan. Mèsi pou sipò w.

Sensèman,

_____ *(Pwofesè)*

Pale avèk yon moun lakay ou. Imajine yo te kite w dèyè pa aksidan nan youn nan kote sa yo:

a. yon zil dezè nan Oseyan Pasifik lan

b. mitan dezè Gobi an

c. nati sovaj frèt Alaska

Chwazi yon zòn: _____

Avèk manm fanmi w, kreye yon twous sivi imajinè.

1. Panse a kisa ou pral bezwen pou siviv nan zòn sa a pandan de semèn, jiskaske yo vin sove w.

2. Fè yon lis 10 bagay.

3. Ranje bagay yo selon enpòtans yo genyen pou sivivans ou. Bagay #1 se bagay ki pi enpòtan. Bagay #10 se bagay ki mwens enpòtan.

4. Pale sou rezon ki fè chak bagay enpòtan.

Twous Sivi

1. _____

2. _____

3. _____

4. _____

5. _____

6. _____

7. _____

8. _____

9. _____

10. _____

Name _____

Date _____

Dear Family,

In class, we learned about journeys. _____ *(student's name)* would like to share with you the stories we read.

I Have No Address, by Hamza El Din This poem is about a sparrow that flies around the world and wishes peace, love, and goodwill for all people.

The Voyage of the Lucky Dragon, by Jack Bennett A family plans a journey to escape from the new government in Vietnam.

The Time Bike, by Jane Langton A boy discovers that his ugly, new bicycle may have the special power of traveling through time.

Why We Can't Get There From Here, by Neil de Grasse Tyson This scientific article explains the difficulties in traveling to other planets and stars.

The California Gold Rush, by Pam Zollman, & **Dame Shirley and the Gold Rush,** by Jim Rawls Searching for gold in 1849 was hard work. A woman makes a difficult journey from New England to a mining camp in California during the Gold Rush.

We would also like you to take a few moments to participate in an interview about journeys to share with the class. Thank you for your support.

Sincerely,

_____ *(Teacher)*

INTERVIEW

1. Name of person being interviewed: _____

2. Question: What is the most memorable journey that you have ever taken? When and where did you go?

   Answer: _____

3. Question: Why did you take this journey?

   Answer: _____

4. Question: What happened on this journey when you arrived at your destination?

   Answer: _____

5. Question: Why is this journey memorable?

   Answer: _____

6. (Student: *Ask one question of your own.*)

   Question: _____

   Answer: _____

Nombre _____

Fecha _____

Estimada familia:

En nuestra clase, aprendimos acerca de viajes. A _____ *(nombre del estudiante)* le gustaría compartir con usted las historias que leímos.

I Have No Address, por Hamza El Din Este poema es acerca de un gorrión que vuela alrededor del mundo, deseando paz, amor y bienestar para todos.

The Voyage of the Lucky Dragon, por Jack Bennett Una familia planea un viaje para escapar de un nuevo gobierno en Vietnám.

The Time Bike, por Jane Langton Un niño descubre que su nueva bicicleta fea puede que tenga el poder especial de viajar a través del tiempo.

Why We Can't Get There From Here, por Neil de Grasse Tyson Este artículo científico explica las dificultades para poder viajar a otros planetas y estrellas.

The California Gold Rush, por Pam Zollman, & **Dame Shirley and the Gold Rush,** por Jim Rawls Buscar oro en 1849 era muy difícil. Una mujer viaja de New England a un campo minero en California durante la Fiebre del Oro.

Ahora nos gustaría que participara en una entrevista acerca de viajes, para luego compartirla con el resto de la clase. Muchas gracias por su apoyo.

Cordialmente,

_____ *[Maestra(o)]*

ENTREVISTA

1. Nombre de la persona siendo entrevistada: _____

2. Pregunta: ¿Cuál es el viaje más memorable que has hecho? ¿Cuándo lo hiciste y adónde fuiste?

   Respuesta: _____

3. Pregunta: ¿Por qué hiciste el viaje?

   Respuesta: _____

4. Pregunta: ¿Qué ocurrió en el viaje cuando llegaste a tu destino?

   Respuesta: _____

5. Pregunta: ¿Por qué fue memorable ese viaje?

   Respuesta: _____

6. (Estudiante: *Haz una pregunta tuya.*)

   Pregunta: _____

   Respuesta: _____

Kính Gởi Phụ Huynh,

Trong lớp, chúng tôi đã tìm hiểu về những cuộc hành trình. _____ *(tên học sinh)* muốn chia xẻ với quý vị những câu chuyện chúng tôi đã đọc.

I Have No Address, tác gia Hamza El Din Bài thơ này nói về một con chim sẻ bay vòng quanh thế giới và ước mong hòa bình, tình yêu, và thiện chí cho nhân loại.

The Voyage of the Lucky Dragon, tác gia Jack Bennett Một gia đình chuẩn bị cho một cuộc hành trình trốn chạy chính quyền mới ở Việt Nam.

The Time Bike, tác gia Jane Langton Một cậu bé khám phá ra chiếc xe đạp mới xấu xí của mình có một quyền năng đặc biệt là du lịch xuyên thời gian.

Why We Can't Get There From Here, tác gia Neil de Grasse Tyson Bài khoa học này giải thích sự khó khăn của việc du hành tới các hành tinh và ngôi sao khác.

The California Gold Rush, tác gia Pam Zollman, & **Dame Shirley and the Gold Rush,** tác gia Jim Rawls Đi tìm vàng vào năm 1849 là một việc rất cực nhọc. Một người đàn bà thực hiện cuộc hành trình gian khổ từ vùng New England đến một trại đào vàng ở California vào thời điểm Đổ Xô Đi Tìm Vàng.

Chúng tôi cũng xin quý vị dành một ít thời giờ để tham gia một cuộc phỏng vấn về các cuộc hành trình nhằm trình bày với lớp học. Xin cám ơn sự hỗ trợ của quý vị.

Trân trọng,

_____ *(Giáo viên)*

PHỎNG VẤN

1. Tên người được phỏng vấn: _____

2. Hỏi: Cuộc hành trình đáng nhớ nhất của quý vị là gì? Quý vị đi đâu và khi nào?

   Đáp: _____

3. Hỏi: Tại sao quý vị thực hiện cuộc hành trình này?

   Đáp: _____

4. Hỏi: Hãy kể những diễn tiến xảy ra trong suốt cuộc hành trình, hoặc sau khi quý vị đến nơi.

   Đáp: _____

5. Hỏi: Tại sao cuộc hành trình này đáng nhớ?

   Đáp: _____

6. (Học sinh: *Tự đặt câu hỏi.*)

   Hỏi: _____

   Đáp: _____

Nyob zoo,

Nyob rau hauv hoob, peb tau kawm txog txoj hauvkev. _____
(Menyuam npe) xav muab cov dab neeg peb tau kawm lawd coj los qhiav rau nej sub nej thiaj tau nrog peb kawm ua ke.

I Have No Address, los ntawm Hamza El Din Zaj lus paivyi no yog hais txog ib tug noog dawbtxia uas ya ncig ntiajteb thiab thov kom muaj kev thajyeeb, kev hlub, thiab kevzoo rau txhua haiv neeg.

The Voyage of the Lucky Dragon, los ntawm Jack Bennett Ib tseneeg npaj txoj hauvkev khiav tsoom fwv tshiab uas tau los kav tebchaws Nyablaj.

The Time Bike, los ntawm Jane Langton Ib tug menyuam tub pom tias tej zaum nws lub luvthij tshiab uas phem ncawb yuav muaj ib qhov hwjchim uas mus hauv caijnyoog rov tom qab thiab pem suab tau.

Why We Can't Get There From Here, los ntawm Neil de Grasse Tyson Tsab ntawv los ntawm kev kawm tshawb nrhiav no piav txog tej kcv nyuab uas mus los rau lwm lub ntiajteb thiab cov hnub qub

The California Gold Rush, los ntawm Pam Zollman, & **Dame Shirley and the Gold Rush,** los ntawm Jim Rawls Nrhiav kub nyob rau xyoo 1849 mas nyuaj heev. Ib tug pojniam txojkev tuaj New England mus rau ib lub chaw khawb kub nyob hauv California lub caij neeg sib xeem tuaj los sis hu hais tias Gold Rush mas yog ib txogkev nyuag kawg.

Ntxiv ntawm no mus peb xav thov nej siv sib hawm ib pliag los koomtes pab teb cov lus nug hais txog txoj hauvkev nyob nram qab no pub rau cov menyuam tau kawm nyob rau hauv hoob. Ua tsaug rau nej txojkev txhawb nqa no.

Xee npe,

_____ *(Xib hwb)*

LUS XAMPHAJ

1. Npe ntawm tus neeg uas pab teb cov lus xamphaj no: _____

2. Lus nug: Txoj hauvkev uas koj nco ntsoov tsi nov qab es tsi muaj ib zaug ntxiv li lawm yog txojtwg? Yog thaum twg thiab yog mus qhovtwg?

   Lo lus teb: _____

3. Lus nug: Yog vim li cas koj thiaj tau taug txoj hauvkev no?

   Lo lus teb: _____

4. Lus nug: Muaj dabtsi tshwm sim thaum tseem sam sim taug txoj hauvkev ntawm no los yog thaum mus txog chaw?

   Lo lus teb: _____

5. Lus nug: Qhov uas ua rau koj nco tsi hnov qab li txog txoj hauvkev ntawm no yog dabtsi?

   Lo lus teb: _____

6. (Rau tug meyuam: *Nug ib lo lus ua koj ntiagtus.*)

   Lus nug: _____

   Lo lus teb: _____

姓名: _____

日期: _____

各位尊敬的家庭成員:

　　在課堂上,我們學習了有關旅行的內容。_____ (*學生名字*)想與各位分享我們上課時讀過的故事。

I Have No Address, by Hamza El Din 這首詩講的是一隻麻雀,飛遍世界各地,為人們祈願和平、愛及友誼。

The Voyage of the Lucky Dragon, by Jack Bennett 一個家庭計劃逃離越南的新政府。

The Time Bike, by Jane Langton 一位男孩發現,他那輛難看的新自行車可能有穿越時間旅行的特殊本領。

Why We Can't Get There From Here, by Neil de Grasse Tyson 這篇科普文章說明了前往其他行星及星球旅行的困難。

The California Gold Rush, by Pam Zollman, & **Dame Shirley and the Gold Rush,** by Jim Rawls 1849 年的尋金者十分辛苦。在淘金熱中,一名女性從新英格蘭一路跋涉到加州的礦場。

　　我們還希望各位能抽出時間參與一項有關旅行的訪問,與全班同學一起分享。感謝各位的支持。

順祝安康,

_____ (*教師*)

訪談

1. 接受訪問者的姓名: _____

2. 問:哪一次旅行是您最難忘的?那次旅行的時間及目的地?

　　答: _____

3. 問:您為什麼要進行那次旅行?

　　答: _____

4. 問:那次旅途中或在抵達目的地後發生了什麼事情?

　　答: _____

_____

5. 問:那次旅行為什麼是難忘的?

　　答: _____

6. (學生:*請提出一個你自己的問題。*)

　　問: _____

　　答: _____

School-Home Connection
Sharing Visions
ជំពូក ៣ ការធ្វើដំណើរ

ឈ្មោះ ______________
កាលបរិច្ឆេទ ______________

ជូនចំពោះគ្រួសារ.

នៅក្នុងថ្នាក់ យើងរៀនអំពីការធ្វើដំណើរ។ ______________ (ឈ្មោះសិស្ស) ចង់និយាយប្រាប់អ្នកពីរឿង ដែលយើងបានអាន។

I Have No Address, by Hamza El Din កំណាព្យនេះសរសេរអំពីសត្វចាបដែលហោះហើរជុំវិញពិភពលោក ហើយបន ស្រន់ឲ្យមាននូវសន្តិភាព.ការស្រឡាញ់.និងការប្រព្រឹត្តល្អ សំរាប់មនុស្សលោកគ្រប់រូប។

The Voyage of the Lucky Dragon, by Jack Bennett
គ្រួសារមួយគំរោងធ្វើដំណើរភៀសខ្លួនចេញពីរដ្ឋាភិបាលថ្មី នៃប្រទេសវៀតណាម។

The Time Bike, by Jane Langton
ក្មេងប្រុសម្នាក់ដឹងថាកង់ថ្មីដ៏អាក្រក់របស់វាប្រហែលជាមានមហិទ្ធិរិទ្ធិពិសេស ដែលអាចធ្វើដំណើរឆ្លងកាត់ពេលវេលា។

Why We Can't Get There From Here, by Neil de Grasse Tyson
អត្ថបទវិទ្យាសាស្ត្រនេះពន្យល់ពីការលំបាក ក្នុងការធ្វើដំណើរទៅកាន់ប្រភពនិងផ្កាយផ្សេងទៀត។

The California Gold Rush, by Pam Zollman, & **Dame Shirley and the Gold Rush,** by Jim Rawls ការរុករកមាសនៅឆ្នាំ ១៨៤៩ ជាការលំបាក។ ស្ត្រីម្នាក់ធ្វើដំណើរយ៉ាងលំបាកមួយពីញូអង់គ្លេស ទៅកាន់ជំរុយករ៉ែនៅ កាលីហ្វរញ៉ា ក្នុងកំឡុងពេល អ៊ឲ្យលដ ស្រហ

យើងក៏ចង់ឲ្យអ្នកចំណាយពេលមួយភ្លែត ចូលរួមសកម្មភាពអំពីការអាថ៌កំបាំង ដើម្បីប្រាប់សិស្សក្នុងថ្នាក់។ សូមអរគុណដល់ការ គាំទ្ររបស់អ្នក។

ដោយសោះស្ម័គ្រ

______________ (គ្រូបង្រៀន)

កាំរៀង

១, ឈ្មោះអ្នកដែលត្រូវគេសម្ភាសៈ ______________

២, សំនួរៈ អ្វីទៅដែលជាការធ្វើដំណើរជាអានុស្សាវរីយ៍ជាងគេដែលអ្នកធ្លាប់មាន? ពេលណានិងកន្លែងណាដែលអ្នកទៅ?
ចម្លើយៈ ______________

៣, សំនួរៈ ហេតុអ្វីអ្នកធ្វើដំណើរនេះ?
ចម្លើយៈ ______________

៤, សំនួរៈ អ្វីខ្លះដែលកើតឡើងក្នុងពេលធ្វើដំណើរនេះ ឬ ពេលណាអ្នកទៅដល់ទីដៅរបស់អ្នក?
ចម្លើយៈ ______________

៥, សំនួរៈ ហេតុអ្វីការធ្វើដំណើរនេះជាអានុស្សាវរីយ៍?
ចម្លើយៈ ______________

៦, សិស្សៈ សួរសំនួរមួយដោយខ្លួនឯង)
សំនួរៈ ______________
ចម្លើយៈ ______________

Non _____

Dat _____

Chè Fanmi,

Nan klas, nou te aprann konsènan vwayaj. _____ *(non elèv lan)* ta renmen pataje avèk ou kèk nan istwa nou te li yo.

I Have No Address, ekri pa Hamza El Din Powèm sa a pale konsènan yon mwano ki vole patou nan lemonn epi li swete lapè, lanmou ak bon antant pou tout moun.

The Voyage of the Lucky Dragon, ekri pa Jack Bennett Yon fanmi planifye yon vwayaj pou l chape anba men nouvo gouvènman Vyetman lan.

The Time Bike, ekri pa Jane Langton Yon tigason dekouvri nouvo bisiklèt lèd li an, ka genyen pouvwa espesyal pou l vwayaje atravaè le tan.

Why We Can't Get There From Here, ekri pa Neil de Grasse Tyson Atik syantifik sa a eksplike difikilte ki genyen nan vwayaje nan lòt planèt ak etwal yo.

The California Gold Rush, ekri pa Pam Zollman, ak **Dame Shirley and the Gold Rush,** ekri pa Jim Rawls Chèche lò nan ane 1849 se te travay ki di. Yon fanm fè yon vwayaj difisil sot Nouvèl Angletè pou l ale nan yon kan minyè nan Kalifòni pandan Gold Rush lan.

Nou ta renmen pou ou pran yon ti moman pou patisipe nan yon entèvyou osijè vwayaj ou ka pataje ak klas lan. Mèsi pou sipò w.

Sensèman,

_____ *(Pwofesè)*

ENTÈVYOU

1. Non moun w ap entèvyoure a: _____

2. Kesyon: Ki vwayaj ki pi memorab ou te janm fè? Kilè epi ki kote ou te ale?

   Repons: _____

3. Kesyon: Poukisa ou te fè vwayaj sa a?

   Repons: _____

4. Kesyon: Kisa ki te rive pandan vwayaj sa a oswa lè w te rive nan destinasyon w?

   Repons: _____

5. Kesyon: Poukisa vwayaj sa a memorab?

   Repons: _____

6. (Elèv: *Poze yon kesyon paw.*)

   Kesyon: _____

   Repons: _____

Name _____

Date _____

Dear Family,

   In class, we learned about cycles. _____ *(student's name)* would like to share with you the stories we read.

   Water Dance, by Thomas Locker This poem describes how water is recycled into different forms.

   Persephone and the Seasons, by Heather Amery This Greek myth explains why the seasons change.

   The Circuit, by Francisco Jiménez A teenager has to change schools just when he is making progress.

   The Elements of Life, by Paul Bennett Everything on Earth is made up of elements. Elements are used over and over again in the cycle of life.

   We would also like you to take a few moments to participate in an activity about cycles to share with the class. Thank you for your support.

                                        Sincerely,

                              _____ *(Teacher)*

Talk with someone at home about life cycles. Choose something that you know about and describe its life cycle. The words in the box can give you ideas. Write the word on the line in the circle.

a flower   a vegetable   an insect   an animal   a butterfly   a tree   a fish

1 _____

6 _____

2 _____

Name the stages in a life cycle of

_____ .

Draw pictures to illustrate the life cycle.

5 _____

3 _____

4 _____

School-Home Connection
Sharing Visions
UNIDAD 4 Ciclos

Estimada familia:

En nuestra clase, aprendimos acerca de ciclos. A _____ *(nombre del estudiante)* le gustaría compartir con usted las historias que leímos.

Water Dance, por Thomas Locker Este poema describe cómo es reciclada el agua de maneras distintas.

Persephone and the Seasons, por Heather Amery Este mito griego explica por qué cambian las estaciones.

The Circuit, por Francisco Jiménez Un joven tiene que cambiarse de escuela, justo cuando estaba comenzando a demostrar progreso en su estudio.

The Elements of Life, por Paul Bennett Todo en el planeta está formado por distintos elementos. Esos elementos son usados una y otra vez en el ciclo de la vida.

Ahora nos gustaría que participara en una actividad acerca de ciclos, para luego compartirla con el resto de la clase. Muchas gracias por su apoyo.

Cordialmente,

_____ *[Maestra(o)]*

Habla con alguien en casa acerca de los ciclos de la vida. Escogan algo que conozcan y describan su ciclo de vida. Las palabras en la caja de abajo les dan algunas ideas. Cuando hayan escogido algo, escriban la palabra en el círculo.

| una flor | un vegetal | un insecto | un animal | una mariposa | un árbol | un pez |

1 _____

6 _____

2 _____

Nombra los pasos en la vida de un(a)

_____ .

Haz dibujos para ilustrar el ciclo de vida.

5 _____

3 _____

4 _____

Tên _____

Ngày _____

Kính Gởi Phụ Huynh,

Trong lớp, chúng tôi đã tìm hiểu về các chu kỳ. _____ (tên học sinh) muốn chia xẻ với quý vị những câu chuyện chúng tôi đã đọc.

Water Dance, tác gia Thomas Locker Bài thơ này giải thích nước được luân chuyển sang các dạng khác nhau như thế nào.

Persephone and the Seasons, tác gia Heather Amery Truyện huyền thoại Hy Lạp này giải thích tại sao mùa lại thay đổi.

The Circuit, tác gia Francisco Jiménez Một thiếu niên bị buộc phải chuyển trường ngay vào lúc cậu đang đạt tiến bộ nửa chừng.

The Elements of Life, tác gia Paul Bennett Mọi thứ trên Trái Đất được cấu tạo bởi các nguyên tố. Các nguyên tố được dùng đi dùng lại trong chu trình cuộc sống.

Chúng tôi cũng xin quý vị dành một ít thời giờ để tham dự một hoạt động về chu kỳ nhằm trình bày với lớp học. Xin cám ơn sự hỗ trợ của quý vị.

Trân trọng,

_____ (Giáo viên)

Hãy thảo luận với một người thân trong nhà về các chu kỳ sống. Chọn một sinh vật em biết rõ và mô tả chu kỳ sống của sinh vật đó. Trong ô dưới đây có một số từ ngữ gợi ý. Viết từ chọn lên đường thẳng trong hình tròn.

một bông hoa   một loài rau   một con côn trùng   một con thú vật   một con bướm   một cái cây   một con cá

1 _____

6 _____

Cho biết các giai đoạn trong chu kỳ sống của

_____ .

Vẽ hình để minh họa chu kỳ sống

2 _____

5 _____

3 _____

4 _____

Npe _____

Vasthib _____

Nyob zoo,

Nyob rau hauv hoob, peb tau kawm txog lub neej ncig mus los. _____
(Menyuam npe) xav muab cov dab neeg uas peb tau kawm no coj los qhia rau nej sub nej thiab tau nrog peb kawm ua ke.

Water Dance, los ntawm Thomas Locker Zaj lus paivyi no piav qhia txog kev lim dej tawm mus ua ntau yam txawv.

Persephone and the Seasons, los ntawm Heather Amery Zaj dab neeg Greek no qhia txog tias yog vim li cas lub ntuj fuabcua thiaj hloov mus rau ntau lub caij.

The Circuit, los ntawm Francisco Jiménez Ib tug tub hluas nim qhuav kawm tau ntawv zog xwb txawm siv yuav tau hloov tsev kawm ntawv tshiab dua lawm thiab.

The Elements of Life, los ntawm Paul Bennett Txhua yam nyob rau hauv lub Ntiajteb no yog muaj los ntawm ntau yam tseemceeb sib sau los ua ke. Ntau yam uas hais ntawm no yeej tau siv mus siv los raws lub li lub neej uas ncig mus ncig los.

Ntxiv ntawm no mus peb thov nej siv sib hawm ib pliag los koomtes pab teb cov lus nug txog qhov kev ncig mus los nyob rau nram qab no rau cov menyuam lubxiv tau kawm nyob rau hauv hoob. Ua tsaug rau nej txojkev txhawb nqa no..

Xee npe,

_____ *(Xib hwb)*

Nrog ib tug neeg tom tsev tham txog kev ua neej ncig mus ncig los. Xaiv ib yam uas koj paub txog thiab piav txog nws lub neej uas ncig mus li cas. Cov lus hauv lub npov nram qab no yuav pab tau tswvyim rau koj. Sau lo lus rau ntawm kab uas khij nyob rau hauv lub vajvoos.

ib lubpaj	ib qhovzaub	ib tugkab	ib tugtsiaj	ib tug npaujnpaim	ib tsobntoo	ib tugntses

1 _____

6 _____

2 _____

Npe ntawm tej theem lub neej ua ncig mus los

_____ .

Kos duab qhia txog lubneej ua ncig mus los

5 _____

3 _____

4 _____

姓名:_____

日期:_____

各位尊敬的家庭成員:

　　在課堂上,我們學習了有關週期循環的內容。_____(學生名字)想與各位分享我們上課時讀過的故事。

　　Water Dance, by Thomas Locker 這首詩描寫了水在循環中的各種不同形態。

　　Persephone and the Seasons, by Heather Amery 這篇希臘神話說明了為何有四季的更替。

　　The Circuit, by Francisco Jiménez 一位少年剛剛取得進步,卻又要換學校了。

　　The Elements of Life, by Paul Bennett 地球上的萬物都是由元素構成的。在生命週期中,元素被一再地重復使用。

　　我們還希望各位能抽出時間參與一項有關週期循環的活動,與全班同學一起分享。感謝各位的支持。

順祝安康,

_____(教師)

與一位家人討論生命週期循環。選擇你所知道的一種生物,描述該種生物的生命週期。框內的名詞可以給你一些啟發。請在圈圈內的線上寫下生物的名字。

| 花 | 蔬菜 | 昆蟲 | 動物 | 蝴蝶 | 樹 | 魚 |

1 _____

6 _____

2 _____

> 寫出該生物在生命週期中的各個階段
>
> _____
>
> 請畫圖說明

5 _____

3 _____

4 _____

School-Home Connection
Sharing Visions
ជំពូក ៤ ការវិលវល

ឈ្មោះ ____________________

កាលបរិច្ឆេទ ____________________

ជូនចំពោះគ្រួសារ.

នៅក្នុងថ្នាក់ យើងរៀនអំពីការវិលវល់។ ____________________ (ឈ្មោះសិស្ស) ចង់និយាយប្រាប់អ្នកពីរឿង ដែលយើងបានអាន។

Water Dance, by Thomas Locker
កំណាព្យនេះរៀបរាប់អំពីរបៀបដែលទឹកត្រូវវិលវល់ចុះឡើងជួរទម្រង់ផ្សេងៗគ្នា។

Persephone and the Seasons, by Heather Amery
រឿងជំនាន់ដើមនៃប្រទេសក្រិកពន្យល់ពីហេតុដែលរដូវផ្លាស់ប_រ។

The Circuit, by Francisco Jiménez ក្មេងជំទង់ម្នាក់ត្រូវប_រសាលា នៅពេលណាវាកំពុងរៀនល្អតលាស់។

The Elements of Life, by Paul Bennett អ្វីៗនៅលើផែនដីនេះ កើតឡើងពីសារធាតុ។ សារធាតុត្រូវប្រើម_ងហើយម_ង ទៀតនៅក្នុងជីវិតវិលវល់ចុះឡើង។

យើងក៏ចង់ឲ្យអ្នកចំណាយពេលមួយភ្លេត ចូលរួមសកម្មភាពអំពីការវិលវល់ ដើម្បីប្រាប់សិស្សក្នុងថ្នាក់។ សូមអរគុណដល់ការ គាំទ្ររបស់អ្នក។

ដោយសេចក្តីគោរព

____________________ (គ្រូបង្រៀន)

និយាយជាមួយនរណាម្នាក់នៅផ_ះអំពីការវិលវល់នៃជីវិតនេះ។ រើសអ្វីមួយដែលអ្នកស្គាល់ ហើយរៀបរាប់ពីជីវិតវាដែលវិលវល់។ ពាក្យនៅក្នុងប្រអប់នេះអាចឲ្យគំនិតដល់អ្នក។ សរសេរពាក្យលើបន_ាត់ជាការវិលវល់។

ផ្កា	បន្លែ	សត្វល្អិត	សត្វជើងបួន	មេអំបៅ	ដើមឈើ	ត្រ

1 ____________________

2 ____________________

3 ____________________

4 ____________________

5 ____________________

6 ____________________

ឲ្យឈ្មោះវគ្គទីមួយ នៃការវិលវល់នៃ

____________________.

គូររូបដែលបង្ហាញពីការវិ ល វិលនេះ

Non _____

Dat _____

Chè Fanmi,

Nan klas, nou te aprann konsènan sik. _____ *(non elèv lan)* ta renmen pataje avèk ou kèk nan istwa nou te li yo.

Water Dance, ekri pa Thomas Locker Powèm sa a dekri kouman dlo resikle nan diferan fòm.

Persephone and the Seasons, ekri pa Heather Amery Mit Grèk sa a eksplike poukisa sezon yo chanje.

The Circuit, ekri pa Francisco Jiménez Yon tigason adolesan chanje lekòl tou jis lè l ap fè pwogrè.

The Elements of Life, ekri pa Paul Bennett Tout bagay sou Latè fèt ak eleman. Yo te itilize eleman yo plizyè fwa nan sik lavi a.

Nou ta renmen pou ou pran yon ti moman pou patisipe nan yon aktivite osijè sik yo ou ka pataje ak klas lan. Mèsi pou sipò w.

Sensèman,

_____ *(Pwofesè)*

Pale ak yon moun nan kay la sou sik lavi a. Chwazi yon bagay ou konnen epi dekri sik lavi li. Mo nan bwat lan ka baw kèk lide. Ekri mo an sou liy nan sèk lan.

| yon flè | yon vejetab | yon ensèk | yon bèt | yon papiyon | yon pye bwa |

1 _____

6 _____

2 _____

Site etap yo nan yon sik lavi

_____ .

Desine foto pou ilistre sik lavi a.

5 _____

3 _____

4 _____

Name _____

Date _____

Dear Family,

    In class, we learned about freedom. _____ *(student's name)* would like to share with you the stories we read.

    Rosa Parks, by Andrea Davis Pinkney Rosa Parks played an important role in the Civil Rights Movement and helped to end segregation in the United States.

    The Gettysburg Address, by Kenneth Richards, including a speech by Abraham Lincoln President Abraham Lincoln gave this famous speech in 1863 to honor soldiers killed in a Civil War battle.

    So Far from the Bamboo Grove, by Yoko Kawashima Watkins A boy crosses the dangerous border between North and South Korea to gain freedom.

    Alone & Samantha's Story, by Samantha Abeel Everyone has special talents as well as things that they are not very good at.

    We would also like you to take a few moments to participate in an activity about freedom to share with the class. Thank you for your support.

Sincerely,

_____ *(Teacher)*

President George W. Bush created the USA Freedom Corps. The USA Freedom Corps is a volunteer program. It helps people get involved with their communities and help their neighbors. They work in the areas listed in the box.

Talk with someone at home about the USA Freedom Corps. Ask these questions.

1. Do you think that volunteering in a program like the Freedom Corps is a good thing to do? Why or why not?

    _____

USA Freedom Corps
Animals & Environment
Arts & Culture
Children & Youth
Civic & Community
Education & Technology
Health
Human Services
Public Safety
Disaster Preparation

2. If you could take the time to do it, what kind of program would you enjoy volunteering for? _____

3. What kind of work would you like to do in this program?

    _____

4. Which type of program would help our community the most? Why? _____

    _____

5. Do you know if our community has any volunteer programs that we can become involved in?

    How can we find out? _____

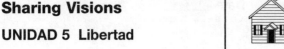

Nombre _____

Fecha _____

Estimada familia:

En nuestra clase, aprendimos acerca de la libertad. A _____ *(nombre del estudiante)* le gustaría compartir con usted las historias que leímos.

Rosa Parks, por Andrea Davis Pinkney Rosa Parks jugó un papel importante en el movimiento por los Derechos Civiles, y en avanzar la causa de poner fin a la segregación en los Estados Unidos.

The Gettysburg Address, por Kenneth Richards, incluyendo un discurso por Abraham Lincoln El Presidente Abraham Lincoln dio este famoso discurso en 1863 para dar honor a soldados que murieron en batallas de la Guerra Civil.

So Far from the Bamboo Grove, por Yoko Kawashima Watkins Para lograr su libertad, un niño cruza la peligrosa frontera entre Corea del Norte y Corea del Sur.

Alone & Samantha's Story, por Samantha Abeel Todos tenemos talentos especiales, así como cosas en las que no somos particularmente hábiles.

Ahora nos gustaría que participara en una actividad acerca de la libertad, para luego compartirla con el resto de la clase. Muchas gracias por su apoyo.

Cordialmente,

_____ *[Maestra(o)]*

El Presidente George W. Bush creó el *"USA Freedom Corps"*, que es una organización de voluntarios. El programa ayuda a que la gente se involucre en sus comunidades y que ayuden a sus vecinos. El programa enfoca su trabajo en las áreas nombradas en la caja.

Habla con alguien en casa acerca del *"USA Freedom Corps"*. Haz estas preguntas.

USA Freedom Corps
Los animales y el medio ambiente
Arte y cultura
Niños y jóvenes
Civismo y comunidad
Educación y tecnología
Salud
Servivios sociales
Seguridad pública
Preparación de desastres

1. ¿Crees que trabajar de voluntario en programas como *"USA Freedom Corps"* es una buena cosa? ¿Por qué sí o por qué no?

   _____

2. Si tuvieras tiempo, ¿en qué tipo de programa de voluntarios te gustaría participar? _____

3. ¿Qué tipo de trabajo te gustaría hacer en este programa?

   _____

4. ¿Qué tipo de programa ayudaría más a nuestra comunidad? ¿Por qué? _____

   _____

5. ¿Sabes si nuestra comunidad tiene programas de voluntarios en que nos podamos involucrar? ¿Cómo lo podemos averiguar? _____

Tên _____

Ngày _____

Kính Gởi Phụ Huynh,

Trong lớp, chúng tôi đã tìm hiểu về tự do. _____ (tên học sinh) muốn chia xẻ với quý vị những câu chuyện chúng tôi đã đọc.

Rosa Parks, tác gia Andrea Davis Pinkney Rosa Parks đóng vai trò quan trọng trong Phong Trào Đòi Quyền Dân Sự và giúp chấm dứt chính sách phân biệt chủng tộc ở Hoa Kỳ.

The Gettysburg Address, tác gia Kenneth Richards, bao gồm bài diễn văn của **Abraham Lincoln** Tổng Thống Abraham Lincoln thuyết trình bài diễn văn nổi tiếng này vào năm 1863 với mục đích ca ngợi những chiến sĩ hy sinh trong cuộc Nội Chiến.

So Far from the Bamboo Grove, tác gia Yoko Kawashima Watkins Một cậu bé vượt qua biên giới nguy hiểm giữa Bắc và Nam Hàn để được tự do.

Alone & Samantha's Story, tác gia Samantha Abeel Mọi người đều có tài năng đặc biệt cũng như những khuyết điểm.

Chúng tôi cũng xin quý vị dành một ít thời giờ để tham dự một hoạt động về tự do nhằm trình bày với lớp học. Xin cám ơn sự hỗ trợ của quý vị.

Trân trọng,

_____ (Giáo viên)

Tổng Thống George W. Bush sáng lập Đoàn Tự Do Hoa Kỳ. Đoàn Tự Do Hoa Kỳ là một chương trình từ thiện. Chương trình giúp cư dân tham gia các sinh hoạt cộng đồng và giúp đỡ láng giềng. Họ làm việc trong các lãnh vực liệt kê trong ô dưới đây.

Hãy thảo luận với người thân trong nhà về Đoàn Tự Do Hoa Kỳ. Đặt các câu hỏi sau đây.

1. Quý vị có nghĩ rằng việc tham gia tình nguyện trong một chương trình như Đoàn Tự Do Hoa Kỳ là một điều nên làm hay không? Tại sao hoặc tại sao không?

   _____

2. Nếu quý vị có thể dành thời giờ tham gia, thì quý vị muốn tình nguyện tham gia chương trình nào?

   _____

3. Quý vị muốn làm công việc gì trong chương trình này?

   _____

4. Loại chương trình nào có ích nhất cho cộng đồng chúng ta? Vì sao?

   _____

5. Theo quý vị biết, cộng đồng chúng ta có chương trình thiện nguyện nào mà chúng ta có thể tham gia không? Làm thế nào để biết được?

   _____

Đoàn Tự Do Hoa Kỳ
Động Vật & Môi Trường
Nghệ Thuật & Văn Hóa
Trẻ Em & Thanh Thiếu Niên
Công Dân & Cộng Đồng
Giáo Dục & Kỹ Thuật Công Nghệ
Sức Khỏe
Các Dịch Vụ Xã Hội
An Toàn Công Cộng
Chuẩn Bị Đối Phó Tai Họa

Npe _____

Vasthib _____

Nyob zoo,

Nyob rau hauv hoob, peb kawm txog kev ywjpheej. _____ *(Menyuam npe)* xav muab tej dab neeg uas peb tau kawm lawd coj los qhia rau nej sub nej thiab tau nrog peb kawm ua ke.

Rosa Parks, los ntawm Andrea Davis Pinkney Rosa Parks yog ib tug uas muaj kev koomtes tseem ceeb nyob rau hauv Civil Rights Movement thiab pab ua rau txojkev sibcais neeg nyob rau hauv United States no los xaus tsi muaj ntxiv.

The Gettysburg Address, los ntawm Kenneth Richards, including a speech by Abraham Lincoln Nyob rau xyoo 1863 nom Abraham Lincoln tau hais zaj lus nto moo qhuas hawm txog cov tub rog uas tau raug phom tuag los ntawm lub tebchaws rov sibtua uas yog Civil War.

So Far from the Bamboo Grove, los ntawm Yoko Kawashima Watkins Ib tug menyuam tub hla tus ciam av tebchaws Kauslim Qaumteb thiab Qabteb uas kab ndas kawg nkaus los mus nrhiav txoj kev ywjpheej.

Alone & Samantha's Story, los ntawm Samantha Abeel Txhua tug puavleej nyias muaj nyias ib qho uas nyias txawj phijxej thiab nyias kuj muaj nyias yam uas paub tsi zoo tib yam nkaus.

Ntxiv ntawm no mus peb xav thov nej siv sib hawm ib pliag los koomtes pab teb cov lus nug txog kev ywjpheej nyob rau nrab qab no pub rau cov menyuam lubxiv tau kawm. Ua tsaug ntau rau nej txojkev txhawb nqa no.

Xee npe,

_____ *(Xib hwb)*

Nom George W. Bush tau tsim muaj lub koos haum USA Freedom Corps. Lub USA Freedom Corps no yog ib tug plahaum ua haujlwm pab dawd. Nws los pab rub tej tib neeg mus koom tes nrog lwm haiv neeg hauv zej zos thiab pab lawv tej neeg zej zos. Lawv ua haujlwm rau cov chaw uas muaj npe nyob rau hauv lub npov tom sab xis no.

Nrog ib tug hauv tsev tham txog USA Freedom Corps. Siv cov lus nram qab no nug.

1. Koj puas xav hais tias ua haujlwm pab dawb nyob rau ib tug plahaum zoo li Freedom Corps puas yog ib qhov zoo? Zoo yog vim li cas los yog tsi zoo no los yog vim li cas?

   _____

2. Yog tias koj nrhiav tau lub sib hawm mus pab ua haujlwm dawb, yuav yog yam plahaum twg koj thiaj nyiam pab?

   _____

3. Tegnum koj xav pab nyob rau hauv tus plahaum no yog dabtsi?

   _____

4. Yam plahaum twg yuav pab tau peb cov neeg hauv zos tshaj plaws? Vim licas? _____

5. Koj puas paub saib nyob rau hauv peb cov neeg puas muaj plahaum pab ua haujwm dawb uas peb yuav mus koomtes pab tau? _____

USA Freedom Corps
Tejtsiaj & Fuabcua cheebtsam
Mojzeeg & Haiv neeg kev cojnoj cojua
Menyuam yaus & Cov hluas
Lub nroog & Cov neeg
Kev kawm ntawv & Tej cuabyeej thevnoblosntsis
Seem rau mob nkeeg
Koos haum pab neeg
Kev puajphais rau tsoomzeej
Kev npaj rau thaum muaj kev puamruaj puagnroog

School-Home Connection
Sharing Visions

第五單元:自由

姓名：_____

日期：_____

各位尊敬的家庭成員:

　　在課堂上，我們學習了有關自由的內容。_____（學生名字）想與各位分享我們上課時讀過的故事。

　　Rosa Parks, by Andrea Davis Pinkney 在民權運動中，羅莎•柏嘉斯扮演了一個重要角色，促使美國廢除了種族隔離制度。

　　The Gettysburg Address, by Kenneth Richards, including a speech by Abraham Lincoln 林肯總統於 1863 年發表了這篇著名的演講，記念在南北戰爭中陣亡的士兵。

　　So Far from the Bamboo Grove, by Yoko Kawashima Watkins 一個男孩穿越南韓與北韓間的危險邊界，投奔自由。

　　Alone & Samantha's Story, by Samantha Abeel 每個人都有特殊的才能，也有不太擅長做的事。

　　我們還希望各位能抽出時間參與一項有關自由的活動，與全班同學一起分享。感謝各位的支持。

　　　　　　　　順祝安康，

　　　　　　　　_____（教師）

喬治•W•布殊總統創建了美國自由團。美國自由團是一個義工組織，幫助人們關心社區，協助鄰里。框內列出了自由團的工作範圍。與家人討論美國自由團，提出以下問題。

美國自由團
動物及環境
藝術及文化
兒童及青年
城市及社區
教育及技術
衛生
人道服務

1. 您認為參與自由團這樣的義工計劃是件好事嗎？為什麼？_____
_____

2. 如果您有時間去做義工，您有意參與哪類計劃？_____
_____

3. 在該計劃中，您願意承擔哪種工作？_____
_____

4. 哪類計劃對我們社區的最有助益？為什麼？_____
_____

5. 您知道我們社區中是否有我們可以參與的義工計劃？_____
我們如何才能找到相關資訊？_____
_____
_____

School-Home Connection
Sharing Visions
ជំពូក ៥ សេរីភាព

ជូនចំពោះគ្រួសារ.

នៅក្នុងថ្នាក់ យើងរៀនអំពីសេរីភាព។ _____ (ឈ្មោះសិស្ស)
ចង់និយាយប្រាប់អ្នកពីរឿង ដែលយើងបានអាន។

Rosa Parks, by Andrea Davis Pinkney រ៉ូស្បា ផាក
មានតួនាទីសខាន់នៅក្នុងចលនាទាមទារសិទ្ធិក្នុងស្រុក
ហើយជួយបញ្ចប់វិយោគកម្មនៅក្នុងសហរដ្ឋ។

The Gettysburg Address, by Kenneth Richards, including a speech by Abraham Lincoln
ប្រធានាធិបតេយ្យ អេប្រាហា លិនកុន ថ្លែងសន_រកថាដ៏ល្បីរបស់គាត់ក្នុងឆ្នាំ ១៨៦៣
ដើម្បីគោរពទាហានដែលស្លាប់ នៅក្នុងសង្គ្រាមក្នុងស្រុក។

So Far from the Bamboo Grove, by Yoko Kawashima Watkins
ក្មេងស្រីប្រុសម្នាក់ឆ្លងទល់ដែនដែលប្រកប ដោយគ្រោះថ្នាក់រវាងកូរ៉េខាងជើងនិងខាងត្បូង
ដើម្បីទៅរកសេរីភាព។

Alone & Samantha's Story, by Samantha Abeel ត្រប់ៗគ្នាមានទេពកោសល្យពិសេស
ក៏ដូចអ្វីៗដែលគេមិន មានការប៉ុនប្រសប់ធ្វើដូចឆ្ពោះដែរ។

យើងក៏ចង់ឱ្យអ្នកចំណាយពេលមួយភ្លេត ចូលរួមសកម្មភាពអំពីការអាថ៌កំបាំង
ដើម្បីប្រាប់សិស្សក្នុងថ្នាក់។ សូមអរគុណដល់ការ គាំទ្ររបស់អ្នក។

ដោយសេាះស័ត្គ្រ

_____ (គ្រូបង្រៀន)

ប្រធានាធិបតេយ្យ ចូច ដេវបែលយូ ប៊ូស បង្កើតឱ្យមានអង្គភាពសេរីអាមេរិក។ អង្គភាពសេរីអាមេរិក
ជាកម្មវិធីសំគ្រចិត_។ វាជួយមនុស្សឱ្យចូលរួមជាមួយសហគមន_របស់គេ និងជួយអ្នកភូមិគេ។
គេធ្វើការទៅតាមផ្នែកដែលចុះក្នុងប្រអប់នេះ។

និយាយជាមួយនរណាម្នាក់នៅទ_:អំពីអង្គភាពសេរីអា
មេរិក។ ស្ទង់សន្ទរទាំងនេះ។

១. តើអ្នកគិតថាការសំគ្រចិត_ចូលក្នុងអង្គភាពបែបនេះជាការ
ល្អមួយឬទេ? ហេតុអ្វីល្អ ឬហេតុអ្វីល្អ?

_____

២. បើអ្នកអាចចំណាយពេលជួយ តើកម្មវិធីបែបណាដែលអ្នករីក
រាយសំគ្រចិត_ជួយ? _____

៣. ។តើកិច្ចការបែបណាដែលអ្នកចង់ធ្វើនៅក្នុងកម្មវិធីនេះ?

_____

៤. តើកម្មវិធីបែបណាដែលអ្នកចង់ជួយសហគមន_ជាងគេ? ហេតុអ្វី?

_____

៥. តើអ្នកដឹងថាសហគមន_យើងមានកម្មវិធីសំគ្រចិត_ណាមួយដែលយើងអាចចូលរួមជាមួយទេ?
តើយើងអាចដឹងដោយរបៀបណា? _____
ចម្លើយ: _____

អង្គភាពសេរីអាមេរិក

សត្វនិងបរិស_ាន
សិល្បៈនិងវប្បធម
កុមារនិងយុវជន
ក្រុងនិងសហគមន_
ការសិក្សានិងបច្ចេកទេស
សុខភាព
កិច្ចបំរើមនុស្ស
សុវត្តិភាពសាធារណ:
ការប្រងប្រៀបនិងមហាន
_រាយ

Non _____

Dat _____

Chè Fanmi,

Nan klas, nou te aprann konsènan libète. _____ *(non elèv lan)* ta renmen pataje avèk ou kèk nan istwa nou te li yo.

Rosa Parks, ekri pa Andrea Davis Pinkney Rosa Parks te jwe yon wòl enpòtan nan Mouvman Dwa Sivil epi nan ede mete fen a segregasyon Ozetazini.

The Gettysburg Address, ekri pa Kenneth Richards, ikonpri yon diskou pa Abraham Lincoln Prezidan Abraham Lincoln te bay diskou selèb sa a an 1863 pou l onore sòlda ki te mouri nan batay Lagè Sivil la.

So Far from the Bamboo Grove, ekri pa Yoko Kawashima Watkins Yon tigason travèse fwontyè danjre ant Kore di Nò ak Kore di Sid pou l jwenn libète.

Alone & Samantha's Story, ekri pa Samantha Abeel Tout moun genyen talan espesyal ansanm ak bagay yo pa tèlman fò ladan yo.

Nou ta renmen pou ou pran yon ti moman pou patisipe nan yon aktivite osijè libète ou ka pataje ak klas lan. Mèsi pou sipò w.

Sensèman,

_____ *(Pwofesè)*

President George W. Bush te kreye USA Freedom Corps. USA Freedom Corps lan se yon pwogram volontè. Li ede moun patisipe nan kominote yo epi ede vwazen yo. Yo travay nan zòn ki site nan bwat la.

Pale avèk yon moun lakay ou konsènan USA Freedom Corps. Poze kesyon sa yo.

1. Èske w panse pote w volontè nan yon pwogram tankou Freedom Corps se yon bon bagay pou fè? Poukisa oswa poukwa pa?

   _____

2. Si w te ka pran tan pou fè sa, ki kalite pwogram ou ta renmen pote w volontè pou fe? _____

3. Ki kalite travay ou ta renmen fè nan pwogram sa a?

   _____

4. Ki kalite pwogram ki ta ka ede kominote w lan plis? Poukisa?

   _____

5. Èske w konnen si kominote nou an genyen pwogram volontè nou ka patisipe ladan yo?

   Kouman nou ka chèche konnen? _____

   Repons: _____

USA Freedom Corps
Zannimo ak Anviwonman
Atizay ak Kilti
Timoun ak Jèn
Sivik ak Kominote
Edikasyon ak Teknoloji
Lasante
Sèvis Imen
Sekirite Piblik
Preparasyon pou katastwòf

Name _____

Date _____

Dear Family,

In class, we learned about visions. _____ *(student's name)* would like to share with you the stories we read.

Mr. Scrooge Finds Christmas, by Aileen Fisher Ebenezer Scrooge learns about charity and kindness through visions of his life in the past, present, and future.

The House on Mango Street, by Sandra Cisneros A girl has a vision of a real house where she wants her family to live.

The Pearl, by John Steinbeck A pearl diver finds the perfect pearl and thinks that it will help his family.

What Will Our Towns Look Like?, by Martha Pickerill Inventions and technology will help make Earth a cleaner and healthier place to live in the future.

We would also like you to take a few moments to participate in an interview about visions to share with the class. Thank you for your support.

Sincerely,

_____ *(Teacher)*

INTERVIEW

1. Name of person being interviewed: _____

2. Question: What vision or goal do you have for the future?

Answer: _____

_____

3. Question: What three things can you do to make the vision or goal become a reality?

Answer: **1.** _____

2. _____

3. _____

4. Question: What is the first step to take?

Answer: _____

5. Decide together on a plan to make the vision or goal a reality. In one month, talk about the vision or goal again.

Question: Are you closer to making the vision or goal a reality? Explain.

Answer: _____

_____

Nombre _____

Fecha _____

Estimada familia:

En nuestra clase, aprendimos acerca de visiones. A _____ *(nombre del estudiante)* le gustaría compartir con usted las historias que leímos.

Mr. Scrooge Finds Christmas, por Aileen Fisher Ebenezer Scrooge aprende sobre la caridad y la bondad a través de visiones de su vida en el pasado, presente y futuro.

The House on Mango Street, por Sandra Cisneros Una niña tiene una visión de una casa real, en donde ella quiere que viva su familia.

The Pearl, por John Steinbeck Un buzo que pesca ostras haya la perla perfecta y cree que ésta le ayudará a su familia.

What Will Our Towns Look Like?, por Martha Pickerill Las invenciones y la tecnología ayudarán a hacer del planeta Tierra un lugar más limpio y más saludable para vivir en el futuro.

Ahora nos gustaría que participara en una entrevista acerca de visiones, para luego compartirla con el resto de la clase. Muchas gracias por su apoyo.

Cordialmente,

_____ *[Maestra(o)]*

ENTREVISTA

1. Nombre de la persona siendo entrevistada: _____

2. Pregunta: ¿Qué vision o qué meta tiene para el futuro?

   Respuesta: _____

   _____

3. Pregunta: ¿Hay tres cosas que puedas hacer para que la visión o meta se vuelva realidad?

   Respuesta: 1. _____

   2. _____

   3. _____

4. Pregunta: ¿Cuál es el primer paso a tomar?

   Respuesta: _____

5. Decidan juntos en un plan para hacer que la visión o meta se vuelva realidad. En un mes, vuelvan a hablar de la visión o meta.

   Pregunta: ¿Estás más cerca ahora de que tu sueño se vuelva realidad? Explica.

   Respuesta: _____

   _____

Tên _____

Ngày _____

Kính Gởi Phụ Huynh,

Trong lớp, chúng tôi đã tìm hiểu về các viễn cảnh. _____ *(tên học sinh)* muốn trình bày với quý vị những câu chuyện chúng tôi đã đọc

Mr. Scrooge Finds Christmas, tác gia **Aileen Fisher** Ebenezer Scrooge học về lòng từ bi và thương người khi thấy ảo cảnh về cuộc sống của mình trong quá khứ, hiện tại, và tương lai.

The House on Mango Street, tác gia **Sandra Cisneros** Một cô bé đặt ra viễn cảnh của một căn nhà thực sự nơi cô muốn sống cùng gia đình.

The Pearl, tác gia **John Steinbeck** Một người lặn tìm được một hòn ngọc trai hoàn hảo và nghĩ rằng ngọc sẽ giúp gia đình mình.

What Will Our Towns Look Like?, tác gia **Martha Pickerill** Các phát minh và kỹ thuật công nghệ sẽ giúp Trái Đất trở thành một nơi sống sạch sẽ và lành mạnh hơn trong tương lai.

Chúng tôi cũng xin quý vị dành một ít thời giờ để tham gia một cuộc phỏng vấn về các viễn cảnh nhằm trình bày với lớp học. Xin cám ơn sự hỗ trợ của quý vị.

Trân trọng,

_____ *(Giáo viên)*

PHỎNG VẤN

1. Tên người được phỏng vấn: _____

2. Hỏi: Quý vị có mục tiêu hay viễn cảnh gì cho tương lai?

Đáp: _____

_____

3. Hỏi: Cho biết ba việc quý vị có thể làm để biến viễn cảnh hay mục tiêu này thành hiện thực.

Đáp: 1. _____

2. _____

3. _____

4. Hỏi: Bước đầu tiên cần thực hiện là gì?

Đáp: _____

5. Hãy cùng nhau vạch ra một kế hoạch giúp biến viễn cảnh hay mục tiêu này thành hiện thực. Một tháng sau đó, hãy bàn thảo lại về viễn cảnh hay mục tiêu này.

Hỏi: Quý vị sắp biến viễn cảnh hay mục tiêu này thành hiện thực được chưa? Hãy giải thích.

Đáp: _____

Npe _____

Vasthib _____

Nyob zoo,

Nyob rau hauv hoob, peb tau kawm txog lub zeem muag. _____
(Menyuam npe) xav muab cov dab neeg uas peb tau kawm lawd coj los qhia rau nej sub nej thiaj tau
nrog peb kawm ua ib ke.

Mr. Scrooge Finds Christmas, los ntawm Aileen Fisher Ebenezer Scrooge kawm txog kev
pub dawb thiab siab zoo los ntawm zeem muag pom txog nws lub neej yav dhau los lawd,
lub neej tam sim no, thiab lub neej yav pemsuab.

The House on Mango Street, los ntawm Sandra Cisneros Ib tug ntxhais muaj lub zeem
muag txog ib lub tsev tiag uas nws xav tau rau nws tsev neeg nyob.

The Pearl, los ntawm John Steinbeck Ib tug txivneej dhia dej nrhiav hlaws qwj thiab nws
nrhiav tau lub zoo heev ces txawm xav tias qhov ntawd yuav pab tau nws tsev neeg.

What Will Our Towns Look Like?, los ntawm Martha Pickerill Tej kev tsim thiab tej
thevnoblosntsis los sis technology yuav pab ua tau rau lub Ntiajteb huv ntxiv tuaj thiab yuav
ua rau qhov chaw huvsiab rau sawv daws nyob lawm yav pemsuab.

Ntxiv ntawm no mus peb xav thov nej siv sib hawb ib pliag los koomtes pab teb cov lus nug txog
lub zeem muag nyob nram qab no pub rau cov menyuam lubxiv tau kawm nyob rau hauv hoob. Ua
tsaug rau nej txojkev txhawb nqa no.

Xee npe,

_____ *(Xib hwb)*

LUS XAMPHAJ

1. Npe tus neeg uas teb cov lus xamphaj no: _____

2. Lus nug: Koj muaj lub zeem muag los yog homphiav li cas rau yav pemsuab?

   Lo lus teb: _____

   _____

3. Lus nug: Peb yam uas koj yuav ua tau los pab rau koj lub zeem muag los sis homphiaj tshwm
   sim tau yog dabtsi?

   Lo lus teb: **1.** _____

   2. _____

   3. _____

4. Lus nug: Thawj ruam yuav ua yog li cas?

   Lo lus teb: _____

5. Txiav txim siab ua ib ke rau tib lub tswvyim los ua kom lub zeem muag los sis lub homphiaj
   tshwm sim taus. Tom qab ib lub hlis lawm, los sib tham txog qhov zeem muag ntawd los sis
   lub homphiaj ntawd ntxiv.

   Lus nug: Koj puas ze zuj zug rau lub zeem muag los sis lub homphiaj tshwm sim taus? Piav
   qhia saib.

   Lo lus teb: _____

   _____

姓名:＿＿＿＿＿＿＿＿＿＿＿＿＿

日期:＿＿＿＿＿＿＿＿＿＿＿＿＿

各位尊敬的家庭成員:

在課堂上,我們學習了有關願景的內容。＿＿＿＿＿＿＿＿(學生名字)想與各位分享我們上課時讀過的故事。

Mr. Scrooge Finds Christmas, by Aileen Fisher 依班尼沙•士谷透過其昨日、今日與明日的人生願景,領悟了慈善與仁慈。

The House on Mango Street, by Sandra Cisneros 女孩有個願景,那是一所真正的房子,她希望她的家人能住在裡面。

The Pearl, by John Steinbeck 一名採珍珠的潛水員發現一顆完美的珍珠,他想珍珠能為家人帶來助益。

What Will Our Towns Look Like?, by Martha Pickerill 技術與發明將使未來的地球成為更潔淨、更健康的居住地。

我們還希望各位能抽出時間參與一項有關願景的訪問,與全班同學一起分享。感謝各位的支持。

順祝安康,

＿＿＿＿＿＿＿＿＿＿＿＿＿＿＿(教師)

訪談

1. 接受訪問者的姓名:＿＿＿＿＿＿＿＿＿＿＿＿＿＿＿＿＿＿＿＿

2. 問:您對未來有什麼樣的願景或目標?

    答:＿＿＿＿＿＿＿＿＿＿＿＿＿＿＿＿＿＿＿＿＿＿＿＿＿＿＿＿

    ＿＿＿＿＿＿＿＿＿＿＿＿＿＿＿＿＿＿＿＿＿＿＿＿＿＿＿＿＿＿

3. 問:要實現願景或目標,您有哪三件事情可以去做?

    答: 1.＿＿＿＿＿＿＿＿＿＿＿＿＿＿＿＿＿＿＿＿＿＿＿＿＿

    2.＿＿＿＿＿＿＿＿＿＿＿＿＿＿＿＿＿＿＿＿＿＿＿＿＿

    3.＿＿＿＿＿＿＿＿＿＿＿＿＿＿＿＿＿＿＿＿＿＿＿＿＿

4. 問:第一步應該怎麼走?

    答:＿＿＿＿＿＿＿＿＿＿＿＿＿＿＿＿＿＿＿＿＿＿＿＿＿＿＿＿

    ＿＿＿＿＿＿＿＿＿＿＿＿＿＿＿＿＿＿＿＿＿＿＿＿＿＿＿＿＿＿

5. 共同商定一個實現願景或目標的計劃。一個月後,再次討論相關的願景或目標。

    問:您是否離實現願景或目標又近了一步?請說明。

    答:＿＿＿＿＿＿＿＿＿＿＿＿＿＿＿＿＿＿＿＿＿＿＿＿＿＿＿＿

    ＿＿＿＿＿＿＿＿＿＿＿＿＿＿＿＿＿＿＿＿＿＿＿＿＿＿＿＿＿＿

ឈ្មោះ _____

កាលបរិច្ឆេទ _____

ជូនចំពោះគ្រួសារ.

នៅក្នុងថ្នាក់ យើងបង្រៀនអំពីការប្រមើលមើលឃើញ។ _____ (ឈ្មោះសិស្ស) ចង់និយាយប្រាប់អ្នកពីរឿង ដែលយើងបានអាន។

Mr. Scrooge Finds Christmas, by Aileen Fisher ឆ្នាំ១៨០៤ អេប៊ីនីស៊ែរ ស្គ្រូច រៀនអំពីទ្បាននិងថ្ងិត_ល្អាមរយៈការ ប្រមើលមើលឃើញនូវជីវិតគាត់ពីអតីតកាល.បច្ចុប្បន្ន.និងអនាគត។

The House on Mango Street, by Sandra Cisneros កេ្មងស្រីម្នាក់ប្រមើលមើលឃើញនូវជ_ ៈពិតមួយដែល នាងចង់ឱ្យគ្រួសារនាងរស់នៅ។

The Pearl, by John Steinbeck អ្នកមុជទឹករករតុងម្នាក់រកឃើញតុចល្អួតតខ្ច្បាៈ ហើយគិតថាវានឹងជួយគ្រួសារ គាត់។

What Will Our Towns Look Like?, by Martha Pickerill ក្រ៉ារកឃើញនិងប្បច្ចេកទេសនិងជួ្ម៉យ៉ែនជឿ ឱ្យ ទៅជាកន្លែងស្នាក់និងមានសុខភាពសំរាប់ការរស់នៅក្នុងពេលអនាគត។

យើងក៏ចង់ឱ្យអ្នកចំណាយពេលមួយភ្លែត ចូលរួមសកម្មភាពអំពីការប្រមើលមើលឃើញ ដើម្បីប្រាប់សិស្សក្នុងថ្នាក់។ សូមអរគុណដល់ការគាំទ្ររបស់អ្នក។

ដោយសេចក្ដីស្មោះត្រង់

_____ (គ្រូបង្រៀន)

គន្លឹះ

១, ឈ្មោះអ្នកដែលត្រូវគេសម្ភាស: _____

២, សំនួរ: តើអ្វីដែលជាការមើលឃើញឬគោលដៅដែលអ្នកមានសំរាប់អនាគត?

ចម្លើយ: _____

៣, សំនួរ: អ្វីបីបែបដែលអ្នកអាចធ្វើដើម្បីឱ្យការមើលឃើញឬគោលដៅទៅអ្នកក្លាយជាការពិត?

ចម្លើយ: ១, _____

           ២, _____

           ៣, _____

៤, សំនួរ: អ្វីដែលជាជំហានទីមួយត្រូវធ្វើ?

ចម្លើយ: _____

៥, សំរេចរួមគ្នាលើកំរោងមួយដើម្បីធ្វើឱ្យការមើលឃើញឬគោលដៅទៅក្លាយជាការពិត។ ក្នុងពេលមួយខែ ត្រូវនិយាយពីការមើលឃើញ ឬពិគោលដៅនេះមតងទៀត។

សំនួរ: តើអ្នកជិតនឹងធ្វើឱ្យការមើលឃើញឬគោលដៅនេះក្លាយជាពិតមែនទេ? ពន្យល់។

ចម្លើយ: _____

Non _____

Dat _____

Chè Fanmi,

Nan klas, nou te aprann konsènan vizyon. _____ *(non elèv lan)* ta renmen pataje avèk ou kèk nan istwa nou te li yo.

> **Mr. Scrooge Finds Christmas,** ekri pa Aileen Fisher Ebenezer Scrooge aprann konsènan charite ak jantiyès atravè vizyon lavi li nan lepase, leprezan ak lavni.

> **The House on Mango Street,** ekri pa Sandra Cisneros Yon tifi genyen yon vizyon yon kay toubonvre kote li vle fanmi l rete.

> **The Pearl,** ekri pa John Steinbeck Yon moun k ap chèhe pèl jwenn yon bon kalite pèl ki pral ede fanmi l.

> **What Will Our Towns Look Like?,** ekri pa Martha Pickerill Envansyon ak teknoloji pral ede moun fè Latè a yon kote ki pi pwòp epi ki pi ansante pou moun rete nan lavni.

Nou ta renmen pou ou pran yon ti moman pou patisipe nan yon entèvyou osijè vizyon ou ka pataje ak klas lan. Mèsi pou sipò w.

Sensèman,

_____ *(Pwofesè)*

ENTÈVYOU

1. Non moun w ap entèvyoure a: _____

2. Kesyon: Ki vizyon oswa objektif ou genyen pou lavni?

Repons: _____

_____

3. Kesyon: Ki twa bagay ou ka fè pou fè vizyon an oswa objektif lan vin yon reyalite?

Repons: 1. _____

2. _____

3. _____

4. Kesyon: Ki premye etap pou pran?

Repons: _____

5. Deside ansanm sou yon plan pou fè vizyon an oswa objektif lan vin yon reyalite. Nan yon mwa, pale konsènan vizyon an oswa objektif lan ankò.

Kesyon: Èske w pi prè pou fè vizyon an oswa objektif lan vin yon reyalite? Eksplike.

Repons: _____

UNIT 1 · MYSTERIES

The Mystery of the Skunk Ape

BOWDEN (REPORTER): Florida's Everglades—as dangerous as they are graceful. But somewhere, hiding deep in the swamps and the palmettos lurks the legend of the Skunk Ape, similar to Bigfoot, or Sasquatch.

MAN #1: A Skunk Ape looks like a man in a monkey suit, so for somebody to say they've seen a man in a monkey suit is ridiculous. That's what a Skunk Ape is.

BOWDEN: But could the Skunk Ape be as close as Myakka State Park in Sarasota's backyard?

MAN #2: This is worth a hoot. I've never heard of any story even remotely similar to having any kind of ape or likeness thereof out here, not even on Halloween.

BOWDEN: But take a look at these photos, now in evidence at the Sarasota Sheriff's Office. Reported as a suspicious incident, these pictures were mailed in by an anonymous woman, a concerned senior citizen living in a wooded area near I-75.

She claims this strange beast traipsed through her yard, eating whole apples that she had left on her back porch. In her letter, she calls the beast an orangutan, 6 ½ to 7 feet tall while kneeling on the ground, a huge animal with an awful smell that lasted long after it was gone, an animal that made a deep "whoomp" noise.

But experts say coming across an orangutan, especially an oversized one anywhere other than the zoo—or Indonesia, where they're from—is very unlikely.

ROTMAN: It just seems—it just seems very bizarre.

BOWDEN: LeAnn Rotman, an assistant curator who's spent more than a decade working with primates, says orangutans are smart and large but look nothing like the photos.

ROTMAN: It just doesn't seem proportional to any of our ape species, whether it be chimpanzees or orangutan. The hair is a little kind of off-color, so yeah, I would say, my guess would be, yes, it would be a hoax.

BOWDEN: So is it just a tall tale, perhaps one with as many holes as the welcome sign at Myakka State Park?

MAN #3: Have you seen any of the notorious Myakka Skunk Ape today?

PARK VISITOR: No. Well—you pulling my leg?

BOWDEN: Maybe, but the truth is out there somewhere.

Deborah Bowden, FOX 13 News.

UNIT 1 · MYSTERIES

Scotland's Loch Ness Monster

GEISLER (REPORTER): The object in the center of this picture might not immediately look like a monster. The trouble is, it doesn't look like anything else. When Bobby Pollack took his family to the Highlands on holiday, he didn't expect to make money, but then, he didn't expect to see a creature rise five feet out of Loch Ness and speed along the surface. The images he filmed aren't exactly conclusive evidence, but they were enough to win him a £500 bounty put up by a chain of bookies for the Nessie sighting of the year.

POLLACK: Well, first of all, I thought it was a man swimming. And then I said, "No, it's too—too big to be a man swimming," because the height of the hill I was up actually was quite high. So I said, "No, it's not a man. It can't be a seal, and I know it wouldn't be a roe deer because I've seen them in the Loch myself, in the past." So basically, it could only be one thing. Could it be Nessie? I don't know. You get a lot of ridicule about this subject, the Loch Ness, a hell of a lot of ridicule about it, so I held onto it for three months before I actually sent it to Inverness.

GEISLER: But it is being taken seriously. Marine mammal experts have studied the tape time and again. They agree the creature is moving too fast to be a seal, but it's far too big to be any of the other known residents of the Loch. Other experts in the field say it's among the best pieces of Nessie footage ever shot. It'll now sit alongside images like these in the Nessie archive, helping keep the legend alive—good news for visitors, Nessie hunters, and small businesses as the tourist season approaches.

Martin Geisler, ITV News.

UNIT 2 · SURVIVAL

Honoring a *Titanic* Survivor

NETTLETON (REPORTER): It's one of those tourist attractions that seems out of place. Here in the Rocky Mountain West, some 2,000 miles from the Atlantic Ocean, is a monument to one of the greatest disasters at sea. But this museum and historic mansion in downtown Denver has strong ties to the *Titanic*. At one time, the Molly Brown House was the fashionable home of one of the sunken ship's most famous survivors.

WOMAN: Really, Molly Brown represents, sort of the, really, the American dream. She was a fairly poor, working-class girl who came and married well. He struck it rich.

NETTLETON: In the late 1800s, the Browns made their fortune off gold discovered high in the Colorado Mountains. In 1894, the family settled in Denver. Molly Brown lived on and off in this house until her death in 1932. In the 1970s, the Victorian mansion was restored to look as it did when the Browns lived here.

TOUR GUIDE: All of the stained glass that you see throughout the house is original.

NETTLETON: Today the Molly Brown House Museum is one of Denver's top attractions. It was Molly Brown's journey onboard the *Titanic* that secured her place in history. Kathy Bates played the role.

BATES'S *TITANIC* CHARACTER: God Almighty.

NETTLETON: The *Titanic* was touted as the grandest ocean liner ever built. But in April 1912, on its inaugural voyage from Europe to North America, the ship hit an iceberg. Within a few hours, it sank in the North Atlantic, taking the lives of 1,500 passengers. Molly Brown was one of the 700 who survived.

WOMAN: She really took charge of her lifeboat, got in there and taught women how to row so they would keep warm.

NETTLETON: And her heroics continued on the rescue ship.

WOMAN: When she got on board the *Carpathia,* she translated for widows and orphans, raised money before she ever docked in New York. She then went to testify in front of the U.S. Senate on maritime reform.

NETTLETON: Broadway and Hollywood made tributes to the Denver socialite. Remember *The Unsinkable Molly Brown?* For 85 years, the *Titanic* has been memorialized in many ways too, perhaps none so opulent as the latest motion picture.

WOMAN: It's just a—it's a really human story, and people just don't seem to tire of it.

NETTLETON: The attention *Titanic* is generating has translated into big business for the Molly Brown House. In the past few weeks, the museum has seen a dramatic increase in visitors, and its Web site has gotten nearly half a million hits. Those impressive numbers should continue as the phenomenon of *Titanic* continues to grip the nation.

Steve Nettleton, CNN, reporting.

UNIT 3 · JOURNEYS

Recreating Ancestral Travels

LOVLER (REPORTER): In these days of high technology, building a boat of reeds like the ones that ancient Polynesian people might have used to set sail to and from Easter Island—one of the most remote places on Earth—might seem a bit strange. But Spanish explorer Kitin Munoz and his small but dedicated group of multiethnic followers don't see things quite that way.

[Kitin Munoz speaking Spanish]

TRANSLATOR: The name of our expedition, which is called Mata-Rangi, unites all these people who are so different. Mata-Rangi means "Eyes of Paradise," because what it hopes to do is look at our planet, which is our paradise.

LOVLER: Kitin has brought a group of Aymara Indians from Lake Titicaca, Bolivia, to work on the project because they alone still master the craft of building reed boats.

This master builder says his father taught him when he was 12 and that he is proud to be carrying on the traditions of his ancestors.

Many of the Bolivians accompanied Kitin on an earlier ocean adventure from Peru to Tahiti. The Rapa Nui participants, or Easter Islanders, are new to this game. They want to revive lost traditions.

[Rapa Nui islander speaking native language]

TRANSLATOR: We want to show our culture. We want to show that before we traveled like this, Hotu Matua, the first king of Easter Island, came here in a boat like the one we are building.

LOVLER: They are gathering reeds from this volcanic lake to build the primitive-style boat on which they will set off in a few months' time. The project has the backing of UNESCO, the Spanish government, the Explorers Club of New York, and a Swiss watch company that is financing the project.

The boat will be patterned on a design found on a petroglyph etched on one of Easter Island's Moai, or giant stone statues.

[Kitin Munoz speaking Spanish]

TRANSLATOR: It is a classic boat based on old designs and prototypes. We are only using our hands and reeds to build the boat. There are no machines involved.

LOVLER: The group is set to depart in February and will make stops in the Marquesas Islands, Tahiti, Australia, and Japan, where other indigenous adventurers will join the crew. It took years for Kitin to get his Mata-Rangi

project off the ground, but now he
and his multiethnic team are about
to start building their boat of reeds.

*Ronnie Lovler, CNN, Anakena, Easter
Island, in the Chilean Polynesia.*

UNIT 4 · CYCLES

The Planet's Pulse

KELLAN (REPORTER): What does a year in the life of planet Earth look like? Well, something like this, say NASA scientists who are using an Earth-observing satellite called SeaWiFS to monitor plant life on land and in the oceans. Now, a year after SeaWiFS started sending back images to Earth, researchers have assembled this movie, showing changing vegetation patterns around the world through an entire cycle of seasons.

SCIENTIST: Like all living things on Earth, the Earth itself has a pulse. It pulses with the sun rising and setting. It pulses with the seasons. It pulses with changes from year to year. What we're able to do now is actually monitor the Earth's pulse, the Earth's living characteristics, from space.

KELLAN: SeaWiFS monitors vegetation on Earth, seen in these images of green, and phytoplankton in the ocean, seen here in shades of green, yellow, and red. Phytoplankton are microscopic plants that form the base of the ocean's food chain.

SCIENTIST: Essentially, all life in the ocean, in one way or another, depends upon the abundance of phytoplankton as a food source. So if we can understand how phytoplankton concentrations change over time and space, we'll be in a much better position to understand how changing fish populations, whales, and birds, how those things which depend, ultimately, on phytoplankton, respond to those changes.

KELLAN: In the past year, SeaWiFS has gathered a wealth of images from all over the world, from Boston to Los Angeles, Europe to Australia. Scientists have been able to monitor fires and natural disasters, like hurricanes, from space. And they've been particularly interested to see how ocean life in the equatorial Pacific, around the Galapagos Islands, has bounced back from the ravages of El Niño.

SCIENTIST: Well, what happened in May: ocean conditions changed very, very dramatically. The cold, nutrient-rich waters returned to the Galapagos, and literally within days, the waters around the Galapagos, hundreds of thousands of square kilometers, just erupted biologically.

KELLAN: SeaWiFS is slated to continue taking the pulse of the planet for another four years.

Ann Kellan, CNN.

UNIT 5 • FREEDOM

The Civil Rights Movement

CHORUS: On the other side. Yes, I want to cross over to see my Lord. Lift every voice and sing. Lift every voice and sing.

NARRATOR: The people of Montgomery are lifting their voices to celebrate the 40th anniversary of the Montgomery bus boycott.

CHORUS: Lift every voice and sing a song.

NARRATOR: Many well-known civil rights activists were there, but the guest of honor was Rosa Parks, known as the mother of the Civil Rights movement. It was Parks' arrest for refusing to give up her seat on a bus in Montgomery that sparked the boycott in December of 1955.

PARKS: I was very determined to let it be known that we as a people and I as an individual had suffered that kind of humiliation far too long.

NARRATOR: Parks has come full circle. Today she is protected, not arrested, by the police. At the outdoor festival, leaders of the movement relived old memories, some good, some bad.

WOMAN #1: When I would come to Montgomery and people had places to go, not riding the bus, I would stop by the station, and I would pick up whoever was going my way.

WOMAN #2: I was just thinking about the calls that we received. Back then, it was the White Citizens' Council, and they were hired to harass us day and night.

WOMAN #3: It was like a moment of truth when I realized that we were part of a—of a worldwide struggle; a struggle that was taking place as if—if it were on the stage of history.

NARRATOR: Alabama was one of the worst states for racial oppression but one of the first to acknowledge its history with a Black Heritage brochure.

MAN: Forty years ago, they were just churches, and they were just streets, and they were just buildings. Today, they are—they're places of interest to people who did not get a chance to—to participate in them in the past.

NARRATOR: In fact, Montgomery has a Black Heritage tour for visitors.

TOUR GUIDE: We usually go to the Capitol first, and we show them where Jefferson Davis was sworn in as president of the Confederacy, and it's also the spot where Martin Luther King spoke after the march from Selma to Montgomery. It also overlooks the Dexter King Memorial Church, Baptist Church, which was Martin Luther King's first pulpit.

NARRATOR: Tourists can also see the site where Rosa Parks was arrested on that day in 1955. One night, as part of the celebration, a 1950s bus was parked in the spot on Montgomery Street where Rosa Parks was arrested. It was popular with visitors who wanted to sit in the same seat Parks sat in. Not far from this site, on South Jackson Street, is the Martin Luther King Home.

KING'S FORMER BARBER: This is the march from Selma to Montgomery.

NARRATOR: Down the street, visitors can view pictures of the movement and talk to King's former barber.

KING'S FORMER BARBER: Well, I knew him, you know, and both sides of him. Before he got to be famous, you know, well, he'd just come 'round the barbershop and have a little rap, a little philosophical conversation.

CHORUS: Lift every voice and sing a song.

NARRATOR: Finally, tourists can visit Montgomery's Civil Rights Memorial, dedicated to 40 black and white Alabamans who died during the civil rights struggle.

UNIT 6 · VISIONS

Observing a Visionary Figure

BATTISTA (REPORTER): He's been dead for more than 200 years now, but Ben Franklin's presence is still very much a fact of life in Philadelphia. And this year, it seems, just about everyone is lining up for a taste of Franklinmania.

PARK RANGER: And this bell had a 90-year working history.

BATTISTA: While the party will run through the end of the year, it's actually part of a celebration that began three years ago with the 200th anniversary of the Constitution and the discovery that selling history means good business.

MAN #1: It's a combination of taking our known strengths in history and theming them in such a way that it makes people feel compelled to come to this city.

BATTISTA: It's also a matter of capitalizing on a captivating personality.

MAN #2: Benjamin Franklin was probably one of the most down-to-earth good ol' boys that you ever saw. People liked him, and he liked people.

BATTISTA: Many events are scheduled at Franklin Court, part of Independence National Park. There, visitors can learn about Franklin the family man and Franklin the

businessman. Chances are, many will be surprised to learn that Ben Franklin and his legacy are as timely today as they were 200 years ago.

When he wasn't busy with his print shop or inventing everything from lightning rods to bifocals, Franklin was founding hospitals or schools, including the University of Pennsylvania, which celebrated its 250th anniversary last month. And when he wasn't founding one thing, he was improving something else. As Philadelphia's postmaster, he set up the first city delivery system and made other improvements as well.

But Franklin wanted his deeds to outlive him, and when he died, he bequeathed the city $5,000 that is still paying dividends today. Part of that money helped the city establish the Franklin Institute, a scientific museum. The Future Center opened there in May, with the express purpose of bringing young people face-to-face with the future.

GIRL: Oh, this is horrible. I look like my mother.

BATTISTA: All of this might make the average person wonder what old Ben would think about a celebration in honor of his death.

MAN DRESSED AS BENJAMIN FRANKLIN: Well, it wasn't the favorite thing that I did a couple hundred years ago. In fact, I was a little disappointed. I found that people wouldn't talk to me anymore. They—they talked about me, but they wouldn't talk to me, so I'm never going to do it again.

BATTISTA: But if he did, chances are Philadelphia would just have one more reason to celebrate.

Bobbie Battista, CNN, reporting.

Name _____ Date _____

UNIT 1 Mysteries

CNN Video

> **Scotland's Loch Ness Monster** A man in Scotland videotaped a strange and mysterious creature. Is it the Loch Ness monster? Make up your mind as you watch the video clip.

Before Viewing

What do you know about the Loch Ness monster? Use a KWL Chart to take notes and organize ideas. Complete the first two columns before you view the video. Then complete the third column after you view and listen to the video.

While Viewing

First Viewing

Watch and listen to "Scotland's Loch Ness Monster." What are the facts? What are the opinions? As you watch the video, take brief notes.

Topic: Loch Ness Monster		
Know What do I already know about the topic?	**Want to Know** What do I want to know about the topic?	**Learned** What did I learn about the topic?

Second Viewing

Make a note for any section that you did not understand. To help you understand the video, read the written text on the screen for the Bobby Pollack.

Third Viewing

1. Listen carefully to learn about what Bobby Pollack was doing in the Scottish Highlands.
2. Do you understand Bobby Pollack's message? If not, ask your teacher for clarification.

After Viewing

Discussion

1. What are the facts and opinions in the video?
2. Is the Loch Ness monster real? What is your opinion of the tape shown in the video clip? Is the creature still a mystery?
3. Use a Venn Diagram to compare and contrast the video "Scotland's Loch Ness Monster" with "The Loch Ness Monster" on page 5 of your textbook. How are they the same? How are they different?

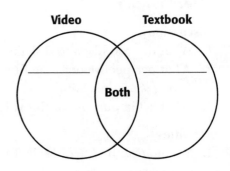

Activities

1. Work with a partner. Compare your opinions of the video clip with your partner's. What did you like or dislike? Use facts to support your opinions.
2. On your own, summarize your list of facts and opinions. What conclusion can you make about the videotape made by Bobby Pollack? Present your summary to the class.
3. Go back to your KWL Chart and complete the third column.

UNIT 2 Survival

Honoring a *Titanic* Survivor A museum in Denver shows the life of a woman named Molly Brown. She survived the greatest sea disaster in history, the sinking of the *Titanic*. This video clip shows how people remember her today.

Before Viewing

Use your prior knowledge to prepare for the video clip. Have you heard of the *Titanic?* Have you ever been to a museum? What do they have there?

While Viewing

First Viewing

Listen and watch for the main events in Molly Brown's life. Write notes that will help you complete the Storyboard.

Second Viewing

Listen carefully to learn about Molly Brown. Write notes to summarize the details about her life.

Third Viewing

1. Listen carefully to connect the main ideas to the details. Use your notes to help you present this information together on the Storyboard.

2. Do you understand the entire video clip? Ask your teacher to clarify any segments that you do not understand.

1. First, _____ _____ _____	2. Second, _____ _____ _____
3. Third, _____ _____ _____	4. Fourth, _____ _____ _____
5. Fifth, _____ _____ _____	6. Finally, _____ _____ _____

After Viewing

Discussion

1. What did you like and disklike about the video clip? Give examples to support your opinion.
2. What perspective does the filmmaker present about Molly Brown? Is she brave? Is she strong, smart, or both?
3. What is the purpose of this video? Does the filmmaker want to influence or to inform?

Activities

1. Summarize the life of Molly Brown. Use details from your Storyboard. Present your summary to a partner.
2. Research the life of Molly Brown. Do online research and use the Web site noted on the video (www.mollybrown.org) to gather more information about her. Choose to write a report, a narrative, a letter, an editorial, a review, or a poem about Molly Brown. Write using a voice and style that is best for your audience and purpose. If appropriate, use transitions such as *first, next,* or *finally.* Present your writing to the class.

UNIT 3 Journeys

Recreating Ancestral Travels This video clip is about a Spanish explorer, Kitin Muñoz, who builds boats based on old designs. Muñoz gathered people from tribes all over the world to build a boat of reeds.

Before Viewing

Work in a small group. Talk about culture and traditions. How do you express or show your culture? Why is culture important?

While Viewing

First Viewing

Watch and listen carefully to learn about the different people and places in the video program. As you watch, think about answers to the questions in a Sunshine Organizer.

Second Viewing

Record your ideas about the people and places in the video in your Sunshine Organizer. Where are these people from? Why is it important to them to save their traditions?

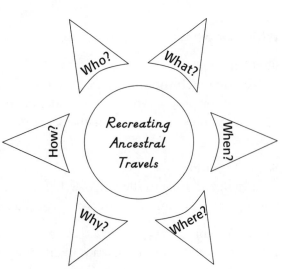

Third Viewing

1. Check your information as you watch the video a third time. Add any missing information.
2. Ask your teacher to clarify any questions you have.

After Viewing

Discussion

1. Who are the people in the video? What are they doing? Where do they live?
2. What is the message of this video? Does the filmmaker want to entertain, to inform, or to persuade?
3. What is culture? How do people show their culture?
4. Connect the information in the video to your own experiences. Do you think people of different cultures work well together? Why or why not? Use information from your Sunshine Organizer to give examples.

Activities

1. Choose to write a narrative, report, or review to present to the class. Write using a voice and style that is best for your audience and purpose. Use the information from your Sunshine Organizer to organize your ideas in a paragraph.
2. Create a class newspaper. Interview and gather information from people who have lived in other countries. Write articles about the cultures and traditions in each country. Use photographs, drawings, and other media to support your articles. Publish your work and display it in your classroom.

UNIT 4 Cycles

CNN Video

The Planet's Pulse This video clip shows pictures of Earth taken from space.
It shows Earth as one big life form with many cycles.

Before Viewing

Think about what you know about animal
and plant life on Earth. Use a two-column chart
to note questions you have about the subject.
Use this chart to prepare for viewing the video.

Animal and Plant Life on Land	Animal and Plant Life in Oceans

While Viewing

First Viewing

As you watch the video clip, take notes on
any words or phrases you do not understand.
Use these notes to prepare for the second
viewing.

Second Viewing

Listen carefully to the video. What are the main ideas? Write them in the
appropriate column of your chart. Write details to support each idea.

Third Viewing

1. As you watch the video, write main ideas about the scientists. What work do they
   do? What do they hope to find?
2. What did you like and dislike about the video clip? Give examples to support
   your opinion.

After Viewing

Discussion

1. What do the pictures from space show you about Earth?
2. What does the video show you about animal and plant life on Earth?
3. How do the pictures from space contribute to the content of the video?

Activities

1. Use your chart to summarize the main ideas and details of the video clip.
   Present your summary to the class.
2. Learn about oceans. Choose to write a report, a narrative, or an editorial about
   the animal and plant life in one of Earth's four major oceans. Select reference
   materials such as the Internet, encyclopedias, and science books as needed for
   your final draft. Research information about the Atlantic, Pacific, Indian, or
   Arctic Ocean. Organize your ideas into paragraphs. Be sure to use transitions
   such as *first, next, finally,* or *in conclusion.* Present your report to the class.

Name _____ Date _____

UNIT 5 Freedom

CNN Video

The Civil Rights Movement Many civil rights events took place in the city of Montgomery, Alabama. This video clip shows the challenges and changes that people faced as they struggled for freedom. It also features Rosa Parks.

Before Viewing

What do you know about civil rights? Who is Rosa Parks? Use a KWL Chart to take notes and organize your ideas. Complete the first two columns now.

Topic: *Civil Rights*		
Know What do I already know about the topic?	**Want to Know** What do I want to know about the topic?	**Learned** What did I learn about the topic?

While Viewing

First Viewing

Watch and listen to learn the main events in the video clip. Note as many things as possible on your KWL Chart.

Second Viewing

Listen for and make note of important dates given in the video. Look and listen for the civil rights leaders referred to in the video.

Third Viewing

1. Write notes about Rosa Parks and other civil rights leaders named in the video.
2. Watch and listen for information that explains how Montgomery changed.

After Viewing

Discussion

1. What does the video teach about the Civil Rights movement?
2. What do you learn about the people of Montgomery? What do the speakers say in the video? What nonverbal messages are shown in the video?
3. How is Montgomery different today?
4. Use a Venn Diagram to compare and contrast "The Civil Rights Movement" with "Rosa Parks" on page 287 of your textbook. How are they different? How are they similar?

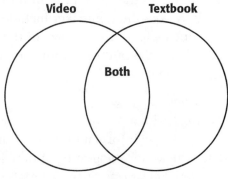

Activities

1. Go back to your KWL Chart. Add information from the discussion to the third column.
2. Work in a small group. Compare your perceptions of the important events.
3. Write a response to the video. Choose to write a letter, an editorial, a journal entry, or a narrative. Select a voice and style that is appropriate to your audience and purpose. Organize your ideas in paragraphs and use transition words.

UNIT 6 Visions

CNN Video

> **Observing a Visionary Figure** Benjamin Franklin helped found the United States over 200 years ago. He lived in Philadelphia, Pennsylvania. This video clip shows how this city remembers him.

Before Viewing

What is vision? What is a visionary? Use a dictionary or ask your teacher.

While Viewing

First Viewing

Listen and watch for ways that people describe Benjamin Franklin. Note these ideas on a Cluster Map.

Second Viewing

Organize ideas and events on the Cluster Map. What did Benjamin Franklin do?

Third Viewing

1. Listen carefully to learn about the city of Philadelphia. Is history important to the people who live here? How do you know?
2. Add more notes to your Cluster Map about Benjamin Franklin.

After Viewing

Discussion

1. How does the video present important ideas about Benjamin Franklin?
2. Why does the filmmaker include an actor in the presentation? How does this contribute to the message of the video?
3. What is the purpose of this video clip? Is it to persuade, to inform, or to entertain?

Activities

1. Work with a partner. Explain why Ben Franklin is a visionary, or man of great ideas. Use information from your Cluster Map in your retelling.
2. Write a short biography of Benjamin Franklin. Use details from your Cluster Map. Select reference materials such as encyclopedias, magazines, or the Internet for your final draft. Organize your information and ideas into paragraphs. Be sure to use transitions such as *first, next, finally,* or *in conclusion.*

Video Answer Key

UNIT 1 MYSTERIES

Before Viewing
Answers will vary but should include that the Loch Ness monster is a strange creature that some people believe lives in Scotland. Some people think it is a joke.

While Viewing

First Viewing
Facts: Man in Scotland named Bobby Pollack videotaped a strange animal. He says it is proof of the monster.
Opinion: It may not be Loch Ness on the tape. It helps attract tourists.

Second Viewing
Answers will vary. Students may say that they have trouble understanding the man on the video clip.

Third Viewing
Answers will vary but may include: 500 lb. bounty for finding Loch Ness; too big to be a man swimming; He held the tape for three months. Experts think the man is moving too fast to be a seal. Other experts say it is the best evidence of Loch Ness monster.

After Viewing
Discussion
1. Facts: The man videotaped a strange animal in Scotland. Experts think it is good evidence of the Loch Ness monster. Opinion: There have been a lot of jokes about Loch Ness. Some people think it is just good for the tourists.
2. Answers will vary.
3. Venn Diagram:
"Scotland's Loch Ness": a videotape shows evidence of a creature; a man sold the tape to experts. Experts think it may be real evidence of Loch Ness.
"The Loch Ness Monster": In 1963, Jim Ayton and his father saw a strange animal in the lake. The text also includes historical information about Loch Ness.
Both: Loch Ness monster may be real.

Activities
1. Students' work will vary.
2. Students' summaries will vary but should include the main events from the video.
3. Students' work will vary.

UNIT 2 SURVIVAL

Before Viewing
Students' work will vary but should include discussion about things to see at a museum or information about the *Titanic.*

While Viewing

First Viewing
Students' storyboards will vary but should include the main events of Molly Brown's life: marriage, trip on the *Titanic,* events after the *Titanic*

Second Viewing
Answers will vary.

Third Viewing
Answers will vary.

After Viewing
Discussion
1. Answers will vary.
2. Molly Brown is shown to be a brave woman.
3. The video's purpose is to inform the viewer about Molly Brown's life.

Activities
1.–2. Students' work will vary.

UNIT 3 JOURNEYS

Before Viewing
Answers will vary but should include examples of culture (food, clothing, music).

While Viewing

First Viewing
Answers will vary but may include the tribal people working in Bolivia. The Spanish explorer, the trip around the world, and Easter Island may be listed.

Second Viewing
The people preserve their culture by building ships made of reeds. This is an old way of making ships.

Third Viewing
1.–3. Students' work will vary.

After Viewing
Discussion
1. The people in the video are tribes that are building ships made of reeds. A Spanish explorer is in the video. The people are trying to preserve their traditions.
2. The filmmaker is trying to inform.
3.–4. Answers will vary.

Activities
1. Answers will vary.
2. Students' work will vary.

UNIT 4 CYCLES

Before Viewing
Answers will vary but may include that Earth is a planet with animal and plant life.

While Viewing

First Viewing
Answers will vary but may include: vegetation, phytoplankton, microscopic, food chain, concentrations, populations.

Second Viewing
Students' work will vary but should include information that scientists are gathering. Scientists learn about sea life and storms from the pictures.

Third Viewing
The scientists gather information. They take the pulse of the planet to better understand life on Earth.

After Viewing
Discussion
1. Answers will vary.
2. Possible answers: The pictures show plants growing. The pictures show storms.
3. The pictures from space show changes on Earth.

Activities
1.–2. Students' answers and reports will vary.

UNIT 5 FREEDOM

Before Viewing
Students' work will vary but should include that Rosa Parks fought for civil rights. She refused to give up her seat on the bus.

While Viewing

First Viewing
Answers will vary.

Second Viewing
Answers will vary but may include Martin Luther King Jr.

Third Viewing
Answers will vary but may include that Montgomery has an African-American heritage tour. Martin Luther King Jr. is another leader who is named.

After Viewing
Discussion
1. Answers will vary.
2.–3. Answers will vary but may include that people were treated poorly. Nonverbal messages include showing anger about the past. Montgomery has changed to promote or show the history that took place there—and represent African-Americans' struggles.
4. Venn Diagram:
"The Civil Rights Movement": shows more civil rights leaders; shows the city of Montgomery; shows Montgomery in the 1950s and today
"Rosa Parks": the biography of Rosa Parks; general information about the civil rights movement Both: Rosa Parks information.

Activities
1.–3. Students' work will vary.

UNIT 6 VISIONS

Before Viewing
Answers will vary but may include that vision has something to do with sight. A visionary is an inventor or founder of something.

While Viewing

First Viewing
Franklin is described as an inventor, founder, and postmaster.

Second Viewing
Answers will vary but should include that Franklin started a hospital, organized the post offices, and left money for a museum.

Third Viewing
1. History is important to the people of Philadelphia. They like to have a party about Benjamin Franklin.
2. Answers will vary.

After Viewing
Discussion
1. Benjamin Franklin was a great man and visionary.
2. The actor showed the viewer what Benjamin Franklin might be like.
3. The video clip is to inform and entertain.

Activities
1.–2. Students' work will vary.

Activity Book Answer Key

UNIT 1 • CHAPTER 1
Build Vocabulary

page 1
A.
1. high-tech
2. murky
3. remote
4. bulky
5. steep
6. tiny

B.
1. apple
2. carrots
3. challenge
4. claim
5. could
6. creature
7. deep

Writing: Punctuation
page 2

A.
1. When scientists used a special computer, this is what they saw.
2. Which discovery amazed them?
3. What did the monster look like?
4. Who saw the monster's flippers?
5. Where is the Loch Ness monster?

B. Answers will vary. Possible responses:
1. Where is the Loch Ness monster?
2. Who saw the Loch Ness monster?
3. How can scientists make clear pictures?

Elements of Literature
page 3

A. Students' stories will vary but should show an order to the events.

B.
1. Students' answers will vary but should describe their drawings.
2. Students' answers should include information about the first event in their stories.
3. Students' answers should include information about the last event in their stories.

Word Study
page 4

The chart should contain the following words. Definitions will vary. The words can be listed in any order.
newspaper; a paper that contains news
bookstore; a store that sells books
waterfall: a place where water falls from a high place
earache: an ache (pain) in the ear
milkshake: a drink that is made with milk and shaken.

Grammar Focus
page 5

A.
1. Underline: He planted the crops in the field; they grew very fast. Circle: and
2. Underline: She worked in the town; she did not work on the farm. Circle: but
3. Underline: They worked in the store after school; they helped at home, too. Circle: and
4. Underline: He sells tomatoes in town; he does not sell apples. Circle: but
5. Underline: She sells shoes in the store; she also sells socks. Circle: but
6. They like to visit the ocean; they do not like to visit the mountains. Circle: but

B.
1. but   3. and
2. but   4. but

Grammar Focus
page 6

A.
1. Everything was quiet at the lake, but then the monster came out.
2. We were scared, and we ran away.
3. We ran into the woods to be safe, but the woods were scary and dark.
4. We searched for the monster, but we never saw it again.
5. We told other people about the monster, but no one believed us.

B.
1. I wanted to go home, my friends wanted to stay.
2. It is usually cold in the winter, but this winter has been warm.
3. My father wants to swim in the lake, but the water is murky.

From Reading to Writing
page 7

Answers will vary.

Across Content Areas
page 8

1. a map
2. an audio CD; an audiocassette
3. a drawing
4. a video
5. the Internet or a CD-ROM

UNIT 1 · CHAPTER 2
Build Vocabulary
page 9

A.
1. modern   2. region   3. symbolize
B.
1. territory   2. embody   3. new

Writing: Capitalization
page 10

1. The Navajo called them ancient enemies.
2. These people settled in Colorado.
3. Katherine lives in Durango, Colorado.
4. The cliff dwellings of Mesa Verde were abandoned.
5. The Pueblo Indians live in Arizona and New Mexico.
6. Leighana Sisneros and Landon Wigton went with her.

Elements of Literature
page 11

A.
1. "I can't go to the movie," Lisa said.
2. Thomas said, "I think it is going to be a very good movie."
3. "I have to clean my room before lunch," said Lisa.
4. "If I help you clean, we can see the movie," Thomas said.
5. Lisa said, "Let's get started."
B. Answers will vary.

Word Study
page 12

A. The chart should be completed to show the following words and definitions:
archaeologist: a person who studies ancient times; geologist: a person who studies geology; biologist: a person who studies biology; guitarist: a person who studies and plays the guitar.

B.
1. guitarist   3. geologist
2. archaeologist   4. biologist

Grammar Focus
page 13

A.
1. Jerry's money is at the bank.
2. My letters are in the mailbox.

3. Kara and Lindsey are at the beach.
4. The lion is sleeping on the large rock.
5. All the snacks are in the jar.
6. My homework is on my desk.

B.
1. Where is Jerry's money?
2. Where are my letters?
3. Where are Kara and Lindsey?
4. Where is the lion sleeping?
5. Where are all the snacks?
6. Where is my homework?

Grammar Focus
page 14

A. Answers will vary, but the prepositional phrases should make sense. Suggested answers follow:
1. The Pueblo people built huge homes in the cliffs.
2. The women cooked corn in pottery.
3. The men planted corn on top of the mesa.
4. Little rain fell in the region.
5. Katherine visited the ruins with her friends from Durango.

From Reading to Writing
page 15

Answers will vary.

Across Content Areas
page 16

A. Venn Diagram should include the following: Encyclopedia article: The Anasazi left due to drought. They moved into the cliffs in A.D. 440.
"Mystery of the Cliff Dwellers": The Anasazi moved into the cliffs in A.D. 550. The Anasazi left due to drought, war, or disease. Both: The Anasazi lived on the sides of cliffs. The Anasazi disappeared.

B.
1. A.D. 440
2. A.D. 550
3. They left due to the drought.
4. They left due to the drought, war, or disease.
5. The Anasazi lived on the sides of cliffs. The Anasazi disappeared.

UNIT 1 · CHAPTER 3
Build Vocabulary
page 17

A.
diary; noun; a written record of a person's feelings, thoughts, and activities
wrist; noun; the joint attaching the hand to the forearm
eardrum; noun; the part inside the ear that moves so that one can hear sound
blood; noun; the red liquid pumped by the heart through the body
B. Answers will vary.

Writing: Spelling
page 18

1. drums, books, heartbeats, muscles

2. brushes, buzzes
3. diaries
4. rodeos

Elements of Literature
page 19

1.–4. Answers will vary but should include use of the pronoun *you* to give instructions.

Word Study
page 20

A.
1. You're tired.
2. It's just a yawn.
3. What's the purpose of yawning?
4. You're bored or sleepy.
5. They'll be sleepy.
6. He didn't stop there.
7. They'll yawn when they stretch.
8. They didn't yawn.

Grammar Focus
page 21

A. 1.–6. Answers will vary but should include dependent clauses beginning with *that*.
B. 1.–5. Answers will vary but should include main (independent) clauses to begin each sentence. Students' sentences should be complete.

Grammar Focus
page 22

A. 1.–5. Answers will vary but should include main and dependent clauses to form complex sentences that make sense.

From Reading to Writing
page 23

Answers will vary.

Across Content Areas
page 24

1. 20 hours   4. 10 hours
2. 25 hours   5. nature videos
3. 30 hours

UNIT 1 · CHAPTER 4
Choose Definitions   page 25
1. a   2. a   3. a   4. b

Writing: Punctuation
page 26

1. Mr. Fink rubbed his chin. "This isn't the briefcase I handed over to the checkroom," he said.
2. The Inspector said, "You told us it was yours. You said it contained only a couple of magazines."
3. "Lucky you," said the Inspector.
4. "I don't mind at all," said Mr. Fink. "I've got nothing to hide," he said.

Elements of Literature
page 27

A. The chart should include the following: **Background:** A policewoman watches a woman run out of a store. **Rising action:** The woman walks out and drives away quickly. The policewoman chases her. **Climax:** The policewoman asks the woman what is in the package. **Resolution:** The woman was rushing home to her sick baby. The policewoman let her go home.

B.
1. two; a policewoman and a woman
2. A policewoman watches a woman run out of a store.
3. Possible response: I thought she took something.
4. The woman went home after she explained.

Word Study
page 28
1. twentieth
2. fourth
3. sixtieth
4. forty-sixth
5. seventh
6. ninetieth
7. sixty-sixth
8. seventieth

Grammar Focus
page 29
A.
1. simple
2. compound
3. complex
4. complex
5. simple

B. Answers will vary but make sure students write in complete sentences and properly identify their sentences.

Grammar Focus
page 30
1. Bansi is going to the dance, or she is going to the movie.
2. Although she is a singer, she gets nervous on stage.
3. The story that the teacher read in class was a mystery.
4. I would like to play soccer today, but I have to help my brother.
5. I will take out the garbage when the rain stops.

From Reading to Writing
page 31
A.–B. Students' work will vary but should include all of the story elements: Characters, Setting, First event, Reaction, Problem, Attempt to resolve problem, Resolution of problem

Across Content Areas
page 32
1. 19–27, 43, and 127
2. 146
3. Crazy Horse National Monument
4. after

UNIT 1 • CHAPTER 5

Build Vocabulary
page 33
1. to
2. one
3. vane
4. would
5. made

Writing: Punctuation
page 34
A.
1. I want to watch a drama, a comedy, or an adventure.
2. Before the first day of school, I bought pens, pencils, and paper.
3. My mother is cooking chicken, potatoes, and corn for dinner.

4. We will paint the house white, green, yellow, or blue.
B. Students' work may include *and* or *or.*
1. I take care of a dog, a cat, and a bird.
2. We picked oranges, lemons, and bananas.
3. She writes poems, plays, and novels.
4. He makes art with paper, paint, and brushes.

Elements of Literature
page 35
A.
1. a
2. e
3. c
4. b
5. d

B. 1.–4. Students' sentences will vary but should show tone. Dialogue should include quotation marks and correct punctuation.

Word Study
page 36
A.
Adjectives
flavorless, without flavor; no taste
worthless, without worth; no value
meaningless, without meaning; no meaning
helpless, without help; no help
humorless, without humor; not funny
effortless, without effort; not difficult
B.
1. humorless
2. flavorless
3. worthless
4. meaningless
5. helpless
6. effortless

Grammar Focus
page 37
1. Jane folded the paper and placed it in a drawer. She is very organized.
2. The girls like karate. They practice twice a day.
3. Ferdinand and I walk to the park. We like to walk together.
4. The machine is fixed. It is very nice now.
5. Thomas, Miguel, and Marsha went to the zoo. They had a good time.
6. Ichabod is not lazy. He works for farmers.
7. Ichabod eats a lot. He is always hungry.
8. The story is scary. I like it.

Grammar Focus
page 38
A.
1. Pablo gave a present to Maria. He gave it to her yesterday.
2. My father painted the house. He made it look very nice.
3. My mother made cookies for the class. She also made brownies for them.
4. My friends are playing the stereo. They are playing it too loudly.
B.
1. He likes them.
2. They enjoy them.
3. Ryan studies it.
4. It lost them.
5. She loves us.

From Reading to Writing
page 39
A.
1. The garden is sweet perfume.
2. Her hair is like a bucket of snakes.
3. That fish is 50 feet long.
4. The waves are as tall as mountains.
B. Students' descriptions will vary but should show hyperbole.

Across Content Areas
page 40
Students' work on the note cards will vary but should be similar to the following:
Research question: What did Washington Irving do for a living? Notes: worked for a newspaper and as a lawyer; wrote important stories: "He wrote two important stories at this time." "Rip Van Winkle" and "The Legend of Sleepy Hollow." Source: Montana, Jack. *Biography of Washington Irving.* Sleepy Hollow Books. New York, NY. 2003.

UNIT 2 • CHAPTER 1

Build Vocabulary
page 41
A.
1. f
2. c
3. d
4. a
5. e
B. Answers will vary. Make sure students' sentences use the vocabulary words correctly.

Writing: Punctuation
page 42
1. I could see the backyard from my bedroom window.
2. Why can't I think of an idea for my novel?
3. I could hear my mother and father talking.
4. She asked him if he thought I would be surprised.
5. What surprise is she talking about?
6. Don't tell me they are planning to send me to camp!
7. How can I get out of it?
8. This is going to ruin my summer!

Elements of Literature
page 43
Possible responses:
1. He gets annoyed when he is disturbed. He does not like to have breakfast with his parents.
2. Jackie's father does not listen to him. He does not think Jackie is too old to have Saturday breakfasts.
3. Jackie does not like muffins. He is an irritable person.
4. Jackie's parents want him to learn. They do not know what Jackie likes.

Word Study
page 44
A.
1. audible
2. deposit
3. capture
4. satisfy
5. tradition

B.
1. tradition
2. satisfy
3. audible
4. capture
5. deposit

Grammar Focus
page 45
A.
Present Progressive
1. is
2. are
3. are
Past Progressive
1. was
2. was
3. were
B.
1. The wind was blowing while we were having a picnic.
2. We are/were waiting for Jackie to finish his lunch.

Grammar Focus
page 46
1. a. Is he playing for our team this summer?
   b. Were they planning for him to begin next week?
2. a. He is not playing for our team this summer.
   b. They were not planning for him to begin next week.
3. a. He isn't playing for our team this summer.
   b. They weren't planning for him to begin next week.

From Reading to Writing
page 47
Answers will vary.

Across Content Areas
page 48
1. Possible response: main types of nutrients that provide energy
2. Type of Nutrient, What It Is Used For, Food That Contains It
3. Proteins, Carbohydrates, Fats
4. Column 3
5. Possible response: the uses of the nutrient
6. Possible responses: meat, fish, milk, eggs

UNIT 2 • CHAPTER 2

Build Vocabulary
page 49
A.
1. swells
2. screeched
3. dusk
4. bridge
5. label
6. fuel
7. helm
B. Noun.

Writing: Punctuation
page 50
A.
1. "Where am I?" he said to the captain.
2. "You are a long way from home," he said.
3. "What's your name?" asked the captain.
4. "My name is David," he said.
5. David asked, "Are they looking for me?"
6. "You bet they are!" answered the captain.
7. "Why are you here?" asked David.
8. The captain said, "We are a whale research ship."

Elements of Literature
page 51

A.

1. external
2. internal
3. external
4. internal
5. internal
6. external

B. Answers will vary. Students' sentences should be complete, and students should correctly identify each sentence as *external* or *internal*.

Word Study
page 52

A.

1. slowly
2. quietly
3. safely
4. roughly

B.

1. slowly
2. roughly

C. Answers will vary.

Grammar Focus
page 53

A.

1. will not
2. I'll
3. will
4. won't
5. will

B. Tomorrow, David will sail at sunrise. His friends and I will have a party for him tonight. We will not see him for a long time. I will get up early to tell him goodbye. He will be away for over two months. We will miss him very much.

Grammar Focus
page 54

A.

1. In July, David will begin his trip.
2. His parents will not leave for home on Saturday.
3. At midnight, the captain will sail from here.
4. He will reach the island in the afternoon.

B. Answers will vary. Students' sentences should correctly use future tense verbs and prepositional phrases of time.

From Reading to Writing
page 55

Answers will vary.

Across Content Areas
page 56

1. south
2. north
3. Los Angeles
4. California
5. Arizona/Nevada
6. Pacific

UNIT 2 • CHAPTER 3

Build Vocabulary
page 57

A.

1. patterns
2. familiarity

B.

1. Meaning 2
2. Meaning 1
3. Meaning 1
4. Meaning 2
5. Meaning 1
6. Meaning 1
7. Meaning 2

Writing: Spelling and Punctuation
page 58

A.

1. I'm very afraid of poisonous snakes.
2. The risk of being bitten by a snake isn't very big.
3. There aren't many poisonous snakes in this area.
4. They're found mostly in the desert.
5. I know it's safe, but flying in an airplane scares me.

B. My parents want me to give up my skateboard. They've read that skateboarding is dangerous. I'm really upset about it. My friends and I are planning to go skateboarding this weekend. There's a new place we've heard about where everyone goes to skateboard. We're planning to ask Felicia and Ena to go. They're sisters, and they've just moved here. I guess I'll have to make some other plans. My parents aren't going to change their minds.

Elements of Literature
page 59

A. One of my favorite things to do is to go on trips to visit my grandmother. <u>Before</u> we begin, my father takes the car to the mechanic to make sure it is working right. <u>Then</u>, on the day of the trip, we wake up early in the morning. <u>First</u> we have a big breakfast. <u>Next</u>, we put all our suitcases and packages into the trunk of the car. <u>Then</u> we are ready to go. We drive all day long. <u>Finally</u>, we arrive at grandmother's house. She has a big dinner waiting for us. <u>After</u> eating, we all sit around the table and tell stories. That is the best part of the day.

B. Answers will vary. Sample answers appear below:
I follow the same steps when I work in the garden. <u>First</u>, I put on my old clothes. <u>Second</u>, I go to the garage where the tools are kept. <u>Third</u>, I pull up all the weeds in the garden. <u>Next</u>, I water all the plants. <u>Then</u>, I put all my tools back in the garage. <u>Finally</u>, I sit next to the garden and drink a big glass of iced tea.

Word Study
page 60

Sentences will vary, but each should include the words listed below.

1. overcooked
2. overcrowded
3. overprotect
4. underdevelop
5. underestimate
6. overpriced
7. overreacted
8. overdressed

Grammar Focus
page 61

A.

1. work
2. works
3. work
4. work
5. works
6. works

B.

1. When it is nice outside, she walks to school.
2. They run when they want to exercise.
3. You play soccer on the weekend.
4. When the weather is bad, he reads a book.
5. We play tennis in the spring and summer.
6. She wants to become a doctor when she gets older.

Grammar Focus
page 62

A.

1. The rattle (make/<u>makes</u>) a soft sound.
2. It (warn/<u>warns</u>) people to stay away from the snake.
3. Spiders (scare/<u>scares</u>) people.
4. People (avoid/<u>avoids</u>) them if possible.
5. Maria (turn/<u>turns</u>) on the light as soon as it gets dark outside.
6. She always (play/<u>plays</u>) the radio when she goes to bed.
7. Johnny (like/<u>likes</u>) to explore caves.
8. He (think/<u>thinks</u>) exploring is a challenge.

B. Sentences will vary, but each should contain a correct use of the verb in parentheses.

From Reading to Writing
page 63

Answers will vary.

Across Content Areas
page 64

1. What Is Psychology?
2. Page 10
3. How Environment Shapes Human Beings
4. Chapter five
5. Chapter four

UNIT 2 • CHAPTER 4

Build Vocabulary
page 65

A.

1. f
2. a
3. c
4. b
5. d
6. e
7. g

B.

1. c
2. f
3. b
4. g
5. e
6. a
7. d

Writing: Punctuation
page 66

A.

1. Early in the morning, she went to search for shellfish.
2. Using her new basket, she collected wood to build a fire.
3. Pulling the bones out one by one, Karana placed them in a pile.
4. Later in the afternoon, she walked down to the water.
5. With its thick, sturdy leaves, the plant made a good covering for the roof.
6. In the floor of her house, she dug a hole for a fire.

B. Corrected paragraph appears below.
Left alone on the island, Karana worked hard to survive. First of all, she had to find shelter. After building a fence, she began to build a house. Every night before bed, she covered the hot embers of her fire. In the morning, she used the embers to start a new fire.

Elements of Literature
page 67

A.

1. Survival: Check *Karana* and *David*
2. Making a home: Check *Karana*
3. Loyalty: Check *David*

B.

1. Check *Karana* and *David*; Check *Survival*
2. Check *David*; Check *Loyalty*
3. Check *Karana*; Check *Making a Home*

C.

1. survival
2. are alone in a dangerous situation
3. make a home
4. builds shelves
5. refuses to leave his boat behind
6. loyalty

Word Study
page 68

A.

1. there
2. There
3. They're
4. Their
5. there
6. They're
7. their
8. their

B. Answers will vary.

1. (Sentence should have *they're* as the subject and verb.)
2. (Sentence should include *their* to show third-person plural possession.)
3. (Sentence should include *there* to begin a sentence where the subject follows the verb, or mean "in that place.")

Grammar Focus
page 69

A.

1. washed, had washed
2. stored, had stored
3. gathered, had gathered
4. quarreled, had quarreled
5. gazed, had gazed
6. deepened, had deepened
7. saved, had saved
8. covered, had covered

B.

1. had covered
2. needed, had saved
3. had gathered
4. had cooked, wanted

Grammar Focus
page 70

Answers should contain the following verb forms:

1. had not gathered
2. did, gaze
3. had, stored
4. didn't cover
5. hadn't, washed

From Reading to Writing
page 71

Answers will vary.

Across Content Areas
page 72

Possible responses:
1. a girl
2. a (whale) bone
3. no
4. a dog or fox; shrubs, cactus, twisted trees
5. Answers will vary.
6. Answers will vary.

UNIT 2 · CHAPTER 5

Build Vocabulary
page 73

A.
1. comets
2. engaged
3. century
4. predict
5. theories
6. catastrophe
7. resources
8. glamorous

B.
Catastrophes
Resources
Theories

Writing: Capitalization
page 74

1. During summer vacation, my family is going to visit the Grand Canyon.
2. The boy told me his name was Robert Munoz.
3. In school today, we learned about the Declaration of Independence.
4. When we went to Chicago, we saw the Sears Tower and Lake Michigan.
5. After school, Ben and his sister went to the family reunion.
6. José's grandparents are coming to visit from Mexico.
7. Mrs. Ortiz, our teacher, said the whole class did well on the tests.

Elements of Literature
page 75

A.
1. deductive
2. inductive
3. deductive
4. inductive

B.
1. **Deductive**
   I think I have a cold.
   My head aches.
   My nose is stuffy.
   My throat hurts.
2. **Inductive**
   My head aches.
   My nose is stuffy.
   My throat hurts.
   I think I have a cold.

Word Study
page 76

A.
1. action
2. prediction
3. connection
4. perfection

B.
1. prediction
2. action
3. perfection
4. connection

C. Answers will vary. Sentences should include the nouns *prediction, action, perfection, connection.*

Grammar Focus
page 77

A.
1. Scientists hope that they can slow down the rate of extinction.
2. Scientists try to convince people that they should help solve the problem.
3. My friend believes that we should start a club to tell people about extinction.
4. She thinks that people should learn about the problem.

B. Answers will vary. Sentences should begin with the words: *Scientists hope that; Scientists try to convince people that; My friend believes that; She thinks that…*

Grammar Focus
page 78

1. complex
2. NOT
3. complex
4. complex
5. complex

B. Answers will vary. Paragraph should have four sentences, including at least one complex sentence.

From Reading to Writing
page 79

Answers will vary.

Across Content Areas
page 80

1. why dinosaurs became extinct
2. Climate Change, Asteroid
3. under Climate Change
4. Asteroid
5. Answers will vary. One sentence should state that dinosaurs could not adapt to a change in the weather. Another sentence should state that the lack of sunlight from the asteroid disaster caused food supplies to die out.

UNIT 3 · CHAPTER 1

Build Vocabulary
page 81

A.
1. growing
2. sword
3. sight
4. quiet
5. noisy
6. dying
7. anger

B. You will not find Utopia on our globe. You will not find it anywhere. It is a made-up place. It means "paradise on Earth." Do you have a longing to go somewhere wonderful? Then you can go to Utopia in your mind. It is a place where humanity rules. Maybe it is a tranquil garden, blooming all year. Or it could be a palace, richly ornamented just for you. Or perhaps it is a beach where you hear the echo of a seagull. Are any of these your idea of Utopia?

Writing: Spelling
page 82

1. having
2. peaceful
3. changing
4. becoming
5. making
6. living
7. shining
8. looseness

Elements of Literature
page 83

Answers in the web will vary but may include the following: **sight:** brush, lace, white, brown, butterflies, manes, teeth, leaves, hooves; **smell:** lace; **taste:** breath, wind; **hearing:** brush, chasing, swirling, gnashing, rush, hooves; **touch:** brush, manes, breath, wind.

Word Study
page 84

A.
1. activity, the condition or state of action
2. oddity, the condition or state of being odd; strange
3. scarcity, the condition or state of being scarce
4. sincerity, the condition or state of being sincere; honest
5. humanity, the condition or state of being human

B.
1. sincerity
2. activity
3. humanity
4. scarcity
5. oddity

Grammar Focus
page 85

A. Some people enjoy traveling for a living. Keisha's job is to find places to shoot movies. She also makes sure the crew's needs are taken care of. The workers' food and living arrangements must be adequate. Suki's job is to find crafts in Asia. Her company's stores sell interesting clothing and home items from all over the world. Suki loves searching in Asia's cities and villages. Brianna travels to her bank's offices in Europe and Africa. In her time off, she especially likes Dakar's music and Paris' fashions.

B.
Sentences will vary.
1. boys'
2. Karl's
3. tree's
4. buildings'
5. Carlos'

Grammar Focus
page 86

1. Many of the women in my family are lawyers.
2. The children in my class like their teacher.
3. My feet hurt after soccer practice.
4. Most of the men in my family are over six feet tall.
5. My mother is afraid of mice, but I think they are cute.
6. I brush my teeth.
7. Where did you put the women's coats?
8. The people work at the restaurant.
9. The dentist said that my teeth are OK.

From Reading to Writing
page 87

Answers will vary. Students' poems should reflect content about a person they know and be in stanza format. The poem should include details about ideas and feelings and examples of possessive forms.

Across Content Areas
page 88

Answers will vary.

UNIT 3 · CHAPTER 2

Build Vocabulary
page 89

A.
1. shrugged
2. rapped
3. gazing
4. nervously
5. steadfastly
6. declared
7. defensively
8. rudely
9. abolished

B.
1. rap
3. gaze
2. rude

Writing: Capitalization
page 90

1. Like several other nations, France had colonies in Asia.
2. During the early 20th century, Vietnam was part of French Indochina.
3. After World War II, many people around the world fought for independence.
4. Many Vietnamese joined the fight against France.
5. French Indochina became four countries: North Vietnam, South Vietnam, Laos, and Cambodia.
6. Communists were in charge of North Vietnam.
7. They wanted to control South Vietnam, too.
8. The United States sent soldiers to help the South Vietnamese.
9. The Chinese sent soldiers to help the North Vietnamese.
10. When the fighting ended, Vietnam became one country.

Elements of Literature
page 91

A. Students' webs will vary.

B. Students' paragraphs will vary. Students' work should show details about a mood based on one of the webs.

Word Study
page 92

A. Possible responses:
1. not aware
2. not usual; strange
3. not comfortable
4. straighten
5. not important
6. not clear
7. not certain
8. not believable
9. not listed
10. do the opposite of lock; undo a lock, open

B. Answers will vary. Possible responses:
1. unaware; I am unaware of any assignment that is due for class tomorrow.
2. unhappy; I am unhappy about the weather.
3. unlock; I will unlock the door.

4. unusual; I think that boy is unusual.
5. unhealthy; Eating too many snacks is unhealthy.

Grammar Focus
page 93

A. Students' work should contain the correct use of the pronouns below.

1. I   2. He   3. She

B.
1. All eyes were fixed on her.
2. The family members did like him.
3. They remembered it.
4. During the Vietnam War, Americans learned a lot about them.

Grammar Focus
page 94

1. I   5. She, I
2. I   6. me
3. her   7. him
4. I, her

From Reading to Writing
page 95

Students' stories will vary but should include the pronouns *I, me,* and *my.* The mood of the story should be happy and upbeat.

Across Content Areas
page 96

1. west   4. northeast, north
2. 65, south   5. southwest
3. southwest

UNIT 3 · CHAPTER 3

Build Vocabulary
page 97

1. phosphorescent 5. nook
2. murmur   6. oval
3. Croquet   7. speedometer
4. mallets   8. fender

Writing: Capitalization and Punctuation
page 98

1. "Let's take a look at that bike," said Uncle Freddy.
2. "I'll bring my wrench set," Eddy answered.
3. "I don't think wrenches will fix what is wrong," Uncle Freddy said.
4. "What do you suggest then?" asked Eddy.
5. Just then they heard a voice call, "Eddy and Freddy! Time for lunch."

Elements of Literature
page 99

1. b   3. a   5. b
2. a   4. b

Word Study
page 100

A.
1. 24
2. Possible response: a wedding between two people from different countries.
3. Possible response: a zebra
4. about 60
5. Possible response: a person

B. Answers will vary. Students' sentences should correctly use each of the words.

Grammar Focus
page 101

1. We're   4. I'll   7. he'll
2. It's   5. I've   8. I'd
3. We've   6. We'll   9. I'd

Grammar Focus
page 102

1. I hadn't gone a step when I heard a strange buzzing.
2. I turned around and couldn't believe my eyes.
3. I didn't know it was going to snow all day long.
4. I wasn't prepared for my math exam today.
5. You aren't going to the movie unless you finish your homework.
6. I couldn't stand sitting inside until the rain stopped.
7. You haven't seen your big sister for a long time.
8. I wouldn't want to take a test like that again.
9. There isn't a place to put the computer.

From Reading to Writing
page 103

A. Answers will vary. Students' cluster maps should present a place of the future and details relating to the five senses.
B. Answers will vary. Students' paragraphs should make use of the items they listed in their cluster maps.

Across Content Areas
page 104

1. three
2. one
3. Answer will vary.
4. 12:00 P.M.
5. 2:00 A.M. on Tuesday

UNIT 3 · CHAPTER 4

Build Vocabulary
page 105

1. c   3. c   5. a   7. b
2. d   4. d   6. b

Writing: Capitalization
page 106

1. The *Voyager* spacecraft explored the outer planets of our solar system.
2. We learned a lot about Jupiter, Saturn, Uranus, and Neptune.
3. The spacecraft did not fly near Pluto.
4. Cameras and computers showed us the planets' moons and rings.
5. We see little of them from Earth because they are far away.

Elements of Literature
page 107

First Venn Diagram:
Under Sari: girl, likes sports, likes math
Under Sari and Sam: same birthday, brown hair and eyes, funny, kind

Under Sam: boy, taller than Sari, likes to draw, likes writing poetry
Second Venn Diagram:
Under Enzo: cat, long hair, sheds a lot, keeps to himself, likes to sleep
Under Enzo and Lucy: same owner; three years old, brown hair
Under Lucy: dog, short hair, does not shed much, loves other animals and people, likes to run and play catch

Word Study
page 108

1. fastest   6. loneliest
2. coldest   7. starriest
3. noisiest   8. biggest
4. strangest   9. emptiest
5. darkest   10. boldest

Grammar Focus
page 109

A.
1. the tallest
2. the most wonderful
3. the warmest
4. the most capable
5. the highest
6. the most amazing
7. the lowest
8. the most surprising

B.
1. most exciting   4. quietest
2. best   5. loudest
3. most interesting 6. greatest

Grammar Focus
page 110

A.
1. Do you wonder which of Mars's two moons is bigger?
2. The astronaut is one of the bravest people in the world.
3. Venus is closer to the Sun than Earth. Mercury is the closest of all the planets.
4. I think space travel is the most fascinating topic in this book.
B. Answers will vary. Make sure students correctly use a superlative adjective in each sentence.

From Reading to Writing
page 111

Answers will vary.

Across Content Areas
page 112

Answers will vary. Possible responses:
1. I could use audio CDs and audiocassettes to play radio transmissions from astronauts in space.
2. I could use videos to show a space shuttle blastoff.
3. I could use the Internet to research a famous astronaut.
4. I could use photographs and drawings to show what planets look like.
5. I could use diagrams and charts to compare distance between planets.
6. I could use CD-ROMs to present on the computer a map of the solar system.

UNIT 3 · CHAPTER 5

Build Vocabulary
page 113

1. sail   4. days
2. road   5. knead
3. feat   6. sight

Writing: Punctuation
page 114

A.
1. breakfast, lunch, and dinner
2. James, Maria, Vince, and Luis
3. movies or music
4. Italian, French, and Spanish
5. roses and tulips

B.
1. Henry entered the dining room carrying a bag and a hat.
2. His clothes were old, dusty, and torn.
3. Everyone in the room was a prospector, a peddler, or a shopkeeper.
4. Henry ate a simple meal of meat, potatoes, gravy, and bread.
5. Daisy, Yuri, and Joe looked at each other while Henry ate.
6. After Henry left, Joe said, "He was either a miner or a visitor."

Elements of Literature
page 115

Answers will vary. For Juan's traits, students might write: likes news, likes to write, likes to draw, curious, creative, intelligent, brave, kind; cares about the feelings of others. For Juan's motivations, students might write: wants to be a journalist, wants to be informed, wants to help people, wants to be like his father.

Word Study
page 116

1. a   3. b   5. a   7. a
2. a   4. b   6. a   8. b

Grammar Focus
page 117

A.
easily   safely   bravely
wonderfully   nervously   tiredly
dangerously   sadly

B.
1. easily   4. tiredly
2. bravely   5. safely
3. nervously   6. sadly

Grammar Focus
page 118

A. I waited <u>patiently</u> for my father to come home. He walked in <u>wearily</u> with a heavy sack on his back. It was the last of the supplies we needed for our trip west. We were leaving <u>immediately</u> for Independence, Missouri. From there, we would travel to San Francisco, California. I shouted <u>loudly</u> at my little sister to hurry up. She was <u>sadly</u> saying good-bye to all the plants and birds around our house. I thought <u>dreamily</u> about what life would be like in San Francisco. I am sure my father was thinking <u>seriously</u> about his new work in a mining camp. My mother bundled us warmly into the wagon. We were finally on our way.

B. Answers will vary. Students should write four sentences. They should include adverbs that describe verbs.

From Reading to Writing
page 119

Answers will vary. Possible responses:

Forty-Niners: most were men
Both: searched for gold, adventurous
Dame Shirley: a woman

In this paragraph, I will compare and contrast the forty-niners and Dame Shirley. The forty-niners are characters from "The California Gold Rush." Dame Shirley is a character from "Dame Shirley and the Gold Rush." The forty-niners and Dame Shirley went to California looking for gold. These characters are similar because they were adventurous and willing to endure hardships. The characters are different because the forty-niners were men. Dame Shirley was a woman.

Across Content Areas
page 120

Answers to chart:
tree; renewable; to make paper
gold; nonrenewable; to make jewelry and coins
coal; nonrenewable; to use for fuel, heating, and to make steel
soil; renewable; to grow crops and plants

UNIT 4 · CHAPTER 1

Build Vocabulary
page 121

A.
1. reappear
2. spiraling
3. sparkles
4. overflow
5. disappear
6. cascade
7. darkened

B.
1. c
2. f
3. d
4. b
5. g
6. a
7. e

Writing: Capitalization and Punctuation
page 122

A.
1. !
2. ?
3. .

B. Sometimes I cascade. I tumble down, down, over the moss-covered rocks, through the forest shadows. I am the mountain stream. At the foot of the mountains, I leap from a stone cliff.

Elements of Literature
page 123

A.
1. smell
2. touch
3. taste
4. hearing
5. sight

B.

Sight	Hearing
shadows	echoing
darkened	ringing
sparkles	banging

Touch	Taste
warm	peppery
wet	sour
cool	mouth-burning

Word Study
page 124

A.
1. connotative definition
2. denotative definition
3. denotative definition
4. connotative definition
5. denotative definition
6. connotative definition

B.
1. golden
2. tumble
3. golden
4. veils
5. tumble
6. veils

Grammar Focus
page 125

A.
1. heavier, heaviest
2. deeper, deepest
3. wider, widest
4. higher, highest
5. funnier, funniest

B.
1. neater, neatest
2. colder, coldest
3. higher, highest
4. busiest
5. happiest

Grammar Focus
page 126

Answers will vary.
1. soft, softer, softest
2. easy, easier, easiest
3. deep, deeper, deepest
4. quiet, quieter, quietest
5. large, larger, largest

From Reading to Writing
page 127

Answers will vary.

Across Content Areas
page 128

1. The article is about the water cycle.
2. It is a cycle because the process is repeated.
3. The part that shows precipitation.

UNIT 4 · CHAPTER 2

Build Vocabulary
page 129

A.
1. antonyms
2. antonyms
3. synonyms
4. antonyms

B.
1. harvests
2. searched
3. roared
4. messenger
5. swallowed
6. reasonable
7. begged

Writing: Capitalization
page 130

A.
1. Mount Rushmore
2. Atlantic Ocean
3. George Washington
4. Texas

B. Corrections are underlined.
"Persephone and the Seasons" is a Greek myth. People in ancient Greece and ancient Rome told many of the same stories, but they often gave different names to the gods and goddesses in their myths. For example, the king of the gods in Greek myths is Zeus, but in Roman myths he is called Jupiter. The messenger of the gods was Hermes to the Greeks and Mercury to the Romans. A few names were the same, though. In the myths of both Greece and Rome, the sun god is named Apollo.

Elements of Literature
page 131

Answers will vary. Be sure students understand the comparisons and contrasts between the seasons and have completed the Venn Diagram accordingly.

Word Study
page 132

1. couldn't
2. wasn't
3. aren't
4. weren't
5. didn't

Grammar Focus
page 133

A.
1. went
2. sang
3. had
4. taught
5. came

B. When Pluto chased Persephone, she ran away as fast as she could. But Pluto caught her and took her to the Underworld. Demeter could not find Persephone anywhere. It broke her heart when she could not find her daughter.

Grammar Focus
page 134

A.
1. I did not have a new bike in the garage.
   I didn't have a new bike in the garage.
2. We did not draw a picture for our presentation.
   We didn't draw a picture for our presentation.
3. They did not go away on the weekend.
   They didn't go away on the weekend.
4. I did not break the dishes while washing them.
   I didn't break the dishes while washing them.
5. She did not sing very loudly.
   She didn't sign very loudly.

B.
1. Did you catch a bad cold?
2. Did they draw from their earlier experiences?
3. Did it run across the yard?

From Reading to Writing
page 135

Answers will vary. Students' summaries should cover all the items in the checklist.

Across Content Areas
page 136

1. Jade Emperor and Zeus are both the rulers of the heavens.
2. "Why the Moon Is Pale" explains the cycle of day and night.

UNIT 4 · CHAPTER 3

Build Vocabulary
page 137

A.
1. accompanied
2. circuit
3. adventure
4. clasped
5. struggled
6. wearily
7. principal

B.
1. circuit
2. accompanied
3. principal
4. struggled

Writing: Punctuation
page 138

A. At my school, a lot of us like to say things like "hello," "goodbye," "yes," and "no" in foreign languages. My friend Anju says "bonjour" every morning. Toni likes to say "adios" when she leaves. My way of greeting people is to say "guten tag." Janice always says "yes" in Japanese, so we hear the word "hai" all day. It's really fun!

B.
1. "*Mi olla*," she used to say proudly.
2. "Yes, I like *corridos*," I answered.

Elements of Literature
page 139

A.
1. First
2. Third
3. Third
4. First

Word Study
page 140

A.
1. clearly
2. proudly
3. gladly

B.
1. quickly, in a fast way
2. pleasantly, in an easygoing way
3. sadly, in an unhappy way
4. smartly, in an intelligent way
5. neatly, in a clean or tidy way

Grammar Focus
page 141

A.
1. As long as we were at the mall, we decided to stop for lunch.
2. My sister swept the sidewalk while I cut the grass.
3. Whenever it snows, ice forms on the edge of our roof.
4. Ever since we changed the tires on my bicycle, it rides much more smoothly.
5. We go skating as soon as the ponds freeze.

B.
1. before she asks the teacher
2. When I see my grandmother
3. When you want to borrow a book
4. when you ride your bike
5. before you try them on

Grammar Focus
page 142

A.
1. dependent clause
2. sentence
3. sentence
4. dependent clause
5. dependent clause

B.

1. While it was raining, we played a game inside.
2. When Melissa arrived, the party started.
3. As long as you are up, please bring me a glass of water.
4. I went to the store after I finished cleaning my room.
5. Before Manolo went to the movie, he ate a sandwich.

C. Answers will vary. Be sure students write complete sentences and correctly punctuate introductory dependent clauses.

From Reading to Writing
page 143

Answers will vary.

Across Content Areas
page 144

Answers will vary.

UNIT 4 • CHAPTER 4

Build Vocabulary
page 145

A.

1. a		3. b		5. a	
2. b		4. a		6. b	

B. Answers will vary. Students should list any process that includes a series of steps.

Writing: Punctuation
page 146

A.

1. do not need commas
2. need commas
3. need commas
4. need commas
5. do not need commas

B. Corrected errors are underlined. Almost everything around you is a compound. Compounds are made of combinations of elements. For example, table salt is a compound of the elements sodium and chlorine. The material used to make paper contains the three elements carbon, hydrogen, and oxygen. The air we breathe has many gases in it, including nitrogen, oxygen, and carbon dioxide, among other gases.

Elements of Literature
page 147

Answers will vary. Make sure students' storyboards accurately reflect the process.

Word Study
page 148

1. finis	3. bio
2. graphein	4. tenere

Grammar Focus
page 149

1. <u>Kareem jumped</u> higher than anyone else at the track meet.
2. <u>We were hired</u> by our neighbor to clean his yard. (circled)
3. <u>The herd of cows walked</u> slowly across the grass.
4. <u>Alexandro threw</u> the stick for the dog.
5. <u>The famous singer was</u> <u>recognized</u> when he walked into the restaurant. (circled)

Grammar Focus
page 150

1. The most interesting gift was given by Jason.
2. My father cleaned my grandmother's gutters.
3. The principal warned the class to stay together.
4. The rabbit was chased by the fox.
5. Everyone admired Sonya's beautiful voice.

From Reading to Writing
page 151

Answers will vary.

Across Content Areas
page 152

Answers will vary. Students' charts should accurately compare and contrast a living thing with a nonliving thing.

UNIT 5 • CHAPTER 1

Build Vocabulary
page 153

A.

1. b		3. f		5. e	
2. a		4. c		6. d	

B.

1. telephone	4. store
2. house	5. puppy
3. car	

Writing: Capitalization
page 154

A.

1. Rosa, Raymond Parks, Fred Gray, John B. Scott
2. Thursday, December
3. Montgomery, Alabama
4. Judge
5. Montgomery Fair

B.

Corrections are underlined.
1. <u>I</u> have never lived outside of <u>N</u>ew <u>Y</u>ork <u>C</u>ity.
2. <u>H</u>ave you ever visited the <u>E</u>mpire <u>S</u>tate Building?
3. <u>P</u>eople come from as far as <u>J</u>apan and <u>C</u>hina to see it.
4. <u>I</u> went to see the <u>S</u>tatue of <u>L</u>iberty with <u>L</u>ouis.
5. <u>P</u>eople like to enjoy the beauty of <u>C</u>entral Park.
6. <u>I</u>n the month of <u>A</u>pril, New York parks bloom with flowers.

Elements of Literature
page 155

A.

1. smart, smooth talking, forthright, persistent
   Possible responses for 2–5:
2. not immediately impressed
3. well-spoken; cared deeply about the plight of black people
4. grateful
5. iron will

B.

1. He was intelligent, and he acted like someone who felt sure of himself.
   Possible responses for 2–5:
2. She did not like him right away.
3. He supported their rights.
4. She felt it was grateful.
5. She would have to show courage and strength.

Word Study
page 156

A.

1. argument, the act of arguing
2. improvement, the act of improving
3. arrangement, the act of arranging
4. movement, the act of moving
5. treatment, the act of treating

B.

1. arrangement	4. treatment
2. movement	5. argument
3. improvement	

Grammar Focus
page 157

A.

1. We stayed at our friend's house.
2. She talked about her love of reading.
3. I chose the red notebook.
4. They worked together at the school.
5. She did many things well.
6. He wore a red shirt and jeans.

B.

1. walked	4. played
2. understood	5. kept
3. won	

Grammar Focus
page 158

1. The trucks carried bales of hay.
2. Molly and Dan shopped in a bakery.
3. The dancers moved to the music.
4. The clowns in the circus juggled oranges.
5. Jana and Shane cried during a sad movie.
6. The cars slipped on the icy roads.

From Reading to Writing
page 159

Answers will vary. Students should write notes in chronological order and check all of the items in the checklist.

Across Content Areas
page 160

Answers will vary. Students may note that they wish to see more parks, less pollution, better schools, more facilities for the disabled, and so on.

UNIT 5 • CHAPTER 2

Build Vocabulary
page 161

A.

1. c		3. a		5. e		7. d	
2. g		4. b		6. f			

Writing: Punctuation
page 162

1. yes: Lincoln said, "I must write a better speech for these men."
2. no
3. no
4. yes: Lincoln thought, "I will make my speech short."
5. no
6. yes: "We will sing a special song," said the choir leader.
7. no
8. yes: One of the people in the crowd shouted, "That was the best speech I have heard in many years!"

B.

Although President Lincoln was busy thinking about the Civil War, he still knew it was important for him to travel to Gettysburg. He said, "I have to honor the brave soldiers who gave their lives." He knew Mr. Everett would be speaking. "I don't want to speak for a long time," said President Lincoln.

Elements of Literature
page 163

A.

1. a		2. b		3. b

B.

1. false	3. false	5. true
2. true	4. true	

Word Study
page 164

A.

actor (a person who acts)
translator (a person who translates)
narrator (a person who narrates)

B.

1. writer   2. buyer   3. painter

Grammar Focus
page 165

1. Verb: expects; Object: me; Infinitive: to visit
2. Verb: needed; Object: James; Infinitive: to hold
3. Verb: asks; Object: Martina; Infinitive: to drive
4. Verb: requires; Object: students; Infinitive: to learn
5. Verb: tells; Object: drummers; Infinitive: to count
6. Verb: allows; Object: him; Infinitive: to use

Grammar Focus
page 166

A.

1. Verb: will meet; Direct Object: mother
2. Verb: found; Direct Object: sweater
3. Verb: bought; Direct Object: gifts
4. Verb: thanked; Direct Object: uncle
5. Verb: saw; Direct Object: lions and tigers

B. Answers will vary. Possible answers are:

1. salads	4. cereal
2. tamales	5. a doctor
3. a CD	

From Reading to Writing
page 167

Answers will vary. Possible responses:

1. I am intelligent, caring, brave, and creative.
2. I come to school on time.
3. We could have a bake sale after school.

4. I will use words like *I am the right choice for Class President; I will make a difference!*
5. I worked with two other people to put up a display for our science project.

Paragraph

Answers will vary but should include information based on answers to the questions.

Across Content Areas
page 168

1. 1704
2. 1/2 hour
3. 14 days
4. 2
5. older than one year by 5 months

UNIT 5 • CHAPTER 3

Build Vocabulary
page 169

A.

1. e	3. b	5. f
2. d	4. a	6. c

B.

1. adjective: bare; noun: trees
2. adjective: falling; noun: snow
3. adjective: red; noun: sleds
4. adjective: soft; noun: bed
5. adjective: quick; noun: breakfast
6. adjective: big; noun: hill

Writing: Spelling
page 170

A.

1. hips	5. Communists
2. soldiers	6. eyes
3. times	7. directions
4. friends	8. bullets

B.

1. gloves	4. girls
2. friends	5. cookies
3. snowballs	6. snacks

Elements of Literature
page 171

Possible responses:
1. He is a generous person who cares about Hideyo.
2. Hideyo needs money and takes it, but he feels bad about it.
3. He is embarrassed.
4. She is sad.
5. He is afraid for his life.
6. He escapes.

Word Study
page 172

A.

1. dismiss	3. motion
2. vision	4. reverse

B. Answers will vary. Sentences should include the words *dismiss, motion, reverse,* and *vision*.

Grammar Focus
page 173

1. He wore dark clothes so that the soldiers wouldn't see him at night.
2. Mrs. Kim gave him food so that he wouldn't be hungry.
3. He moved silently so that no one would hear him.
4. His friends gave him a map so that he wouldn't get lost.

5. Mrs. Kim put the rucksack in a bag so that Hideyo would look like a Korean.

Grammar Focus
page 174

A.
1. (until) I come home from school
2. (until) my family comes into the house
3. (because) he has been many times before
4. (while) I am at school
5. (if) he hears the mail carrier
6. (after) the mail carrier walks away

B. Answers will vary.

From Reading to Writing
page 175

Answers will vary.

Across Content Areas
page 176

Answers will vary. Students should include two sentences that are questions and two sentences that are exclamations.

UNIT 5 • CHAPTER 4

Build Vocabulary
page 177

Answers will vary. Sentences should include the words *disabilities, refuge, illusion, critiquing, obscure, afloat*.

Writing: Punctuation
page 178

A. Samantha had been having a difficult time in school. She didn't do well in almost every subject. However, she enjoyed her creative writing class. There she was allowed to write in whatever way she wanted. It was a chance for her to feel successful. Once people realized she was learning disabled, her teachers could help her learn in a better way. She still writes today and teaches others about what it's like to be learning disabled.

B. I tried to work on my math lesson, but I felt really sick. I asked my teacher, Ms. Lopez, if I could see the nurse. "Of course," Ms. Lopez said. I then went to visit Mr. Clark, the school nurse. He examined me and told me that I had a fever. He called my mother and said that she should take me to our family's doctor. My mother answered, "Thank you for calling, Mr. Clark. I will make an appointment with Dr. Jackson right away."

Elements of Literature
page 179

A. Answers will vary. Sample answers below:
1. A tall, beautiful tree in the nighttime moonlight. There is a glow around the tree and the stars are shining above it.
2. A man or woman confidently and happily singing.

3. A plane flying above a dense layer of fluffy clouds that look like the waves of the sea.
4. A basketball player jumping very high with a ball in his or her hand. The player is going toward the net with the ball.

B. Images will vary.

Word Study
page 180

A.

1. sunlight	4. lightly
2. moonlight	5. lighter
3. delightful	6. enlighten

B.

1. sunlight	4. moonlight
2. enlighten	5. lighter
3. delightful	6. lightly

Grammar Focus
page 181

A.

1. nicest	5. cleanest
2. brightest	6. largest
3. finest	7. youngest
4. sunniest	8. friendliest

B.

1. brightest	4. youngest
2. clearest	5. friendliest
3. sunniest	

Grammar Focus
page 182

A.

1. nicer	5. shorter
2. cleaner	6. longer
3. sleepier	7. later
4. sunnier	8. quiet

B.
1. Kayla ran fast, but Marco ran faster. Ava ran the fastest.
2–5. Answers will vary.
6. Answers will vary but should include *quiet, quieter, quietest*.

From Reading to Writing
page 183

A. Answers will vary. Answers should include the name of any place and words that describe the place.

B. Answers will vary. Poems should be made up of at least four lines and can include rhyming or non-rhyming words.

Across Content Areas
page 184

1. Autobiography	4. Biography
2. Fiction	5. Fable
3. Drama	6. Poetry

UNIT 6 • CHAPTER 1

Build Vocabulary
page 185

A.
1. Her fancy clothes are extravagant.
2. The carpenter is showing his apprentice how to build a wooden table.
3. People try to reform laws that are unfair.
4. My mother likes to furnish hot chocolate after we play in the snow.

5. The circus always has a festive group of clowns and jugglers.
6. I tried hard, but I could save only a meager amount of money.
7. Mark shows his benevolence by feeding stray cats.
8. We will find a time to meet that is convenient for both of us.

Writing: Punctuation
page 186

1. Cratchit—why are you using coal at this time of day?
2. But, sir—I cannot write well when my fingers are so cold.
3. Merry Christmas, uncle—you look just as pleased as usual.
4. We would like you to come for dinner—that is all I came to ask.
5. We would like to ask you to make a donation—just a small amount.
6. You have to be joking—do you think I just give money away?

Elements of Literature
page 187

1. a. Bob is very cold.
2. b. Scrooge is angry that Bob wants to take time off of work.
3. a. Scrooge is angry.
4. a. Bob is embarrassed about his action and afraid that Scrooge will be angry.
5. a. The solicitor is offended.

Word Study
page 188

A.

1. I couldn't	5. he'll
2. I didn't	6. I'm not
3. he's not	7. he's
4. we'd	8. they're

B.

1. I'm	4. wasn't
2. I'll	5. he's
3. didn't	6. he'll

Grammar Focus
page 189

A.

1. has	4. have
2. have	5. have
3. have	

B.

1. has worked	4. has done
2. has known	5. have walked
3. have eaten	

Grammar Focus
page 190

1. Have they been in the library for an hour?
2. I haven't lived here for two years.
3. John and Judi haven't eaten at home all week.
4. Have you known about the party for a week?
5. They have not/haven't gone to this school for a long time.

From Reading to Writing
page 191

Answers will vary.

Across Content Areas
page 192

Answers will vary. Students' stories should correspond to the storyboards they filled in.

UNIT 6 • CHAPTER 2

Build Vocabulary
page 193

1. c   3. b   5. f   7. g
2. e   4. a   6. d

Writing: Capitalization
page 194

1. I wanted to go to Simpson Street to shop for fabric.
2. My friend Susan wanted to make clown clothes for our school circus.
3. We took the Chicago Avenue bus to get to the fabric store.
4. Our friends José and Mark met us there.
5. They are going to enter a clown contest in Florida.
6. Mark told me they won a contest in California last month.

Elements of Literature
page 195

1. Limited Third Person—uses *he, she,* or *they* but does not know what characters think
2. Omniscient Third Person—uses *he, she,* or *they* and knows what characters think
3. First Person—uses *I, me, we,* and *us* and the narrator is a character in the story

Word Study
page 196

A.
1. Inuit   3. Italian
2. Spanish   4. French

B. Answers will vary. Students' sentences should correctly use the words from other languages.

Grammar Focus
page 197

A.
1. their   4. There
2. They're   5. there
3. their   6. They're

B.
1. They're going to the park to play a game of soccer.
2. Pablo and Seth are bringing their soccer balls.
3. There will also be a barbecue.
4. The kids will have their parents pick them up after the game.
5. My parents will already be there.

Grammar Focus
page 198

A.
1. wives   5. boxes
2. tomatoes   6. beaches
3. churches   7. shelf
4. thieves   8. brush

B.
1. I need to go to the store to get some tomatoes.
2. In the fall, all the leaves from the trees fall to the ground.
3. During the flood, there were many heroes.
4. Some people say that cats have nine lives.
5. One of my jobs at home is to wash the dishes after dinner.

From Reading to Writing
page 199

Answers will vary. Students should add details to all sentences.

Across Content Areas
page 200

A. Answers will vary. Students should choose a habitat from the reading and write details in the appropriate spots in their cluster maps.

B. Answers will vary. Students' paragraphs should correspond to their cluster maps.

UNIT 6 • CHAPTER 3

Build Vocabulary
page 201

1. flitted   4. covered
2. clusters   5. gloating
3. strewn   6. clinging

Writing: Spelling
page 202

1. heaviness   9. drier
2. heavier   10. merriment
3. oiliness   11. payment
4. oilier   12. flier
5. readiness   13. enjoyment
6. steadiness   14. appliance
7. silliness   15. fogginess
8. healthier   16. defiance

Elements of Literature
page 203

Background and Conflict: Kino and Juana are a poor couple with a sick baby. To earn money, Kino dives for pearl oysters.
Rising Action: While he is underwater, Kino knows that Juana is praying in the boat. She prays for something to heal their baby, Coyotito. Kino sees a large oyster lying by itself.
Climax: He picks this oyster. Kino thinks it may have a pearl inside. In the boat, Kino opens the oyster. Inside, he finds a large pearl.
Falling action: Kino and Juana are excited.
Resolution: The baby is already getting better.

Word Study
page 204

1. b   4. j   7. a
2. e   5. c   8. i
3. d   6. h   9. f

Grammar Focus
page 205

1. and   3. or   5. or
2. but   4. but   6. but

Grammar Focus
page 206

A.
1. Emil is the best student in math, but he is not the best student in science.
2. Ivana works at the library, and she also works at the school.
3. Tina likes the guitar, but she does not like the piano.
4. Does Youssouf speak French at work, or does he speak English?
5. When Rosa writes to her cousin, she writes letters or she writes E-mails.
6. Irina calls us in the morning, but she does not call us in the evenings.

B. Sentences will vary but should include conjunctions and the correct use of commas.

From Reading to Writing
page 207

Answers will vary.

Across Content Areas
page 208

1. North America, Europe, and Asia
2. Atlantic Ocean
3. Pacific Ocean and Indian Ocean
4. Answers may vary but should include one of the following: Australia, Asia, South America, and North America
5. Atlantic Ocean and Indian Ocean
6. Pacific Ocean and Atlantic Ocean

UNIT 6 • CHAPTER 4

Build Vocabulary
page 209

1. a   4. c   7. d
2. e   5. f
3. b   6. g

Writing: Punctuation
page 210

A.
1. rivers, streams, and oceans
2. working, playing, and raising families
3. fruits, grains, and vegetables
4. coal, oil, and gas
5. plants, fish, snails, and bacteria

B.
1. They will grow fruit, grains, or vegetables.
2. They travel in cars, trucks, or trains.
3. Energy will flow from windmills, panels, and cells.
4. Plants, fish, and snails purify the water.
5. Our power comes from oil, coal, or gas.
6. Work, food, and shopping will change.

Elements of Literature
page 211

A.
1. to inform   4. to inform
2. to persuade   5. to inform
3. to entertain   6. to entertain

B. Answers will vary. Paragraphs should give the author's purpose and support it with examples.

Word Study
page 212

A.
1. a captain of a team with someone else
2. to own a business with someone else
3. an organizer of a new organization with someone else
4. a host of a party or a show with someone else
5. to be a leading actor in a play or movie with someone else

B.
1. cocaptain   4. colead
2. cohost   5. coown
3. cofounder

Grammar Focus
page 213

A.
1. I will go to college after high school.
2. I won't be late.
3. This game will be interesting.
4. This soup will taste very good.
5. We won't finish our report tonight.

B. Answers will vary. Possible answers are:
1. Cheng will buy a hotdog and a soda
2. she will go to bed
3. she will invite him another time
4. they will miss the bus

Grammar Focus
page 214

1. pulled   5. smiled
2. will play   6. asked
3. will wave   7. will open
4. talks   8. closed

From Reading to Writing
page 215

Answers will vary. Students' letters should be based on the information from their charts.

Across Content Areas
page 216

Possible answers for chart:

Air Pollution (Solutions):

Cars and trucks will run on clean, hydrogen-powered fuel cells.
We'll often travel on old-fashioned, earth-friendly bicycles.
Our power will come from sources cleaner than coal, oil, and gas.
Some energy will flow from windmills.
Rooftop solar panels will supply electricity.

Water Pollution (Solutions):

Since the farms will use natural forms of pest control, there will be far fewer chemicals in the food supply.
Plants, fish, snails, and bacteria will purify wastewater.

Both (Solutions):

The mall will be one big recycling operation.

Air Pollution (Examples):

Electric heat and light made our homes warm and welcoming but also burned up limited coal and oil.

Water Pollution (Examples):

Factories revolutionized the way we worked, but industrial waste trashed rivers, streams, and oceans.

Both (Examples):

Answers will vary.